ADOLESCENT LITERACY

GARLAND REFERENCE LIBRARY
OF SOCIAL SCIENCE
(VOL. 828)

ADOLESCENT LITERACY
What Works and Why

Second Edition

Center for Early Adolescence
The University of North Carolina at Chapel Hill

Judith Davidson
and
David Koppenhaver

GARLAND PUBLISHING, INC. • NEW YORK & LONDON
1993

Library of Congress Cataloging-in-Publication Data

Davidson, Judith, 1953–
   Adolescent literacy : what works and why / Judith Davidson and
David Koppenhaver. —2nd ed.
      p.   cm. — (Garland reference library of social science : vol.
828)
   Includes bibliographical references and index.
   ISBN 0-8153-0877-9 (alk. paper)
   ISBN 0-8153-0920-1 (pbk. alk. paper)
   1. Project on Adolescent Literacy (U.S.) 2. Reading (Adult
education)—United States. 3. Reading—United States—Remedial
teaching. 4. Literacy—United States. I. Koppenhaver, David,
1956– . II. Title. III. Series: Garland reference library of
social science; v. 828.
LC5225.R4D38 1993
428.4'071'2—dc20   92–13812
                                                            CIP

Printed on 250-year-life, acid-free paper
Manufactured in the United States of America

CONTENTS

FOREWORD

In schools across the country, adults are playing a game of make-believe with young people. They say, in effect, "We will make believe we don't know that you can't read, if you will make believe that you can." Motivations for maintaining this mutual deception range from apathy to cynicism to despair. Lacking training, tools, and, too often, vision, the adults charged with preparing our youth for enriched and enriching futures condemn them to a game of chance more cruel than the classroom charade: a life spent impoverished by functional illiteracy.

In this second edition of *Adolescent Literacy: What Works and Why,* the authors remind us that our concern about unmet literacy needs must not rest with "how many adolescents are at risk of illiteracy" but must be expanded to the more daunting question, "How many young adolescents will acquire adequate literacy skills?" Asking this ambitious question thrusts *Adolescent Literacy* into the public-policy arena, considering issues of poverty and race and of their powerful interrelationship. As the authors say, "By and large, the majority of those who are not gaining these critical literacy skills and the positive attitudes toward literacy that accompany accomplishment are young adolescents living in poverty. Low literacy achievement is part of the web of problems economically disadvantaged youth face, and it is both a cause and a consequence of many other problems they encounter."

In its 1987 report, *Children in Need: Investment Strategies for the Educationally Disadvantaged,* the Committee for Economic Development (CED) warned its fellow corporate executives that:

> [d]emographic trends dramatize the need to address seriously the plight of the disadvantaged; the sheer numbers and the growing proportion of the U.S. population that they represent are staggering. The percentage of both poor children and minorities in the United States has been rising

> steadily in recent years and will continue to climb in the
> foreseeable future. . . . In 1985, minorities represented about
> 17 percent of the total U.S. population. By the year 2020, this
> proportion is expected to rise more than one-third; if current
> demographic trends continue, a larger proportion of this
> group will be children from disadvantaged homes. (p. 9)

CED sounded an alarm that "the demographic imperative" required
aggressive intervention because our schools perform least well with
exactly the children whose numbers are rising: African-American
and Hispanic children living in poverty. Likewise, this second
edition of *Adolescent Literacy: What Works and Why* presses its readers
to take vigorous action in both policymaking and program
implementation.

This book results from an investigation of reading programs
that refuse to tolerate acquiescence to the inevitability of reading
failure. This rich but readable, optimistic but wary book is utterly
pragmatic. It lives up to its title. It tells us what works and why,
through case studies and through observations gleaned from
hundreds of days of exhaustive literature searches and exhausting
site visits.

The authors' message is deceptively simple: "Prominently
characteristic of each of these successful programs is a firm belief by
teachers and administrators in each young person's right and ability
to learn to read, an emphasis on the importance of literacy, and a
large proportion of instructional time devoted to actual reading and
writing." They derived this message by asking deceptively simple
questions: "Are the students reading and writing? What are they
reading and writing? Can they talk about the books they have read
and describe the kinds of writing projects they have completed? Are
the teachers instructing, not just managing or evaluating? Are the
students learning, not just complying? . . . How do the participants
feel about the program?"

Preceding the articulation of those questions were months
spent combing research on reading in early adolescence, numerous
conversations with the nation's leading literacy experts, and
discussions among members of the Center for Early Adolescence's
literacy team that acknowledged few time or physical limitations.
The mission of the Center for the past fourteen years has been to
alert adults to the quality of young adolescents' lives as they

negotiate the various challenges of their development and to strengthen the institutions established ostensibly to ease and enrich that development. As a result, the Project on Adolescent Literacy looked not only at schools but at nonschool and summer literacy programs as well. Some children spend their days in homes and schools filled with people who read for pleasure and livelihood, surrounded by book-filled rooms sending visual messages about the centrality of reading in their lives. For youngsters in literacy-impoverished homes—and in some cases schools—out-of-school programs can become a critical factor in decisions to stay in school or to learn in an alternative institution. These investigators found out-of-school literacy programs that are changing the lives of young adolescents, who become eager readers rushing to find new books, to read to younger children, and even to serve as reconnectors to the schools they have rejected. A sampling of several excellent programs reveals, once again, a simple, underlying goal: to help students have a good experience with a book.

Adolescent Literacy: What Works and Why is an optimistic book, assuring us that "good early adolescent literacy programs can make readers and writers out of students who school and community have despaired would ever learn." It urges us forward: "The results of these successful programs can be replicated, and the techniques and methods for doing so can be learned and shared." It presses for the adoption of a variety of policy recommendations that would help young people make the transition from beginning-level to proficient readers and writers—and thus would help break the stranglehold relationship between poverty and reading failure.

Some of the authors' conclusions are sobering. For instance, the Project on Adolescent Literacy team found no successful after-school literacy programs or summer-literacy programs designed specifically for the early adolescent age group. They also found communities mired in the debate about whether schools should provide services to beginning English-speakers, or who in the community is responsible for doing so. Even in some of the best programs, they found ardent people engaged in a complex endeavor, hampered by staff uninformed about theory and practice, lacking access to expert guidance and inspiration, too often hearing the sirens of packaged materials or computers that can never substitute for the expert instruction of an inspired teacher. They were sobered by a flagging federal commitment to compensatory education at a time when increasing numbers of children live in poverty. "Put bluntly, there is not only less to share, but more who need help."

Nonetheless, despite the paucity of literacy programs for the age group, the very existence of excellent programs bears witness to their feasibility. Heroes and heroines documented in this book teach and learn together, using the best of what is known about literacy and early adolescence. The teachers "possess a deep curiosity toward the world and a special thoughtfulness toward the presentation of that world to young people." The students "catch" that enthusiasm. In perhaps their most ingenuously moving line, the authors report that, in these best of classes, "students explore new topics and concerns with courage and vigor, building conceptual information while improving basic skills." Courage abounds in this book: the courage of researchers to maneuver in the white waters of a complex and often contentious academic and public-policy field; the courage of adults who insist that every child experience the thrill of extracting meaning from print; and the courage of young adolescents to expose themselves to the vulnerability of effort and hope.

Read on.

Then take action.

Joan Lipsitz
Program Director, Education
Lilly Endowment Inc.

ACKNOWLEDGMENTS

The Project on Adolescent Literacy (PAL) owes much to many, but none more than Joan Lipsitz, former director of the Center for Early Adolescence, who realized that the need for improved basic skills instruction at the middle-grades level would soon become a matter of national concern. Young adolescents without good basic skills face a bleak future and are at great risk of dropping out, becoming teenaged parents, involving themselves in crime, or slipping into drug and alcohol abuse. Lipsitz saw improving basic skills in the middle grades as a natural outgrowth of the Center's previous work in promoting school and community programs and agencies that are responsive to the characteristics and needs of young adolescents.

With Leah Lefstein, associate director of the Center, and Betsy Riesz, educational consultant to the project, Lipsitz established the philosophy, goals, and methodology that have guided the project through the publication of its findings. Although Lipsitz left the Center at the end of 1985 to accept another position, her creative influence is still the driving force behind this work.

Reviewing the literature, contacting programs, interviewing busy program directors over the phone, and arranging site visits: all these jobs and more were skillfully carried out by Rosalyn Rossignol, project coordinator, and David Koppenhaver, project researcher. Susan Rosenzweig, the Center's director of information services, helped to set up a database for information on programs, people, and organizations concerned with promoting adolescent literacy and, with her staff, spent innumerable hours tracking down materials and leads for the PAL team.

An advisory board composed of the following people provided invaluable guidance for the development of the literacy project: Richard Allington, State University of New York at Albany; James W. Cunningham, University of North Carolina at Chapel Hill; Michael Graves, University of Minnesota; Jerome C. Harste, Indiana

University at Bloomington; Linda Meyer, University of Illinois at Urbana-Champaign; Charlene Rivera, Development Associates; Jacqueline Cook, Literacy Assistance Center; Mary Beth Curtis, Boys Town Literacy Center; William S. Hall, University of Maryland; Reynaldo F. Macias, University of Southern California; Victoria Risko, Vanderbilt University; and Nancy Rogers-Zegarra, Charlotte (N.C.) Public Schools.

Lipsitz, Lefstein, Koppenhaver, Rossignol, and Rosenzweig made the first round of site visits, which spanned the months from April 1985 to the summer of 1986. In September 1986 Judith Davidson joined the team as the new project director. Lefstein, Koppenhaver, and Davidson spent many days crossing the country on a second round of site visits that fall.

At each site the teams visited on their two rounds, they were greeted with gracious hospitality. The staff, students, and parents involved in each program eagerly answered their myriad questions. This desire to share both their concerns and their hopes made each visit exciting and gratifying.

Sites in Order of Visits

Griffin Middle School, High Point, North Carolina

Hill Learning Development Center, Durham Academy, Durham, North Carolina

The Kenosha Model, Chapter 1, Kenosha Unified School District, Kenosha, Wisconsin

Morris Brown Reading Academy, Los Angeles, California

BASIC, California Demonstration Project in Reading, Benjamin Franklin Middle School, San Francisco, California

ESL Immersion, Lafayette Elementary School, Lancaster, Pennsylvania

HILT (High Intensity Language Training), El Paso Independent School District, El Paso, Texas

Marlboro Homework Helper, Brooklyn, New York

Learning to Read through the Arts, Public School No. 9, New York, New York

STAR (Structured Teaching in the Areas of Reading and Writing), Community School District No. 4, New York, New York

Na Pua a Pauahi Program, Kamehameha Schools, Honolulu, Hawaii

Caswell County Chapter 1, Yanceyville, North Carolina

Basic and Vocational Skills Program, Burlington City Schools, Burlington, North Carolina

Chapter 1—Project CPR, Taunton Public Schools, Taunton, Massachusetts

McCormack Middle School, Dorchester, Massachusetts

Targeted Reading Program, Boston Public Schools, Boston, Massachusetts

Highline Indian Tutoring Program, Highline City Schools, Seattle, Washington

Middle School Reading Laboratory, Jefferson County School District, Louisville, Kentucky

Tucson Unified School District (bilingual and ESL program), Tucson, Arizona

Chapter 1, Starpoint Central School, Lockport, New York

Adventures in Excellence, Behrman Middle School, New Orleans, Louisiana

The Cross-Age Tutoring Program, Literacy Council of Alaska, Fairbanks, Alaska

Goals for Boston, Boston Public Schools, Boston, Massachusetts

STEP (Summer Training and Education Program), Boston, Massachusetts

Fourth Church Summer Day Program and After-school Program, Fourth Presbyterian Church, Chicago, Illinois

MARC (Mathematics, Arts, and Reading Camps), Greater Philadelphia Federation of Settlements, Philadelphia, Pennsylvania

Theodore Gathings Junior High School, I.S. 158, Bronx, New York

The Friendly Place (sponsored by the American Reading Council), New York, New York

Montgomery Ward-Cabrini Green Tutoring Program, Chicago, Illinois

North Bronx Family Service Center After-school Tutoring Program, Bronx, New York

The PAL team managed, quite conveniently, to make it back to home base in North Carolina in time for the birth of Daniel August Koppenhaver in December 1986. David's wife, Janice, is one of the unsung heroes of the project. Daniel's birth, as much as any other event, marked the team's shift from gathering facts to sifting and analyzing them and preparing and writing up the findings.

As the writing proceeded, team members were once again thankful for the extraordinary patience of the staff at the different sites they had visited, who were willing to answer follow-up questions, find more statistics, and share new developments in their work.

Others working in the literacy field who were helpful in sharing their experience and expertise with the PAL team included Mary Jean LeTendre and her staff at the United States Department of Education, Richard Long and Alan Farstrup of the International Reading Association, Evelyn Shaevel of the Young Adult Services Division of the American Library Association, and Harry Singer at the University of California-Riverside.

At the Center, many aided the team in making the first edition of this publication a reality. Leah Lefstein, the Center's acting director and the project's principal investigator, also served as editor, fund raiser, and thoughtful mentor; Monica Jacoby, communications manager, edited and negotiated with our publisher; Gayle Dorman, former director of educational services, generously shared with PAL staff important insights from her experience; Suzanne Rucker, operations manager, kept the team afloat, organizing help when needed; Jan Touma, Terry Hammersley, Lois Hewett, and Sarah Clark provided the project's clerical needs; Sarah Clark also filled in frequently as editorial and research assistant; Barbara Mineiro, information manager, helped fill information requests; and Denise Allen, with never a word of complaint, faithfully transported carloads of books back and forth between the library and the office. Bobbie Sanders provided excellent technical support on the computer, and Laura Oaks edited the final draft of the manuscript.

Special thanks must also go to those who assisted with the preparation of the second edition of this book. Joan Lipsitz graciously wrote the foreword to the second edition. Judith Erickson of the Indiana Youth Institute provided assistance researching the history of community-based organizations' literacy work. We are also grateful to Jack Humphrey, director of the Middle Grades Reading Network at the University of Evansville, to advisory board members Linda Meyer, Mary Beth Curtis, and Victoria Risko, and to Susan Rosenzweig, former director of information services, for their insightful comments on drafts of this manuscript. Center staff members were also an integral part of producing the second edition. Janice Britson, project secretary, provided clerical and editorial support for the project; Roberta Lloyd, information specialist, verified citations; and Robin Pulver, director of educational resource development, prepared the final draft of the manuscript for publication.

At Garland Publishing, Marie Ellen Larcada graciously shepherded the manuscript through the final stages of production on both editions of the book.

We are most grateful for the financial support we received for the project. The Carnegie Corporation of New York, the Mary Reynolds Babcock Foundation, and Lilly Endowment Inc. provided funding for the project. The Bowne Foundation also provided assistance for visiting literacy programs in New York City. Vivien Stewart at the Carnegie Corporation of New York, William Bondurant at the Mary Reynolds Babcock Foundation, William Bonifield and Susan Wisely at Lilly Endowment, Inc., and Dianne Kangisser at the Bowne Foundation deserve special thanks for their support of the project's work.

With the publication of the second edition, we continue the task of disseminating to others the lessons the team has gleaned about successful literacy programs for young adolescents.

INTRODUCTION TO THE SECOND EDITION

In 1988 the Center for Early Adolescence released the findings of its three-year national study of successful compensatory literacy programs in the book *Adolescent Literacy: What Works and Why*. The opening chapter of the study was titled "Adolescent Illiteracy: A National Problem."

At that time we wrote:

> There are 27 million illiterate adults in America. An additional 47 million are considered functionally illiterate: that is, they would have difficulty reading a newspaper article, deciphering the warning on a medicine bottle, or writing a note to their child's teacher.[1] Illiteracy is a word we usually apply to adults, but the problem begins earlier. By early adolescence the future illiterates and functional illiterates (often defined as reading below 6th-grade level) of the adult statistics have already begun to diverge from the mainstream. They are the 13-year-olds who cannot read the social studies textbooks, the 6th-graders who cannot do their math homework because they cannot read the story problems, and the high-school freshmen who are chronically truant because they have lost all hope that they will be able to learn.[2]

It is significant that the opening chapter to the second edition has been retitled "Adolescent Literacy Today." The new title is symbolic of new and emerging definitions and frameworks for understanding literacy. It is also symbolic of an enlarged concern about the unmet literacy needs of our nation's 10- to 15-year-olds. The question today is not how many adolescents are at risk of illiteracy, but rather how many young adolescents will acquire adequate literacy skills.

It is not only the reconceptualization of terms that has implications for this second edition. Since we made our site visits and wrote about our findings, much has also changed in the national political context, as well as in schools and youth programs.

Children now represent the largest single age-group living in poverty, and immigrant children continue to swell the ranks of schools. Although educators and policymakers have turned increased attention to the needs of young adolescent learners, particularly the disadvantaged, it remains to be seen if this trend is only a passing fad or if the issue will be institutionalized as a permanent concern.

Some things remain constant. The values and standards that are characteristics of successful compensatory literacy programs have not changed. The case studies presented in this book continue to serve as beacons for those who are searching for ways to effectively address the literacy learning needs of disadvantaged youth. Through them we can learn much about the thoughtful process that goes into developing and honing good educational environments. The leaders in these programs skillfully balance academic goals and objectives with responsiveness to the joys and concerns of the young adolescent. The effect is sculptural beauty— one part engineering and one part aesthetic. The lessons to be learned from these examples are still, and will continue to be, valid. Thus, for the purposes of the second edition of *Adolescent Literacy: What Works and Why*, the case studies remain constant, but our discussion of the circumstances surrounding them has broadened and enlarged.

In the first edition we titled our concluding chapter "Policy Implications." We have titled the concluding chapter of the second edition "Translating What Works into Programs and Policies." The change in title here is also significant because experience has reshaped our recommendations in firmer form. In this chapter we discuss the findings of our study in light of the many changes that have occurred in the realm of educational policy and in light of the implications of shifting economic and political tides for the lives of young people, their families, teachers, and youth workers. Here we present an updated agenda for action that we believe will alleviate the serious conditions young adolescents struggle against in their attempts to develop their full potential as literacy learners.

Joan Lipsitz, who initiated the Project on Adolescent Literacy (now called the Youth Literacy Initiative) at the Center for Early Adolescence, "recontributed" a foreword for this edition. The second edition also contains a new resource list focusing on the practical needs of administrators, teachers, and youth workers. It is designed to provide answers to the questions What do I do next? Where do I go from here? How do I set about improving my program? We are fortunate that there has been a boom in publishing concerning issues related to literacy and young adolescents, and there are many excellent resources available that were not present at the time of the first edition.

In preparing this second edition we were filled again with admiration for the young people, teachers, youth workers, principals, and parents profiled in this book. We applaud their thoughtfulness, conviction, and accomplishments. They are the ones to whom we dedicate this work.

Notes

1. U.S. Department of Education, Clearinghouse on Adult Education, press release, June 1983, on file at the Center for Early Adolescence.

2. National Assessment of Educational Progress (NAEP), *The Reading Report Card: Progress toward Excellence in Our Schools; Trends in Reading over Four National Assessments 1971–1984,* Report no. 15-R-01 (Princeton: Educational Testing Service, 1985), 15–16, 20.

ADOLESCENT LITERACY

ADOLESCENT LITERACY TODAY

Becoming a fully proficient literacy user in a literate society is a complex and time-consuming task. Members of our society explore, practice, and consolidate critical literacy skills during the early adolescent years. Reading and writing become tools for inquiry, enjoyment, reflection, and solace. If this narrow window of opportunity is missed, it will be difficult, if not impossible, to attain this learning at a later point in life.

Many 10- to 15-year-olds are passing through the middle grades without obtaining the attitudes and skills that are essential for becoming proficient and adept literacy users. These are the 11-year-olds who cannot read the textbook, the 13-year-olds who cannot go beyond the information given in the textbook, and the 14-year-olds who do not know how to read and compare sources, take notes, or write a simple report based on original research. These young people may not have discovered that there are books written about subjects of interest to them or that one can escape deep into reading when tired, when seeking excitement, or when curious about a new subject. For them, writing is an unnatural and painful act undertaken only on request.

By and large, the majority of those who are not gaining these critical literacy skills and the positive attitudes toward literacy that accompany accomplishment are young adolescents living in poverty. Low literacy achievement is part of the web of problems economically disadvantaged youth face, and it is both a cause and a consequence of many other problems they encounter. This should be a matter of grave concern, given the recent drastic rise in the numbers of young people living in poverty.

Although the problem is worsening in many ways, there is also cause for hope: we know what works. From research and exemplary practice, we know much about the characteristics of a successful literacy curriculum and successful instruction for young adolescents. We know how to shape these ideas and techniques into

programs that young adolescents like and want to attend—
programs in which they learn the literacy skills they need.

We look to schools primarily, but also to community agencies
and the programs they support in the after-school and summer
hours, in order to provide special educational assistance to these
young people, who would otherwise fail. Schools and community
agencies have had varying degrees of interest and success in the
area of compensatory literacy services. Their difficulty in
responding to the special literacy needs of this age-group is closely
connected to a larger set of questions about the ways we envision
and organize young adolescents' educational experiences.

In 1985 the Center for Early Adolescence, through its Project
on Adolescent Literacy (PAL), began to investigate the special
needs of young adolescents who, because of their failure to gain the
levels of literacy achievement expected of their age or grade, were
in jeopardy of academic failure and of exposure to the subsequent
dangers attached to such failure. Project staff identified, studied,
and analyzed successful compensatory literacy programs sponsored
by schools or community agencies. We gleaned lessons that could
be shared with others—shared in the hopes that this information
could improve programs, could stimulate the development of new
and better literacy supports, and ultimately could improve the
futures of young people. This book reports the findings of that PAL
study conducted from 1985 to 1988.

This chapter provides background information for
understanding the problems and the solutions discussed in the
findings. The first section reviews the state of adolescent literacy,
the link between poor literacy achievement and poverty, and the
growing crisis the nation faces in this arena. The second section
discusses the nature of literacy, our expectations for young people's
literacy achievement, and ways to promote this achievement. The
third section examines the roles that schools and community
agencies have chosen to play in providing compensatory literacy
assistance to young adolescents.

Providing all young adolescents with the supports they need
to become fully literate in a highly literate society is a serious
challenge. In *Lives on the Boundary*, an autobiographical essay,
author and literacy specialist Mike Rose describes his struggle to

achieve those skills and the life he has spent assisting others to do the same:

> We are in the middle of an extraordinary social experiment: the attempt to provide education for all members of a vast pluralistic democracy. To have any prayer of success, we'll need many conceptual blessings: A philosophy of language and literacy that affirms the diverse sources of linguistic competence and deepens our understanding of the ways class and culture blind us to the richness of these sources. A perspective on failure that lays open the logic of error. An orientation toward the interaction of poverty and the ability that undercuts simple polarities, that enables us to see simultaneously the constraints poverty places on the play of the mind and the actual mind at play within these constraints.[1]

The educators, youth workers, young people, and parents profiled in this book have taken on that challenge and have been successful. Their examples can lead the way for others.

Section I. Adolescent Literacy: A Compelling Case for Compensatory Literacy Supports

The State of Adolescent Literacy

In 1988 the National Assessment of Educational Progress (NAEP) conducted a series of comprehensive assessments of young people's reading and writing achievement. The NAEP results demonstrated that 99.8 percent of 13-year-olds had acquired rudimentary reading skills and strategies, and 95.1 percent had attained the next level, basic skills and strategies. The 6 percent of students with only rudimentary or basic skills would undoubtedly face serious academic problems related to their reading deficits.[2]

Fifty-eight percent of 13-year-olds had obtained the intermediate level of reading skills and strategies. In other words, they were able to read articles written at the level of newspaper difficulty, search for and identify information correctly within a text, and elaborate somewhat on the information they had read. While having these reading skills may sound like a given, it is not. Many of the students reading at the intermediate level have difficulty with the texts and reading tasks assigned in the eighth grade. They do not have the skills to read complicated texts, either fiction or nonfiction, and they lack sensitivity to many features of the text—genre, form, and rhetorical features—that distinguish adept and advanced-level readers.

The 1988 NAEP showed reading achievement among young adolescents to be stronger than writing achievement. The test interpreters wrote:

> Levels of writing performance in 1988 appeared to be substantially the same as in 1974. Many students continued to perform at minimal levels on the NAEP writing assessment tasks, and relatively few performed at adequate or better levels.[3]

One of the characteristics of the transition young people are making during early adolescence is their growing ability to consider the long-term effects of their own strengths and weaknesses. Although young adolescents who do not read and write, or who read or write far below expectations for their grade level, may be unaware of their shortcomings or of the cumulative effect of those shortcomings, those who are aware begin to believe they will never be able to learn to read and write well enough to meet the responsibilities expected of adults in our society.

The Link between Literacy Achievement and Poverty

Although people with low levels of literacy can be found at any level in society, the problem is largely concentrated among the poor, in pockets of urban and rural poverty. The nation enjoys higher literacy rates than ever before, but literacy expectations are climbing. Not only is there a greater and more diverse population expected to become literate than in previous decades, but also the levels of literacy that are desired or needed have increased.

Without special assistance, youth in poverty will have the most difficulty meeting these rising expectations for reading and writing achievement. The 1988 NAEP data, as well as other studies, make this dramatically clear. "At all three grade levels assessed, there were large differences in reading proficiency according to socioeconomic status. Twelfth-grade students from disadvantaged urban schools performed, on average, below the level of eighth-grade students from advantaged urban schools."[4] The Children's Defense Fund reports in its 1990 annual report, "Poor teenagers are four times more likely than nonpoor teens to have below-average basic academic skills. According to data from the National Longitudinal Survey of Young Americans, more than half of the 15- to 18-year-olds from families with incomes below poverty had reading and math skills that placed them in the bottom 20 percent of all teens."[5]

Young adolescents living in poverty are more likely than other young people to lack grade-level literacy skills and, as a consequence, are more likely to be tracked into a less challenging academic sequence, to be held back a grade, and ultimately to drop out of school. Lack of literacy skills is not the only reason students drop out of school, but poor skills in reading and writing are inextricably linked with dropping out.

A traditional remedy for assisting students who are falling behind in their academic studies is to "track" them, to place groups of students of similar achievement levels in the same classes for the purpose of enhancing learning. Students who achieve are assigned to classes with other students who excel and enjoy reading and writing, and students who do not achieve are assigned to groups or classes with others who do not read or write well and who often do not like to read or write. Tracking, although originally conceived with young people's needs in mind, results in separate and unequal educational experiences, with lower-achieving students receiving less challenging and less meaningful instruction. Poor and minority students were more likely than affluent and white students to be placed in the lower academic tracks.[6]

Young people who are reading below grade level may also be held back a grade. Being retained one grade increases the risk of being a dropout later by 40 to 50 percent. Being held back for two years increases that risk to 90 percent.[7] The more difficult it becomes for students to achieve—or to believe they will achieve—in school, the more likely it is for them to decide to drop out.

Until recently, dropout statistics were compiled and reported only for high school students. Yet many students make the *decision* to drop out while they are still in the middle grades, long before they actually drop out.[8] The links between literacy problems in early adolescence and dropping out at a later age are only now just beginning to be realized.

Dropout rates among youth in poverty are far higher than among other students. The Children's Defense Fund reports:

> Among 16-year-olds who have lived at least half of their lives in poverty, four out of ten have repeated at least one grade— twice the repetition rate for 16-year-olds whose families have never lived in poverty. . . . Regardless of race, poor youth are almost three times more likely than their more well-off peers to drop out of school.[9]

Indeed, poverty seems to be a greater factor than race or ethnicity in the decision to drop out. In low-income neighborhoods, for instance, whites drop out at a higher rate than blacks. Nevertheless, because of the rapidly increasing minority youth population and the concentration of poverty in minority neighborhoods, minority students are those most at risk of dropping out.[10]

Given this situation, it is not surprising that statistics show discrepancies in the literacy skills of white and minority groups. According to the most recent NAEP data, despite significant gains during the 1980s, black students still score far below their white counterparts. Hispanic students' achievement also falls far below that of white students. *Hispanic Education: A Statistical Portrait* offers this interpretation of the NAEP reading scores for 8th-grade students:

> Only about one in five Hispanics (20.5%) and less than one in five Blacks (18.3%) scores at an advanced level, compared to 38.9% of Whites. About one-tenth of Whites (10.4%) score at a below-basic level, compared to one-fifth of Hispanics (21.0%) and nearly one-fourth of Blacks (23.6%).[11]

Dropping out is not the only problem associated with low levels of literacy skills. In a recent analysis of research on at-risk youth, Dryfoos confirms the hypothesis that many educators and youth-serving professionals have long held: academic failure is closely related to many dangerous and self-destructive youth behaviors. These include early sexual activity and teen pregnancy, smoking, alcohol and drug abuse, and juvenile delinquency. This study concludes that "enhancement of early schooling and prevention of school failure should receive high priority not only from those interested in lowering the dropout rate but also from those interested in preventing substance abuse, pregnancy, and delinquency."[12]

Unfortunately, the problems associated with low levels of literacy achievement in adolescence do not magically cease as young people mature. Throughout adulthood this problem will shackle the lives, energy, and potential of those who have not learned to read and write. The toll on the individual and on society is high. Of the more than 600,000 persons incarcerated in U.S. prisons, 60 percent lack adequate literacy skills. Two-thirds of these inmates have not finished high school; one-fourth have not finished elementary or junior high school.[13] Forty percent of adults whose annual incomes are less than $5,000 are functionally illiterate—in contrast to 8 percent of those whose annual incomes are above $15,000.[14] *Education Week* reported in 1984 that the Department of Labor had estimated that "up to 75 percent of the 8 million unemployed in 1982 lacked basic reading and writing skills needed to enable employers to train them."[15]

Moreover, illiteracy perpetuates itself among children born to parents with poor reading skills. Parents' reading levels have a strong positive correlation with the reading levels their children attain.[16] Of the 3.6 million children who began school in the fall of 1986, 10 percent have poorly educated or illiterate parents.[17] Without help, there is little chance that these children will succeed where their parents have failed.

The Growing Crisis the Nation Faces

More than 12.6 million U.S. youngsters—nearly 20 percent of all children under the age of 18—are poor. Thus one in five American children goes to bed hungry or sick or cold.[18]

The well-substantiated relationships among poverty, lack of literacy skills, and young people's future life outcomes should be cause for great alarm because the number of youths living in poverty is increasing rapidly. In 1989 *Education Week* reported, "Children are the poorest segment of the United States population, a position once held by the elderly."[19] Between 1979 and 1983 the number of poor children under six years of age increased by about 50 percent, and these young people are now entering their adolescence.[20]

The inner-city neighborhoods of our largest American cities have experienced extreme increases in poverty levels. In the nation's five largest cities—New York, Chicago, Los Angeles, Philadelphia, and Detroit—the plight of the poor is even more intense.[21] Cities are not the only places where poverty abounds; America's rural areas face a similar alarming increase in the numbers of poor. According to *Poverty in Rural America,* a 1987 report released by the Center on Budget and Policy Priorities, "Some 16.9 percent of rural Americans of all races had income levels below the poverty line, a rate almost as high as the 18.6 percent poverty rate in the central cities."[22]

Minorities, particularly blacks and Hispanics, are represented in disproportionate numbers in these statistics. Almost half (45.6 percent) of black children under 18 years of age are poor.[23] "Nearly two of every five Hispanic children live in poverty."[24]

Conspicuously missing from many current reports and discussions of youth, poverty, and education is mention of the plight of American Indian youth. Although Native Americans comprise only 0.8 percent of the population, as a group they fare far worse than many other ethnic minorities. "American Indians live at a poverty level double the national average."[25] On some reservations, unemployment rates are as high as 90 percent. Not surprisingly, low levels of literacy achievement, elevated school dropout rates, high levels of drug and alcohol abuse, and teen suicide are also prevalent among Indian youth.[26]

It is estimated that nearly 100,000 children under the age of 16 are homeless.[27] Some of these children are lodged in temporary shelters, both in urban and rural settings, but others sleep in abandoned buildings, cars, and public places. Regular school attendance is difficult, if not impossible, for these young people. One study demonstrated that almost 60 percent of the homeless children studied were reading below grade level.[28]

The growing body of our population living in poverty includes many young adolescents. Obtaining the strong literacy skills necessary for success in high school and beyond may be one of the many frills of adolescent life they will have to forego in the pursuit of the real basics: food, clothing, shelter, medical care, and employment.

The future outlook for these young people is grim. Over the next decade, business researchers predict that changing economic conditions will further decrease the number of jobs for workers with low-level literacy skills, while jobs for better educated workers will continue to increase.[29] The majority of today's workers encounter on a regular basis texts written at 9th–12th grade levels, and the amount of text and the level at which it is written will undoubtedly increase over time.

> Workers spend an average of one and one-half to two hours per workday engaged in reading forms, charts, graphs, manuals, computer terminals, and so on.[30]

Compounding the crisis the nation faces is the exponential increase of immigration. Beginning in the late 1960s and continuing through today, the United States is experiencing one of the largest migrations of immigrants in its history. Forced from their native countries by economic and political upheavals, millions have entered the United States seeking the promise of safety, employment, and an education for their children. The majority come from Mexico, Central and South America, the Caribbean, and Asia, and as many as 2.7 million of these new immigrants are school-aged.[31]

Although many young people are literate in their native languages, many of the young adolescent immigrants are not literate even in their own languages. Again, the poverty linkage is evident: if the immigrants were old enough to attend school in their own country, their families may have been too impoverished to send them to school, if schools existed. Less often, illiteracy occurred because their culture did not have a tradition of written literacy.

For the young immigrants to succeed in school and beyond, it is imperative that they learn to speak English, as well as read and write it at the same levels as their English-speaking peers. This has presented formidable challenges to American schools, most of which were unprepared for the rapid influx of new students. Educators, parents, and policymakers struggle with the question of how to provide equitable educational opportunities and retain cultural values.

Conclusion

Many of today's young adolescents face extraordinary pressures in their attempts to obtain adequate literacy. The special needs they present to educators and communities are dizzying in their variety and number. These needs require extraordinary responses to overcome the barriers these young people face. Clearly, there is a compelling case for the existence and growth of compensatory literacy programs for this age-group. The next section provides the background for understanding young adolescent literacy learners and the kinds of literacy learning supports that will make it possible for them to overcome the educational barriers before them and help them to achieve their goals.

Section II. Promoting Young Adolescents' Literacy Learning

If educators and youth workers are to help young adolescent literacy learners succeed, they need knowledge of three things: What is literacy? Who are young adolescent literacy learners? and What are the best ways to promote young adolescents' literacy development?

What Is Literacy?

> Literacy is the complex, dynamic, interactive, and developmental process of making meaning with text.[32]

Literacy has multiple origins. Its roots began thousands of years ago in different cultures around the world, and these roots have nourished each other in many ways—in India with the writers of Sanskrit, in China with the writers of characters, in Egypt with the advent of pictographic script, and in Phoenicia and Greece with the beginnings of a new alphabetic system. The history of writing systems is diverse and complex, calling into consideration the numerous personal and social functions that writing can serve for individuals, institutions, and society.

In today's literate world, people make and convey meaning with text in ways as diverse as reading the daily newspaper, answering a query on electronic mail, filling out an insurance form, or immersing oneself in a mystery book at the end of a hard day. From the perspective of proficient readers and writers, these tasks may seem effortless, but in truth, each of the components is complex, requiring the integration of many pieces of knowledge and information and guided by a strategic plan that is both purposeful and flexible.

Who Are Young Adolescent Literacy Learners?

Early adolescence represents a critical time in the development of the literate individual, as the young person hones important skills, learns new strategies, and becomes familiar with a range of conventions and shared cultural understandings related to our literate past, present, and future. Young adolescents, even in the most homogeneous circumstances, differ widely in the experience and knowledge they bring to literacy tasks. Despite these differences, there is also a core of common characteristics underlying their literacy development. Exploration of this common core reinforces the fact that the literacy learning required of young adolescents occurs in a context. For each individual young adolescent, that context is tempered and shaped by his or her own physical, cognitive, and socioemotional development. Early adolescence is a time of rapid, but not synchronous, growth in each of these areas. The rate of growth varies among, as well as within, individual young people.

Early adolescence is the only time in the human life cycle when the growth rate accelerates.[33] Because there is such a wide variation in the onset of this growth spurt, chronological age is sometimes a poor indicator of physical maturity. In one classroom, students of the same chronological age may easily differ as much as six to eight years in physical maturity.[34] During early adolescence, young people experience a number of physical changes that have an impact on their perceptions of themselves and others. One aspect of growth that is particularly important to young adolescents is the emergence of secondary sex characteristics, including breast development, growth of pubic hair, and enlargement of the testes. Accompanying these developments are those changes that mark the capacity for sexual reproduction: genital growth and first ejaculation in boys, and the onset of menstruation in girls.

Just as young adolescents differ when their physical growth spurts begin and end, their cognitive and linguistic development also varies greatly. Much less is known about the unfolding of their thinking than about their physical growth. More and more researchers are discovering evidence of a qualitative shift in thinking that occurs during early adolescence, but its manifestations seem as variable as the physical changes of the body: the shift can appear at different ages in different individuals, can occur in thinking related to some academic subjects and not to others, or may be promoted by socialization that is specific to particular cultural groups.[35] In other words, in any given classroom the students' cognitive and linguistic abilities will be as diverse as their relative levels of physical and emotional maturity.

The psychologists Jean Piaget and Lev Vygotsky, pioneers in the study of child development, both described the shift in cognitive abilities that tends to occur between childhood and adolescence. Their views of this shift differed in many respects, but both were convinced that a significant qualitative reorganization takes place. Piaget refers to it as the onset of "formal operational" thought; Vygotsky perceives it as the newly acquired ability to form "true concepts."[36]

One of the major changes linked to this shift in cognitive development is that young adolescents gain the ability to hypothesize. As they develop a richer and deeper sense of time—the past, the present, the future—they can use their expanded understanding to consider issues in a much broader context than younger children can. No longer bound by a linear concept of events, they are better able to relate their thoughts to the larger world around them.

Because of this new ability to hypothesize and predict, many young adolescents become concerned not only with "Who am I?" but also with "Who can I become?" During these years, they begin to define their interests and strengths, and some may begin apprenticeships in the fields they hope to enter. Future scientists may spend summers working as unpaid assistants in a laboratory. Young dancers, musicians, and artists may spend long hours perfecting their craft. Mechanically inclined young people may spend hours every day tinkering under the hood of a car or discussing gadgetry with other aficionados. Often these interests, so intensely pursued at this age, become a lifelong commitment.

Because of the dynamic relationship between thought and language, cognitive changes also have a direct bearing on linguistic development.

> The relation of thought to word is not a thing but a process, a continual movement back and forth from thought to word and from word to thought. In that process the relation of thought to word undergoes changes which themselves may be regarded as development in the functional sense. Thought is not merely expressed in words; it comes into existence through them.[37]

Just as cognitive stages have been studied and described, so have the related linguistic stages. Linguistic development in early adolescence is more complex than simply adding more words to a structure that has already been defined. The structure and complexity of language abilities are being shaped in crucial ways during this stage of life.

Young adolescents have the ability to increase their knowledge of vocabulary and concepts. Linguistic encounters have new depth: young people become aware that words have multiple meanings and that the ordering of words can change the meaning of a sentence. Relationships among words gain importance.

The ability to hypothesize means that young adolescents are also able to compare and integrate information from their own experiences and learning, and to make inferences based on that knowledge. They do this with new information in the subject areas (sometimes called "content areas"), such as social studies or science, but they also do it with language itself. That is, they become able to view language as an object that they can hold at arm's length, examine, describe, and play with, just as they do with other ideas. They enjoy analyzing the rules and regulations that affect words and their meanings.[38]

Having acquired new abilities to manipulate language, young adolescents respond with energy and enthusiasm to using language. Talk assumes a new importance—on the telephone, in groups of friends, by the lockers, after school, and in the classroom. A new understanding of the social implications that underlie speech affects how young adolescents talk and what they talk about. They may spend a great deal of time relating their encounters with friends, family, or teachers, often describing in great depth the scene, the gestures, and the words each person used. One important function of these narrative reviews is that they provide an opportunity for role playing, since the narrator assumes the roles of his or her interlocutors throughout the retelling. These detailed accounts also permit an intense scrutiny of motives.

Humor is an important element of linguistic competence, and anyone who works with young adolescents knows how they revel in their jokes. Early adolescence is also the time when a true sense of irony begins to appear.[39] Young adolescents are able to bring their new cognitive and linguistic awareness to bear on literature. Able to appreciate an author's construction of a story, they can also criticize the work from many levels.[40]

Physical, cognitive, and linguistic changes occur at the same time that young people experience social and emotional changes. "Am I normal?" is a question young adolescents frequently ask as their bodies change and as they observe the changing bodies of their friends and classmates. They also compare, contrast, and weigh their own morals and values, along with those of their parents, against those of their friends. Although still closely connected to home and family, their social world and responsibilities expand to include new friendships with peers as well as friendships or acquaintances with different kinds of adults: employers, youth workers, and teachers. During early adolescence, young people will develop increasing autonomy and responsibility for personal behavior and goals. Although eager to be independent, "like adults," young adolescents continue to seek reassurance from caring adults.

Because young adolescents in this society are growing, changing, thinking, and reflecting within a literate world, literacy— reading and writing—becomes an important tool in that process. For young adolescents, as for other age-groups, the purposes and outcomes of literacy cannot be separated from the developmental context that serves as a backdrop for their use.

What Are the Best Ways to Promote Young Adolescents' Literacy Learning?

Recent research and accounts of exemplary practice indicate that young adolescents need four things if they are to develop into proficient or adept literacy users. These are:

• Literacy instruction organized around a positive vision of literacy as a meaningful activity;

• Instruction that is responsive to their developmental needs;

• Instruction that is academically effective; and

• Access to the world of the written word.

A Vision for Literacy Instruction

The ways that we teach young adolescents, whether in formal or informal settings, are structured by assumptions. This is as true with reading and writing as it is with science, ballet, or mechanics. We develop assumptions from our own childhood or adolescent experiences with the subject, formal training, informal guidance, and the continuing reflective process of our own minds. The definition of literacy provided earlier in this chapter reflects the assumptions regarding literacy held by today's researchers and exemplary practitioners.[41]

If literacy is the complex, dynamic, interactive, and developmental process of making meaning with text, the structure of instructional activities should proceed around this assumption. Such a learning environment will, by necessity, focus on reading and writing as meaningful processes, will show an understanding of the process of the learner, and will demonstrate the dynamic interaction among various literacy skills. These are the very kinds of practices and approaches that have been validated to be most effective.

Underlying good practice is a thoughtful understanding of the beliefs and assumptions that guide instruction and curriculum. Even teachers who protest that they do not have a philosophy and that they "just do what works" are, in actuality, working from a structured philosophical base. Teacher educators and researchers place increasing weight on the importance of a teacher's understanding and explicating their assumptions.[42] These educators and researchers believe it is critical that those involved with the literacy education of young adolescents develop a positive philosophy of literacy as a meaningful activity.[43]

Developmentally Responsive Literacy Education

For 10- to 15-year-olds, as for younger and older people, the diverse functions of literacy that they encounter in school and in other environments cannot be separated from the developmental characteristics that are the fabric of their being. Thus, academically effective education—one that promotes exploration of the diverse functions of literacy—is also developmentally responsive education. The importance of developmental responsiveness as a key factor in successful school and out-of-school programs for youth has surfaced again and again in research conducted by the Center for Early Adolescence, leading Center staff to synthesize a framework for understanding the developmental needs of young adolescents.[44] This framework of adolescent developmental needs undergirds discussions of development throughout this book. According to this perspective, young adolescents need opportunities for:

1. *Competence and achievement.* Rapid and varied physical, cognitive, and emotional growth often causes young adolescents to feel self-conscious or unsure of themselves. Young people need opportunities to demonstrate their competence and realize that what they do is valued by others.

2. *Self-exploration and definition.* In early adolescence, just as young people develop new physical abilities, they also develop new cognitive and linguistic abilities. They need chances to flex their mental muscles and to explore the ways in which they may use these new capabilities in their future adult roles.

3. *Positive interaction with peers and adults.* As their new capabilities emerge, young adolescents' relationships with family and friends acquire new meaning, and new friendships with peers and adults are established. The rapid and sometimes uneven development that occurs at this time also makes young adolescents extremely vulnerable in their relationships. Therefore, a positive social network of peers and adults is essential for healthy development.

4. *Physical activity.* Because of their diversity in size, strength, and endurance, young adolescents need access to a variety of physical activities for daily exercise, as well as time to relax and reflect.

5. *Meaningful participation in school and community.* Growing in social and intellectual sophistication, young adolescents need opportunities for meaningful participation in their schools and communities that allows them to demonstrate their ability to assume responsibility, and to act upon their desire to serve others.

6. *Structure and clear limits.* Although young adolescents are able to make more decisions about their lives than are younger children, and are clearly capable of taking on more responsibility, they lack the adult sense of judgment that only experience can bring. To develop those decision-making skills, they need support, guidance, and clear limits set by caring adults.

7. *Diversity.* The wide variation in growth at this age is reflected in the incredible diversity of young adolescents' abilities, interests, and pursuits. Some will spend hours every day playing basketball; others may focus their attention on chess, talking with friends, or reading science fiction. Some favor quiet, independent activities, but others delight in social activities that bring them into contact with many kinds of people. Good environments for young adolescents allow for diversity.[45]

The developmental needs can be translated into effective literacy instruction in diverse ways. By helping young people to gain new reading and writing skills, young people gain a sense of efficacy, competence, and achievement. Individual reading periods, during which students read self-selected books from the school library, provide opportunities for self-exploration and definition as young people explore issues of great personal concern and interest. A workshop-like setting that integrates literacy activities ranging from individual writing to paired or small-group work and large-group discussion allows students greater freedom of movement than do class times that consist solely of teacher lectures.

Academically Effective Literacy Education

An academically effective literacy education is one in which students gain new reading and writing skills, making significant progress over time. In such programs, young people read and write frequently, undertaking progressively more difficult tasks and texts. Over time they develop a deeper reflective understanding of the processes involved in reading and writing.

In seeking to understand the research base for an academically effective literacy education, particularly for those with compensatory needs, one should pay special attention to three areas: (*a*) reading practices, (*b*) writing practices, and (*c*) assumptions about lower achievers. A review of the findings in these three areas not only demonstrates that we do know "what works" but also indicates that many young people do not have access to "what works."

Reading Practices

The International Reading Association (IRA) recently released an edited volume titled *Reading in the Middle School*.[46] The authors and articles presented in this volume represent a diverse yet consistent perspective on current effective practices in middle-grades reading. The practices they recommend support the viewpoint that reading is a meaningful process and one that must be taught with attention to the developmental concerns of young adolescents. Samples of the practices they advocate include:

- Teaching reading comprehension strategies essential for reading content-area materials;
- Teaching skills in context;
- Assisting students to learn how to monitor their own reading processes and to become active problem solvers as readers;
- Providing students with ample time every day for independent reading;
- Providing students with opportunities to use literacy as a tool to meet a broad range of personal, social, and curricular functions;
- Integrating reading and writing across the curriculum;
- Challenging *all* students to become reflective readers; and
- Assisting students to develop positive attitudes toward reading—do not ignore how young people feel about reading.

The items listed previously are examples of effective practices and are not meant to be inclusive of all effective practice. However, looking at even this small sample of recommendations, there is evidence that many of these suggestions are not being implemented in schools. For example, the 1988 NAEP data found that "at all three grade levels, approximately half the students reported reading ten or fewer pages each day for their schoolwork across all curriculum areas."[47] The same report found that only one-fourth of 8th-graders reported reading for pleasure on a daily basis.

An important recommendation of the IRA publication, and one that is echoed by many others in the field, is the need to teach middle-grades students how to read for meaning from increasingly complex subject-area texts. Unfortunately, researchers have found that few of the methods acknowledged as promoting these goals are being used in middle-grades classrooms.[48] Although teachers state that "word-level instruction ought to be replaced by text-level comprehension in the upper grades," observations demonstrate that this does not occur.[49]

In a study of the school lives of 12 middle-grades students attending three middle schools and the ways that reading was taught across the curriculum, Allington and his colleagues found the following:

> Most of the academic work required students to work alone, reading a text and responding to tasks that required them to simply locate or remember literate information from the text base. With the text in front of them these students performed a variety of tasks ranging from "copying out" text information to supplying missing words, selecting the appropriate multiple-choice response, spelling from memory, computing math problems, or answering teacher questions about the text. The students were as likely to read these texts aloud as silently. The texts read, which tended to be short, dominated the instructional tasks . . . the fragmentation of the curriculum was nearly complete, with rare evidence of instruction in one class being linked with another.[50]

Writing Practices

The identification of effective practices in the teaching of writing has also received close attention in recent reports, action research projects, and descriptions of exemplary practitioners.[51] Examples of the kinds of practices advocated by these authors include:

- Providing ample time for writing in the school day;
- Allowing students to write about self-selected topics;
- Focusing on the process of writing, not just the product;
- Teaching skills in context;
- Providing students with opportunities to write for real audiences and real purposes; and
- Showing students how writing can serve as a tool for inquiry in all curricular areas.

Many classrooms and teachers have embraced these methods. An example of the importance of these ideas and their influence is the vitality of the National Writing Project, a grass roots staff development project, which has trained and supported thousands of composition teachers across the nation to take risks and endorse new ideas.

The benefits of these effective practices, however, have not extended to all students, as the most recent NAEP data demonstrate. That 1988 study found that writing instruction in middle-grades schools is limited. Most students receive less than an hour a week, and that is restricted to standard assignments of one to two paragraphs. Fewer than half of the students surveyed received assignments to write analytic or interpretive themes, imaginative pieces, or to use writing as a tool for reflection in journals or learning logs.[52]

Assumptions about Low Achievers

To speak of the implementation of effective practices in general terms assumes that, once implemented, all students will receive the benefit from the practice in an equitable fashion. There is evidence, however, that classroom teachers teach good readers and poor readers differently. For example, starting from the first grade, the more competently the student reads, the more likely it is that he or she will be assigned silent reading and be monitored orally less often. One study of 600 reading-group sessions found that "low ability readers at the first-grade level read orally (round robin) during about 90 percent of the time allocated to the lesson, while high-ability first-graders read aloud about 40 percent of the time. By Grade 5, low-ability groups spent somewhat over 50 percent of the time reading aloud whereas high-ability groups averaged less than

20."[53] Although reading aloud may be an important learning strategy for beginning readers with rudimentary skills, round robin read-aloud sessions do not provide as much practice for students as sustained silent reading. Thus, at the upper-grade levels it appears that better readers are actually getting more practice time than the poorer readers.

Moreover, when teachers interrupt to correct good readers who are reading aloud, the corrections often refer to the meaning of the passage; for poor readers, the corrections often refer to pronunciation. The latent message to good readers is that reading is a meaningful activity; the message to poor readers is that reading is saying words correctly. It is not surprising that students in adult literacy programs, who are the former remedial students of our schools, often initially express deep concern about their oral reading skills and correct pronunciation and see success in those areas as the primary attribute of good readers.[54]

In a recent review, policy analyst Rexford Brown contends that assumptions about low-achieving students are powerful in shaping the form and content of both mainstream and compensatory programs.

> Three points about the assumptions undergirding compensatory education are especially important. First, the research overwhelmingly concentrates on the weaknesses of poor children; very little research has been done on their strengths. Second, these weaknesses are deficiencies in terms of the traditional organization and content of schooling. Very little thought has been given to the idea of changing schooling to accommodate new kinds of students; all the effort has gone to changing the students so that they will fit into the schools. In essence, what compensatory education tries to do is make poor children into middle-class children in their experiences, attitudes, values, and performance. Third, the underlying assumptions about poor students' motivation, language, and conceptual development have militated against offering them a literacy of thoughtfulness and have favored a low-level, atomized, concrete, basic-skills curriculum. The language of that curriculum has been so simplified that it is both boring and artificial. It has been stripped of richness and context and made fundamentally meaningless, which is to say

unabsorbable by normal people, except through memorization, whose effects last only for a few hours or days.[55]

Access to the World of the Written Word

One of the most accurate predictors of reading achievement is the amount of time young people actually spend reading. Young people who read more read better. Better readers are likely to visit the public library regularly and read frequently for pleasure.[56]

Excellent classroom, school, and public library collections are important resources for supporting reading habits. Strong fiction and nonfiction collections encourage young people to turn to literacy as an essential tool for learning, from reading for pleasure and gathering information to exploring new curriculum topics and investigating questions of concern.

The American Association of School Librarians has a saying, "two to maintain and three to build." This means that school libraries should be purchasing two books per student per year to maintain their collections, and to build collections they should purchase three books per student per year. Few school libraries meet this standard. A national survey of junior high school libraries revealed that the national mean for school library book expenditures is $6.09 per student per year. Although some states spend more (North Dakota spends $13.64 per student per year) and some spend much less (Washington, D.C., spends $1.97 per student per year), there is no state, given the high price of trade books, that can boast of an adequate budget that will allow them to meet these standards.[57]

Limited budget conditions over long periods of time cause library collections to become dated.

> The average school library is adding less than one-half book per student each year. Assuming that this number has been added each year for the past 10 years, a school with 500 students would have purchased about 2,500 books. There may be 10,000 books in the library, but many of the 7,500 books purchased over 10 years ago may be of little value to students.[58]

Such conditions cause damage to both fiction and nonfiction collections. Recognizing the need for up-to-date reference materials and the necessity for materials that will support current curriculum, school librarians may place more of their small resources toward the purchase of books that meet those purposes. Consequently, fiction sections in junior high libraries may look alarmingly dated despite the recent explosion in publishing for young adults.[59] Without books and other materials on topics of interest to young adolescents, it will be difficult to support independent reading programs.

Not surprisingly, researchers find that student reading in school is often limited to the textbook and other commercial materials. Richard Allington found, "The most striking aspect of the experiences of students in middle school is the frequent reliance on work sheets and textbooks to teach."[60]

The lack of access to diverse and interesting materials is particularly devastating to students from disadvantaged circumstances. Unlike their more advantaged counterparts, they may not have other materials to read at home and their neighborhoods may be isolated from public libraries and bookstores. Thus, they rely heavily on school to provide them with access.

Conclusion

Young adolescents develop reading and writing skills best in environments that organize literacy instruction around positive definitions of literacy, provide instruction that takes into account the complex developmental characteristics of the age-group, implement what works in literacy instruction in equitable fashion, and provide young people with access to the world of the written word. While all young adolescents can benefit from more and better literacy learning supports, there is indisputable evidence that there are many young adolescents in desperate need of intensive compensatory literacy services. It is imperative that these special services provide them with "more and better" rather than "separate and unequal."

Section III. Schools and Community Agencies:
Their Roles in Providing Compensatory Literacy Assistance
for Young Adolescents

There are large numbers of 10- to 15-year-olds who are falling between the cracks because they are failing to gain the reading and writing skills they will need for the future. However, knowledge is available of the kinds of practices, materials, and experiences that will allow these young people to succeed. While schools are central to literacy instruction at the middle grades, community agencies (such as public libraries, after-school and summer recreation programs, religious programs, and many others) also play important roles. Community agency programs can be instrumental in motivating young people to read and write, enriching the skills and understandings they already possess, and providing assistance to young people who need special help. In the next section, what is known about school-based compensatory literacy programs is examined, and the important, but often invisible, role that community agencies have played in supporting young people's literacy development is discussed.

School-Based Compensatory Literacy Programs for Young Adolescents

The notion of compensatory literacy programming presumes that acknowledged literacy standards are not being met. Today's compensatory literacy programs are based on a standard of literacy far beyond that required a century ago, when signing one's name was ample proof of literacy achievement. As standards of literacy performance have risen, so, too, has the need for supports that will aid young people in meeting these new standards. In conjunction with rising standards, over the last several decades the nation has also opened educational opportunities to many who were previously barred from participation. Furthermore, the rising tide of immigrants has brought many students who need special assistance into the school systems. Thus, a 20 percent high-school graduation rate that was acceptable 50 years ago is unacceptable as a high school dropout rate today. Schools are at the heart of efforts to provide compensatory literacy programs.

In the majority of schools, compensatory assistance is provided by special programs rather than by schoolwide approaches. Recent studies conducted by the Center for Research on Effective Schooling for Disadvantaged Students (CDS) provide detailed information on the organization of these approaches.

> The most common remedial activities are to assign students extra work or homework (in 56% of the schools that contain 8th-graders), to provide a pull-out program in reading or English (50%), after- or before-school coaching classes (46%), peer tutoring (45%), pull-out programs in math (43%), and summer school (41%). Schools are less likely to offer students adult tutors to work with them one-on-one (35% in math, 34% in English) or an extra subject period in lieu of an elective or exploratory course (17%), and rarely offer remediation through mentoring programs (6%) or Saturday classes (3%).[61]

The CDS analysis indicates that pull-out programs, peer-tutoring, and before- or after-school coaching are effective ways of increasing reading achievement, but to date the gains are modest and much could be done to increase the positive effects of programs that employ these methods.[62]

The largest school-based compensatory literacy program is the federally funded Chapter 1 program, which serves thousands of children. National reviews of Chapter 1 disclose that "while Chapter 1 had been effective in raising the achievement of the disadvantaged students it served, it had not been effective in closing the gap between Chapter 1 students and their more advantaged counterparts."[63] Even more discouraging for those who work with young adolescents is the news that "Chapter 1 itself has few effects beyond the third grade."[64]

Researchers have also examined the overarching administrative and curricular relationships among regular classroom and compensatory classroom and the instructional practices in compensatory classrooms. Their findings suggest the need for improvement in this area. For instance, they found that school administrators often make decisions about compensatory education programs based on scheduling and eligibility rather than on the effectiveness of the program itself. Often there is little collaboration between the classroom and the special program, and little effort is made to ensure that the two present a consistent reading philosophy to the student.[65]

Although practice is necessary to become adept at any new skill, students in remedial classes actually read very little. When they do read, they are generally given words in isolation or short passages taken out of context.[66] Hence these students seldom have the chance to read stories that develop character, plot, or setting in exciting or varied ways, nor are they exposed to nonfiction writing of quality and depth. It is no wonder that many lack a basic understanding of the purposes and functions of literacy. These kinds of reading tasks are assigned from textbooks and workbooks and do not provide young people with opportunities to pursue trade books, magazines, and other print formats.

Overlapping general compensatory literacy programs in schools are the special supports provided to young adolescents who are second-language learners. Much of this strand of compensatory literacy support also comes from federally funded programs through the Bilingual Education Act.

Like other compensatory programs, those for second-language learners face controversy from conflicting political agendas, expectations, and the diverse needs and perspectives of participants and providers. For instance, should the purpose of these programs be to move children into English as soon as possible or should educators build initial literacy learning on the foundation of the first language? How far should schools go in providing special support to second-language learners? If students can converse fluently, is that enough, or is more needed? What is the best way to teach English to students in a school where forty different language groups are represented? What is different about second-language instruction for young children and for young adolescents? Where does one draw the line between young people's educational needs and the demands of immigration officials to identify, report, and return illegal aliens? These are only some of the legal, ethical, and research questions facing the field, making second-language learning one of the biggest "hot potato" issues in education.[67]

Community Agencies: The Unacknowledged Educators

For over a century, community agencies—providing services to youth in the after-school and summer hours and sometimes even during school hours—have played an important but generally unacknowledged role in the compensatory literacy arena. Unlike schools, with their clearly defined mission to provide formal education, community agencies providing nonformal education are staggeringly diverse in their missions, resources, the roles they select to fill, and the communities with which they interact. These players include public libraries, settlement houses, religious institutions, churches, national youth organizations such as Boy Scouts and Girl Scouts, comprehensive social service organizations, newspapers, and many more. As literacy supporters, these organizations have provided young people with motivation, enriched young people's reading skills, reached out to make readers and writers of young people whom schools have failed, provided access to books and other materials, and advocated rights and services that would make it possible for young people to obtain an education. Whereas schools have tended to focus on the mastery of clearly defined content areas, community agencies have tailored their educational approaches to young people's immediate needs or problems.

One of the earliest organized attempts at providing compensatory literacy education in out-of-school settings occurred in the Sunday schools of the 1800s. Originally designed to bring the Bible into the lives of working children of industrial England and America on their one day off, the Sunday schools also provided literacy instruction. Settlement houses, first established in the U.S. in the 1860s, also promoted early adolescent literacy learning. They developed lending libraries and reading clubs, conducted classes, and provided homework assistance. As advocates, they helped immigrant parents and students make sense of the U.S. school system, pressured schools for better services, and even took policy roles. For example, Jane Addams, founder of Hull House in Chicago, served on the local school board.[68]

Not all literacy support was tied to the neighborhood, however. For instance, city and regional newspaper clubs played a role as out-of-school literacy supports for some young people with few other resources. Popular across America during the late 1800s and early 1900s, they enrolled large numbers of young people, providing them with reading, writing, and artistic opportunities. The Junior Birdmen, aviation clubs sponsored by the Hearst chain of papers, at one time registered over 500,000 members. Other clubs included the Junior Journal Club sponsored by the *Minneapolis Journal,* The Little Mother's Club in the *Minneapolis Tribune,* The Wide-Awake Club of the *Daily News* of Chicago, and the Cousins Club of the *Washington Post.*[69]

Since the 1960s, national youth organizations such as Boy Scouts of America, Girl Scouts, Camp Fire, Inc., YMCA, and YWCA have struggled to reach out to a broader audience, seeking to include a greater number of minority and disadvantaged children in their programming.[70] A consequence of this drive for a more diverse membership has been an increasing awareness and concern about the reading and writing needs of young people. Youth organizations have responded to these needs in different ways. Girl Scouts recently introduced a literacy program for all levels of scouts, designed to involve members in reading and writing activities, as well as develop an awareness of the importance of literacy in their lives and provide opportunities for young people to learn about and reflect on the reasons that others might not have developed these skills. Boy Scouts and 4–H have taken another tactic by developing special easy-to-read, interesting curriculum materials designed to develop reading skills in the context of teaching skills and ideas of interest to young people.[71]

Research conducted by the Center for Early Adolescence demonstrates the many important ways community agencies continue to support and enrich young people's literacy development and how these agencies provide compensatory literacy supports.[72] For instance, they provide enrichment experiences and life-skill classes that deepen young adolescents' formal educational experiences. Through art, drama, and other offerings, young people use their communication skills to convey ideas. Trips to the public library provide access to books. Homework helper programs, SAT preparation classes, and tutoring programs assist young people with special educational needs. Youth workers, counselors, and program directors often serve as advocates at school for young people and their families, identifying students with potential or needs, translating school values to immigrant families, and pressuring schools to provide needed services.

Little explicit research has been done regarding the role community agencies have played in providing support for compensatory literacy needs. Little information exists on the number of programs, the number of young adolescents served, and the organization, staffing, and efficacy of these programs. By including a look at community agencies' role in compensatory literacy programming, this study represents a new step in understanding and defining the field.

Conclusions

Young adolescents' unmet literacy needs should be a matter of serious concern to us all. Many young adolescents are caught in a dangerous whirlpool of social and political conditions that threaten to pull them under; solid literacy skills are critical. Intensive compensatory literacy supports are essential for these young people.

Many young adolescents in this country face serious reading and writing problems that are connected to many other problems they face: poverty, crime, drug and alcohol abuse, and high teenage pregnancy rates. Many young adolescents are not able to keep up with the increased and varied literacy demands of the middle grades, and reading and writing instruction in the middle grades is not meeting their needs. The disparity between the need for instruction and the continuing lack of instruction exacerbates the situation.

Fortunately, we are knowledgeable of what works in helping young adolescents with reading and writing needs to succeed. Successful literacy learning environments are powered by a positive vision of literacy; they are responsive to young people's swiftly changing moods and diverse needs; they are academically challenging; and they provide 10- to 15-year-olds with access to the world of the written word through books, magazines, posters, computers, and many other formats. These are the general principles behind successful literacy practice, but how do these ideas manifest themselves in the real schools and programs with real kids? Understanding this question is the purpose behind the study that became this book. *Adolescent Literacy: What Works and Why* shares the lessons that we learned from our visits to a variety of exemplary literacy programs. Whether they operate during the school day, after school, or during the summer, these programs are distinguished by their success in helping their students improve their reading and writing skills and by their ability to foster their students' return to the mainstream of school life.

The next chapter, "Methodology" describes the way the Center for Early Adolescence translated these principles into guidelines for our research study of successful compensatory literacy programs. In this chapter the search for programs is also discussed and the protocol used on site visits is included. The several chapters following "Methodology" profile school and community compensatory literacy programs that have put these principles to work. In the chapter titled "What Works and Why" the findings are reviewed and common themes, concerns, and strategies for success are pulled together. The final chapter, "Translating What Works into Programs and Policies," is an unabashed call for action. This section gives recommendations for ways that administrators, policymakers, and others can work to make it possible for programs like the ones described in this book to flourish.

It is on a note of hope that we continue our work to help teachers, parents, youth workers, and others combat the problem of adolescent illiteracy and to learn, from what is being done, what is effective and why.

Notes

1. Mike Rose, *Lives on the Boundary: The Struggles and Achievements of America's Underprepared* (New York: The Free Press, 1989).

2. Ina V.S. Mullis and Lynn B. Jenkins, *The Reading Report Card, 1971–88: Trends from the Nation's Report Card* (Princeton, N.J.: National Assessment of Educational Progress, 1990).

3. Arthur N. Applebee, Judith A. Langer, Ina V.S. Mullis, and Lynn B. Jenkins, *The Writing Report Card, 1984–88: Findings from the Nation's Report Card* (Princeton, N.J.: National Assessment of Educational Progress, 1990), 6.

4. Judith A. Langer, Arthur N. Applebee, Ina V.S. Mullis, and Mary A. Foertsch, *Learning to Read in Our Nation's Schools: Instruction and*

Achievement in 1988 at Grades 4, 8, and 12 (Princeton, N.J.: National Assessment of Educational Progress, 1990), 7.

5. Children's Defense Fund, *A Vision for America's Future: An Agenda for the 1990s: A Children's Defense Budget* (Washington, D.C.: Children's Defense Fund, 1989), 69.

6. Jeannie Oakes, *Keeping Track: How Schools Structure Inequality* (New Haven, Conn.: Yale University Press, 1985).

7. Dale Mann, "Can We Help Dropouts? Thinking about the Undoable," *Teachers College Record* 87 (1986): 307–23.

8. Anne Wheelock and Gayle Dorman, *Before It's Too Late: Dropout Prevention in the Middle Grades* (Carrboro, N.C.: Center for Early Adolescence, University of North Carolina at Chapel Hill; Boston: Massachusetts Advocacy Center, 1988).

9. Children's Defense Fund, *A Vision for America's Future*, 69–70.

10. Jerold M. Starr, "American Youth in the 1980s," *Youth and Society* 17 (June 1986): 323–45.

11. Denise De La Rosa and Carlyle E. Maw, *Hispanic Education: A Statistical Portrait 1990* (Washington, D.C.: National Council of La Raza, 1990), 27.

12. Joy G. Dryfoos, *Adolescents at Risk: Prevalence and Prevention* (New York: Oxford University Press, 1990), 110.

13. "The Main Basic Skills Programs: An Introduction," *Business Council for Effective Literacy: A Newsletter for the Business Community* 1 (September 1984): 8.

14. Stanley N. Wellborn, "Ahead: A Nation of Illiterates?" *U.S. News and World Report* (May 17, 1982): 53–56.

15. Thomas Toch, "America's Quest for Universal Literacy," in "Cracking the Code: Language, Schooling, Literacy," *Education Week* (September 1984): 5.

16. Mullis and Jenkins, *The Reading Report Card, 1971–88.*

17. David Fleming, "Challenge from the Inner City," *Youth Policy* 8, no. 6 (June 1986): 3.

18. Sally Reed and R. Craig Sautter, "Children of Poverty: The Status of 12 Million Young Americans," *Phi Delta Kappan* 90, no. 10 (June 1990): K3.

19. "Children in Poverty," *Education Week* (1 November 1989): 3.

20. National Center for Children in Poverty, *Five Million Children: A Statistical Profile of Our Poorest Young Citizens* (New York: National Center for Children in Poverty, Columbia University, 1990), 16.

21. William Julius Wilson, *The Truly Disadvantaged: The Inner City, the Underclass, and Public Policy* (Chicago: University of Chicago Press, 1987), 46.

Mark Alan Hughes, *Poverty in Cities* (Washington, D.C.: National League of Cities, 1989).

22. Kathryn H. Porter, *Poverty in Rural America: A National Overview* (Washington, D.C.: Center on Budget and Policy Priorities, 1989).

23. "Economic Disparity Gap between Blacks and Whites Widens: Blacks Share Less of Economic Growth," *American Family* 12, no. 1 (January 1989): 20.

24. De La Rosa and Maw, *Hispanic Education*, 13.

25. Liz Schevtchuk Armstrong, "Census Confirms Remarkable Shifts in Ethnic Makeup," *Education Week* (20 March 1991): 1, 16.

26. Ellen L. Beckerman, "Who Put the Bureaucracy in the Bureau: Federal Involvement in Indian Education," *Future Choices* 1, no. 2 (Fall 1989): 8.

27. Lisa Klee Mihaly, *Homeless Families: Failed Policies and Young Victims* (Washington, D.C.: Children's Defense Fund, 1991).

28. "Homeless Children in School," *Aware* (Virginia Department for Children) 13, no. 9 (December 1989): 4.

29. William B. Johnston and Arnold H. Packer, *Workforce 2000: Work and Workers for the Twenty-first Century* (Indianapolis: Hudson Institute, 1987).

30. Carol Nasworthy and Magdalena Rood, *Bridging the Gap between Business and Education: Reconciling Expectations for Student Achievement*, Critical Issues in Student Achievement, no. 4 (Austin, Tex.: Southwest Educational Development Laboratory, 1990), 11.

31. Joan McCarty First and John Willshire Carrera, *New Voices: Immigrant Students in U.S. Public Schools* (Boston: National Coalition of Advocates for Students, 1988), 5–13.

32. Judith Davidson and Robin Pulver, *Literacy Assessment for the Middle Grades: User's Manual* (Carrboro, N.C.: Center for Early Adolescence, University of North Carolina at Chapel Hill, 1991), 13.

33. J.M. Tanner, *Foetus into Man: Physical Growth from Conception to Maturity* (Cambridge, Mass.: Harvard University Press, 1978), 6–7.

34. Gayle Dorman, Dick Geldof, and Bill Scarborough, *Living with 10-to 15-Year-Olds: A Parent Education Curriculum*, 2d ed. (Carrboro, N.C.: Center for Early Adolescence, University of North Carolina at Chapel Hill, 1984).

35. Howard Gardner, *Developmental Psychology: An Introduction*, 2d ed. (Boston: Little, Brown, 1982), 518.

36. Howard E. Gruber and J. Jacques Voneche, eds., *The Essential Piaget* (New York: Basic Books, 1977).
L.S. Vygotsky, *Thought and Language* (Cambridge, Mass.: MIT Press, 1962).

37. Vygotsky, *Thought and Language*, 125.

38. Paula Menyuk, *Language and Maturation* (Cambridge, Mass.: MIT Press, 1977), 97–149; Elisabeth H. Wiig and Wayne Secord, "Linguistic Competence in Early Adolescents with Learning Disabilities: Assessing and Developing Strategies for Learning and Socialization," in *Early Adolescent Transitions*, ed. Melvin D. Levine and Elizabeth R. McAnarney (Lexington, Mass.: Lexington Books, 1988), 209–26.

39. Gardner, *Developmental Psychology*, 429–31.

40. Arthur N. Applebee, *The Child's Concept of Story: Ages Two to Seventeen* (Chicago: University of Chicago Press, 1978).

41. P. David Pearson, "Broad Trends in Reading Research during the 1980s," *Encyclopedia of Educational Research* (1992).
James Flood et al., eds., *Handbook of Research on Teaching the English Language Arts* (New York: Macmillan, 1991).

42. Jerome C. Harste and Carolyn L. Burke, "A New Hypothesis for Reading Teacher Research: Both Teaching and Learning of Reading Are Theoretically Based," in *Reading: Theory, Research, Practice*, ed. P. David Pearson and Jane Hansen (Clemson, S.C.: National Reading Conference, 1977), 32–40.
Gerald G. Duffy, ed., *Reading in the Middle School*, 2d ed. (Newark, Del.: International Reading Association, 1990).

43. Davidson and Pulver, *Literacy Assessment for the Middle Grades*.

44. Joan Lipsitz, *Successful Schools for Young Adolescents* (New Brunswick, N.J.: Transaction Books, 1984).
Leah M. Lefstein and Joan Lipsitz, *3:00 to 6:00 P.M.: Programs for Young Adolescents*, 2d ed. (Carrboro, N.C.: Center for Early Adolescence, University of North Carolina at Chapel Hill, 1986).
Gayle Dorman, *Improving Middle-Grade Schools: A Framework for Action* (Carrboro, N.C.: Center for Early Adolescence, University of North Carolina at Chapel Hill, 1987).

45. Gayle Dorman, *Middle Grades Assessment Program: User's Manual*, 2d ed. (Carrboro, N.C.: Center for Early Adolescence, University of North Carolina at Chapel Hill, 1984).

46. Duffy, *Reading in the Middle School*, 37.

47. Langer et al., *Learning to Read in Our Nation's Schools*, 18.

48. Dolores Durkin, "What Classroom Observations Reveal about Reading Comprehension Instruction," *Reading Research Quarterly* 14 (1978–79): 526.

49. Jana Mason and Jean Osborn, *When Do Children Begin "Reading to Learn"? A Survey of Classroom Reading Instruction Practices in Grades Two through Five*, Technical Report no. 261 (Champaign, Ill.: Center for the Study of Reading, University of Illinois at Urbana-Champaign, 1982).

50. Richard L. Allington, "What Have We Done in the Middle?" in *Reading in the Middle School*, ed. Gerald G. Duffy, 2d ed. (Newark, Del.: International Reading Association, 1990), 34–35.

51. See, for example, Nancie Atwell, ed., *Coming to Know: Writing to Learn in the Intermediate Grades* (Portsmouth, N.H.: Heinemann, 1990); Nancie Atwell, *In the Middle: Writing, Reading, and Learning with Adolescents* (Portsmouth, N.H.: Heinemann, 1987); Lucy McCormick Calkins, *The Art of Teaching Writing* (Portsmouth, N.H.: Heinemann, 1986); Jane Hansen, *When Writers Read* (Portsmouth, N.H.: Heinemann, 1987); Thomas Newkirk and Nancie Atwell, eds., *Understanding Writing: Ways of Observing, Learning, and Teaching K–8*, 2d ed. (Portsmouth, N.H.: Heinemann, 1988); Sondra Perl and Nancy Wilson, *Through Teachers' Eyes: Portraits of Writing Teachers at Work* (Portsmouth, N.H.: Heinemann, 1986).

52. Arthur N. Applebee, Judith A. Langer, Lynn B. Jenkins, Ina V.S. Mullis, and Mary A. Foertsch, *Learning to Write in Our Nation's Schools: Instruction and Achievement in 1988 at Grades 4, 8, and 12* (Princeton, N.J.: National Assessment of Educational Progress, 1990).

53. Richard L. Allington, "Amount and Mode of Contextual Reading as a Function of Reading Group Membership" (paper presented at the National Council of Teachers of English, Washington, D.C., 1982), cited in Richard C. Anderson et al., *Becoming a Nation of Readers: The Report of the Commission on Reading* (Washington, D.C.: National Institute of Education, 1984), 52.

54. Richard L. Allington, "Teacher Interruption Behaviors during Primary-Grade Oral Reading," *Journal of Educational Psychology* 72 (1980): 371–77.

55. Rexford G. Brown, *Schools of Thought: How the Politics of Literacy Shape Thinking in the Classroom* (San Francisco.: Jossey-Bass, 1991), 139–40.

56. Richard Anderson et al., *Becoming a Nation of Readers.*

Barbara Heyns, *Summer Learning and the Effects of Schooling* (New York: Academic Press, 1978).

Arthur N. Applebee, Judith A. Langer, and Ina V.S. Mullis, *Who Reads Best?: Factors Related to Reading Achievement in Grades 3, 7, and 11* (Princeton, N.J.: National Assessment of Educational Progress, 1988).

57. Howard D. White, "School Library Collections and Services: Ranking the States, " *School Library Media Quarterly* 19, no. 1 (Fall 1990): 13–26.

58. Jack W. Humphrey, "Do We Provide Children Enough Books to Read?" *The Reading Teacher* 44, no. 2 (October 1990): 94.

59. Linda Cornwell, Director of Reading Excitement and Paperback Project and consultant, Indiana State Department of Education, telephone conversation with author, June 1991.

60. Allington, "What Have We Done in the Middle?" 33.

61. Douglas J. MacIver, "Helping Students Who Fall Behind: Remedial Activities in the Middle Grades," CDS Report no. 22 (Baltimore: Center for Research on Effective Schooling for Disadvantaged Students, Johns Hopkins University, 1991): 2.

62. MacIver, "Helping Students Who Fall Behind," 14.

63. Thomas W. Fagan and Camilla A. Heid, "Chapter 1 Program Improvement: Opportunity and Practice," *Phi Delta Kappan* 72 (1991): 583.

64. Robert E. Slavin, "Chapter 1: A Vision for the Next Quarter Century," *Phi Delta Kappan* 72 (1991): 587.

65. Richard L. Allington, "How Well Are the Remedial and Special Education Programs Working in Your School?" *School Administrator* 1 (1988): 33–34.

Richard L. Allington and Peter Johnston, "Coordination, Collaboration and Consistency: The Redesign of Compensatory and Special Education Interventions," in *Preventing School Failure: Effective Programs for Students at Risk,* ed. R. Slavin, N. Madden, and N. Karweit (Boston: Allyn & Bacon, 1989).

Arthur A. Hyde and Donald R. Moore, "Reading Services and the Classification of Students in Two School Districts," *Journal of Reading Behavior* 20, no. 4 (1988): 301–38.

Brian Rowan and Larry F. Guthrie, *The Quality of Chapter 1 Instruction: Results from a Study of 24 Schools* (San Francisco: Far West Laboratory for Educational Research and Development, 1988).

66. Richard L. Allington, "If They Don't Read Much, How They Ever Gonna Get Good?" *Journal of Reading* 21 (1977): 57–61.

67. See, for example, "EPIC Events," newsletter of the English Plus Information Clearinghouse, 220 I Street, NE, Suite 220, Washington, DC 20002, (202) 544–0004; *Bilingual Education: A New Look at the Research Evidence*, Briefing Report to the Chairman, Committee on Education and Labor, House of Representatives, March 1987, GAO/PEMD-87-12/BR, U.S. General Accounting Office, P.O. Box 6015, Gaithersburg, MD 20877; Kenji Hakuta and Laurie J. Gould, "Synthesis of Research on Bilingual Education," *Educational Leadership* 44, no. 6 (March 1987): 38–45; James Crawford, "Bilingual Education: Language, Learning, and Politics," *Education Week* 1 April 1987.

68. Joseph F. Kett, *Rites of Passage: Adolescence in America—1790 to the Present* (New York: Basic Books, 1977).

Judith B. Erickson, expert on the history of American youth organizations, Indiana Youth Institute, conversation with author, 6 June 1991.

Robert A. Woods and Albert J. Kennedy, *The Settlement Horizon: A National Estimate* (New York: Russell Sage Foundation, 1922).

69. Judith B. Erickson, "Of Dicky Birds, Go-Hawks, and Junior Birdmen of America: Periodical-Sponsored Clubs for Children. Part I: Newspapers," (St. Paul: Center for Youth Development and Research, University of Minnesota, 1983, draft copy).

70. Judith B. Erickson, "Non-Formal Education in Organizations for American Youth," *Children Today* 15, no. 1 (January–February 1986): 17–25.

71. See, for example, Gail Smith Chesson and Ed Maxa, *River's Edge: A 4-H Environmental Science Adventure*, N.C. Agricultural Extension Service, P.O. Box 7606, Raleigh, NC 27695-7606; Milly Hawk Daniel and Martha Jo Dennison, *Right to Read: Contemporary Issues: Literacy*, Program Office, Girl Scouts of the U.S.A., 830 Third Avenue, New York, NY 10022; Nancy Cowles, *A Teacher's Guide for Environment Skill Book* (Irving, Tex.: Boy Scouts of America, 1980).

72. Lefstein and Lipsitz, *3:00 to 6:00 P.M.*

METHODOLOGY

The Project on Adolescent Literacy focused a wide lens on the problem of the adolescent's unmet literacy needs and how to solve it. PAL's goal was to find literacy programs that succeed in helping young adolescents, particularly those at risk of failure, master reading and writing skills. Because teaching and promoting literacy is a major function of schools, these institutions require careful consideration in any study of successful programs. However, the project's plans also included investigations into the contributions that after-school and summer programs—both school-based and community-based—make toward helping young adolescents attain the reading and writing competencies expected of their age and grade levels. From a nationwide study of general after-school programming for young adolescents conducted by the Center for Early Adolescence in 1982, researchers were aware of the enormous and valuable effect that after-school programs can have on young adolescents' development. Consequently, for the PAL study of literacy programs, staff were especially curious to discover how many and what kind of after-school literacy resources existed for young adolescents, and how young adolescents responded to literacy instruction outside school.

The Ground Rules

Much effort and thought went into the initial planning of the project and the establishment of the ground rules for the study. PAL staff read widely and deeply and discussed their ideas and findings with a number of experts. The first chapter of this book describes the background issues staff researched in order to develop the ground rules for identifying and studying successful compensatory literacy programs for young adolescents. The following are the simple, underlying principles:

1. Successful compensatory literacy programs for young adolescents are responsive to the developmental needs of young adolescents.
2. They are also academically effective.

At the time the study began PAL staff assumed that "vision"— a program's underlying philosophy and definition of literacy—was a part of a program's academic effectiveness. They also assumed that access to the printed word was an attribute of academic effectiveness. Although these two items—vision and access—were considered critically important, they were subsumed under the title "academic effectiveness" in the initial design of the project.

This chapter describes the ground rules and definitions under which PAL staff labored. It also provides information on the process and methods by which staff arrived at their conclusions.

Developmental Responsiveness

The literacy project built upon the existing base of research on young adolescents and their families, schools, and communities. As mentioned in the first chapter, one of the most significant findings that had emerged from the Center's studies of successful schools and after-school programs was the importance of attentiveness to the physical, socioemotional, and cognitive needs of the early adolescent age-group.[1] Thus PAL staff established that developmental responsiveness would be a key feature of any successful program that works with young adolescents. Staff adopted the seven developmental needs, described earlier, as their framework for studying responsiveness to young adolescents' developmental characteristics in the sites they would visit. These needs are:

1. Competence and achievement
2. Self-exploration and definition
3. Positive interaction with peers and adults
4. Physical activity
5. Meaningful participation in school and community
6. Structure and clear limits
7. Diversity

Successful programs for young adolescents—regardless of aim, focus, or content—attend to these developmental needs, using them as a guide for shaping the program's growth.

Academic Effectiveness

Successful literacy programs for young adolescents must demonstrate their responsiveness to these seven developmental needs, but they must also demonstrate an ability to assist young adolescents in achieving higher levels of literacy. To assess a program's success in meeting this second goal, PAL staff, with input from Center for Early Adolescence staff members and outside professional advisers, formulated the following threshold criteria for including a program in the study:

1. The program must have clearly defined goals, and evidence to show that those goals are being met.
2. Evidence of effectiveness must include one or more of the following:
   a. Measures of progress on standardized reading tests.
   b. Measures of progress in academic achievement on standardized tests in at least one subject area, such as social studies or science.
   c. Documentation that students are reading more.
   d. Powerful anecdotal evidence that goals are being met.
   e. Measures of progress on tests developed to evaluate the program's own stated goals (criterion-referenced tests).

Any one of these five latter criteria (2*a–e*) in isolation would be highly controversial. For example, some researchers are reluctant to rely exclusively on scores from standardized tests as a gauge of any program's success in fostering student achievement; others, by contrast, would consider anecdotal evidence (students' enthusiasm for books or success in specific subject areas) as too nebulous to be of any value. Taken as a group, however, the five criteria permitted PAL researchers to examine the complex dimensions of literacy assistance to young adolescents over a wide variety of promising programs. Using multiple measures is in keeping with a "portfolio" approach to evaluating programs, which is widely recommended by authorities on reading assessment.[2]

The advisers' reasons for recommending that PAL staff not accept or reject a program on the basis of any single criterion were solidly grounded in their own experience and research. For instance, some advisers strongly recommended that acceptable evidence of a program's success not be limited to that documented by standardized test scores. The wide amount of variance in such scores results in part from factors such as IQ, perseverance, and prior test experience; standardized tests often are not sensitive to the effects of instruction.[3] Effects must be very large before results are evident through standardized test scores.

Standardized tests have other limitations. Scores may be elevated by teachers who "teach to the test" or by noninstructional strategies used to ensure improved performance.[4] Or a student might, for example, obtain an artificially low score because of lack of experience with the content of a particular test passage.[5] Moreover, because they are composed of short, discrete passages, standardized reading tests do not measure ability to comprehend content from longer passages, such as those that students are commonly expected to read in a novel, a nonfiction book, or a textbook.[6] Students who are just beginning to gain reading fluency may be able to read the passage, but grasping the content with only a minimum of meaningful text on which to base their assumptions may prove too great a challenge.

By including progress in academic achievement (criterion 2*b*), PAL researchers wished to emphasize that a primary goal of reading instruction is developing the ability to read to gain knowledge about a variety of subjects.[7] If one looks only at reading scores, one cannot assess students' ability to perform in the subject areas. Hence the decision to seek evidence of academic achievement in at least one subject area, and to use results on standardized tests as a measure despite controversy about their adequacy.

PAL staff anticipated that some successful programs might be using unconventional approaches in nontraditional settings, which might not be fairly or usefully assessed by standardized tests designed to measure the results of traditional classroom reading instruction. For instance, after-school and summer literacy programs might use different models of instruction than those found in school programs, or their time frames, generally six or eight weeks as opposed to nine months, might skew standardized test results. Because of these limitations and the possibility that standardized test results simply might not be available from some highly successful settings, qualitative and anecdotal items (2*c* and 2*d*) were included on the list of criteria.

Advisers also suggested including item 2*e*, measures of progress on (criterion-referenced) tests developed to evaluate a particular program's stated goals. This permitted PAL staff to include in their research programs whose progress might not be revealed by standardized tests but was nevertheless demonstrable. As the study progressed, the necessity for two of these criteria, 2*c* and 2*d*, became increasingly apparent. "Documentation that students are reading more" and "powerful anecdotal evidence that goals are being met" were truly hallmarks that distinguished successful programs, with a comprehensive approach to the complex task of literacy learning, from merely effective programs, which focused (with success) on cultivating specific aspects of reading and writing.

Researchers found that some widely acclaimed programs, boasting high test scores, may address the skills needed to perform specific literacy tasks in one context but may ignore the variety of contexts in which students will need to exercise those skills. For instance, students who are carefully drilled in the decoding skills used on a certain test may perform well on that test but may not be able to transfer that decoding knowledge to literacy tasks outside the test format.[8]

Comprehensive programs, in contrast, help students improve their skills while providing them with a rich variety of experiences within different literacy contexts. It is these contexts that create the need to use literacy. Some of these contexts are mundane—reading a recipe, writing a telephone message, or filling out a job application. Others, however, are more esoteric—writing a novel, a play, or poetry. In programs that take a more comprehensive view of their mission, students see literacy as more than just getting the right answer or filling in blanks in workbooks. Instead, literacy is viewed as an intrinsically meaningful act of communication. The skills used in one literacy context are applied and integrated into other settings.

In search of the elusive evidence of a program's success, PAL researchers repeatedly asked themselves several straightforward questions: Are the students reading and writing? What are they reading and writing? Can they talk about the books they have read and describe the kinds of writing projects they have completed? Are the teachers instructing, not just managing or evaluating? Are the students learning, not just complying? One of the most important considerations was the "happiness quotient": How do the participants feel about the program?

The Students in the Programs: Defining "Compensatory"

The threshold criteria also defined eligibility for inclusion in the study in terms of the kinds of young adolescents that a program might serve—what specialists would call the program's "population." The programs considered for this study all serve young adolescents who are reading two or more years behind grade level, including the following three categories:

1. Severely disadvantaged students.
2. "Bilingual" students, who must approach English as a second language.
3. Students whose reading difficulties are not the result of physical or other exceptional limitations (see below).

The study does not include programs for students diagnosed as mildly mentally retarded, emotionally and behaviorally disturbed students, learning-disabled students, and students with specific handicapping conditions such as auditory, visual, and motor disorders.

The Case Study Approach

PAL researchers decided on the case study approach as the best method of presenting a full picture of how successful literacy programs respond to developmental needs while helping students to achieve improved academic skills. Indeed, the case study approach is perhaps the only method of capturing and describing the complex of factors that create the environments of successful literacy programs, from program philosophy, instructional techniques, and curriculum to the classroom climate, staff preparation and development, and the organization and administration of the school or agency sponsoring the program. The picture created from the case study approach allows educators and youth workers to "see" the programs described, so that a reading of the research findings can serve as a "field trip" for busy professionals and volunteers.

Selecting the Programs

Although PAL researchers would meet inspired, sensitive, and creative professionals and volunteers in visits to adolescent literacy programs across the nation, their main goal was to find successful programs, not outstanding individuals. Programs are made up of a group of instructors and administrators working together to create a shared reality of literacy curriculum and instruction. They replicate that reality through their practice; they transmit their vision to their students and immediate community. The existence of successful programs should prove that others can learn and replicate the elements that go into good literacy practice.

Identifying successful programs was a longer and more arduous process than had been anticipated. Staff sent thousands of recommendation forms to educators, youth workers, and policymakers, but only a few knew of programs to recommend. PAL project members also distributed recommendation forms at the annual conference of the International Reading Association, the country's largest gathering of reading professionals. They combed the literature on literacy, compensatory education, and effective schooling, seeking leads to successful programs. Despite these efforts, recommendations only trickled, rather than flowed, into the Center for Early Adolescence.

Thinking that libraries would be an excellent location for adolescent literacy programs, PAL staff engaged the help of the American Library Association, which contacted its membership about the existence of such programs. That search uncovered no adolescent literacy programs located in public libraries.

Upon receiving a completed recommendation form, PAL researchers sent a written questionnaire to the recommended program. Staff members reviewed each returned questionnaire to ascertain that the program met the threshold criteria and, if so, arranged a telephone interview with the program's director as the final verification of the match between the program and the threshold criteria for inclusion in the study.

A frequent reason for rejection was that the program simply didn't address the study's targeted age-group. Such recommendations were often accompanied by a note saying something to the effect that "this is a great program, and I am sure it could be adapted to work with young adolescents." It became apparent early on that there were far more services for younger children, older adolescents, and adults than there were for young adolescents.

The nationwide search ultimately netted fewer than 350 recommendations, and this number dwindled after the initial screening. Only 50 programs reached the stage of the telephone interview. From that number, staff chose 32 programs to visit: 17 in-school programs, 9 after-school programs, and 6 summer programs.

Visiting the Programs

The staff members who had developed the written and telephone questionnaires from the threshold criteria now carefully planned a comprehensive set of questions for researchers to ask in interviews at each program to be visited (the site visit protocol). These questions were designed to assess how effectively skills were taught, the functions of literacy in the program, the critical features of the program's literacy environment, the program's responsiveness to the young adolescent age-group, and the relative impact of those features on all program participants.

The questions fell into thirteen general categories:

1. *Delivery system.* Is the scope of the program school-based, district-based, community-based? Is instruction in reading provided in a remedial model or a developmental model?

2. *Population.* What special populations, if any, are targeted for reading instruction? What selection criteria are used to determine which students receive instruction? What ages and grades are served?

3. *Philosophy.* What are the program's theoretical assumptions about reading? What is the program's primary intent? Does the program address a wide range of personal and family problems as well as reading concerns?

4. *Development and administration.* What is the program's history? What level of commitment to the teaching of literacy skills is

evidenced by central administration? Is there strong leadership support or direction at the school level? What are the costs per pupil, budget, fees, and sources of funding?

5. *Classroom organization.* Is grouping heterogeneous or homogeneous? In other words, are students of the same reading level grouped together, or are groups composed of students with mixed reading levels? Are students grouped by chronological age? Are classes team-taught or taught by individual teachers?

6. *Instructional techniques.* What instructional methodologies are used? What strategies are used to overcome lack of prior knowledge? Does the instructional methodology offer students a variety of repetitions? Do teaching techniques stress transfer of skills to other areas? What role is given to concepts, interconnections among ideas, and inferences?

7. *The learning environment.* Is the environment respectful of human dignity? Is the environment sensitive to racial and cultural differences? Is the environment responsive to characteristics of early adolescent development? What are staff perceptions and expectations about students' reading?

8. *Materials.* Are the materials congruent with the stated philosophy and objectives of the program? Is there a rich, varied diet of materials and approaches, or one chosen text or method? Does the curriculum demand different kinds of activities from the students?

9. *Staff.* What categories of staff are involved in program implementation—speech therapists, psychologists, classroom teachers, volunteers, reading specialists? Are there institutional rewards for staff members?

10. *Assessment of reading problems.* Does the program attempt to define the origin of each student's reading problems?

11. *Population-specific questions.* (Examples here are given only for Limited English Proficiency [LEP] students, those who are learning to speak English as well as to read and write.) Where are these students placed? Is the goal flawless pronunciation, or comprehension? Is the program sensitive to culture-based behavior? Is the environment language-rich? Does the instructional methodology stress interactive language-learning strategies, or grammar and translation?

12. *Evaluation.* How does the program monitor student progress? What criteria, procedures, and staff does it use? In what ways do

evaluation techniques match the stated program objectives? For
what purposes is the resulting information used?

13. *Relationship to the community*. Is the program sensitive to the racial
and ethnic concerns of the community? To what extent are
parents involved in the program? Are community volunteers
involved?

As is apparent from the wording of the protocols, PAL staff
viewed "reading" as the central component of compensatory literacy
programs. This view, like others, was also to undergo transformation
over time and through experience.

After choosing the sites and developing the site visit
protocols, PAL researchers scheduled a one- or two-day visit at each
site. In almost all cases more than one PAL staff member took part
in the visit, thus ensuring a richer and more varied perception of
the program. After these first visits were completed, a handful of
promising programs were selected for repeat visits of four or five
days.

Reporting the Findings

This book, which the authors and the members of PAL's
advisory board have reviewed and reworked through several drafts,
serves as a final report of the study described above. It has been
written with the broadest possible audience in mind. Research for
the study revealed that among professionals in education there is
great frustration over solutions to the crisis in reading and writing
instruction and that many dedicated teachers and administrators
are eager for practical information that they can apply immediately
in their school situations. No less interested are various public
interest groups, including literacy councils, child advocacy
organizations, and public officials in whose care lie any number of
social responsibilities, from public instruction to social services to
cultural resources. Many of the youth workers in these agencies are
not education professionals but simply love to help young people.
Though aware of young adolescents' literacy needs, they lack
information on the specific things they can do to assist those who
need help. If they are made aware of the issues and viable
possibilities for improvement, they will certainly rise to the
challenge.

This book, then, seeks to review in a manageable and practical form, from its original conception to its results and their implications for all concerned, literacy programs for young adolescents that do work, that have been observed in operation, and that can be replicated or used as starting points for designing new programs. Except for the first chapter, discussion of theoretical literature is largely subordinated to the notes; the bibliography at the end of the book is comprehensive, containing material that is not mentioned specifically elsewhere. The annotated reading guide is designed to highlight publications of the most general usefulness for practitioners.

The authors have not attempted a review of legislation concerning compensatory education and related issues. Readers will soon observe that many of the school-based programs discussed in this book either began, or continue to operate, under Chapter 1 of the federal Education Consolidation and Improvement Act. Those who are interested in further information on legal authority for programs concerning minorities, especially Native Americans and resident aliens, should consult their local librarians and public officials with specific questions.

The aim of reaching a broad audience necessarily involved the authors in many doubts about suitable terminology. The "jargon" of specialized literature is in many cases necessitated by extremely important but very nuanced differences in meaning; on the other hand, some of the most ordinary terms have acquired a loaded sense that nonspecialists may not recognize. Most of these problems have been resolved with an eye toward the general reader; it is hoped that professionals will bear with a few enormities in the interest of airing the subject. Two sets of terms nevertheless deserve brief discussion here.

The first set involves the typology of the programs discussed. School-based and community-based programs are clearly mutually exclusive. After-school and summer programs can be either school-based or community-based. School-based programs that occur during the regular school day during regular term times have been referred to as "in-school" programs, to distinguish them from after-school and summer programs, sponsored by schools or otherwise. In-school programs that occur in the regular classroom, rather than in special classrooms or other out-of-classroom settings, are simply termed "classroom programs" (although they are sometimes called in-school programs in the professional literature).

The second set of terms includes the appropriate descriptors for programs that teach students for whom English is a new or second language. In standard journalistic reportage the most common term for these programs is "bilingual education." To the general public this term refers to any and all special programs for students whose first language is not English. Educators, however, draw strict distinctions between bilingual programs, in which subject area classes are taught in the students' primary language and students are gradually introduced to the English language, and English as a Second Language (ESL) or English for Speakers of Other Languages (ESOL) programs, whose primary focus is on teaching students to speak, read, and write English. The authors have tried to retain this distinction in terminology where appropriate, but in more general discussions "bilingual" may be assumed to refer to the issue as a whole.

Conclusions

Looking at the programs PAL researchers visited, the diversity of responses to the problems of adolescent compensatory literacy needs is striking—and encouraging. Even more exciting are the common themes that appear and reappear in each successful program, demonstrating that there is a common body of knowledge and practice that informs those who create and work in successful literacy programs for adolescents. The findings of this study prove that good literacy programs for young adolescents can make readers and writers out of students that school and community have despaired would ever learn.

Notes

1. Gayle Dorman, *Middle Grades Assessment Program: User's Manual,* 2d ed. (Carrboro, N.C.: Center for Early Adolescence, University of North Carolina at Chapel Hill, 1981).

Leah M. Lefstein and Joan Lipsitz, *3:00 to 6:00 P.M.: Programs for Young Adolescents,* 2d ed. (Carrboro, N.C.: Center for Early Adolescence, University of North Carolina at Chapel Hill, 1983).

2. See P.D. Pearson, "Assessment, Accountability, and Professional Prerogative," presidential address at the meeting of the National Reading Conference, Austin, Texas, December 1986; R.C. Anderson et al., *Becoming a Nation of Readers: The Report of the Commission on Reading* (Washington, D.C.: National Institute of Education, 1984); R. Farr and R.F. Carey, *Reading: What Can Be Measured?* 2d ed. (Newark, Del.: International Reading Association, 1986); P.H. Johnston, "Assessment in Reading," in *Handbook of Reading Research,* ed. P.D. Pearson (New York: Longman, 1984), 147–82; S. Valencia and P.D. Pearson, "Reading Assessment: Time for a Change," *The Reading Teacher* 40 (1987): 726–32.

3. See J.J. Tuinman, "Determining the Passage Dependency of Comprehension Questions in 5 Major Tests," *Reading Research Quarterly* 9 (1974): 206–23.

4. Farr and Carey, *Reading: What Can Be Measured?*

5. Mary Dupuis, professor of reading, Pennsylvania State University, telephone interview, 15 March 1985.

6. Anderson et al., *Becoming a Nation of Readers.*

7. Harold Singer, professor of reading, University of California-Riverside, personal interview, 31 January 1985.

8. Farr and Carey, *Reading: What Can Be Measured?*

THE KENOSHA MODEL:
ACADEMIC IMPROVEMENT THROUGH
LANGUAGE EXPERIENCE

The shades of the Washington Junior High School resource room are drawn, the lights turned off. It's Halloween, and six 8th-graders are seated around a circular table, in the middle of which a skull-shaped candle drips red wax. They are listening to a reading of "The Dead Man's Brains."[1]

Scott Cleveland, a teacher in the Kenosha Model: Academic Improvement through Language Experience, the Kenosha, Wisconsin, Chapter 1 program, begins.

"Once in this town there lived a man named Brown. It was years ago, on this night, that he was murdered out of spite. We have here his remains.

"First, let's feel his—"

He pauses and turns to the aide, Ellen Binninger, whose silhouette is framed in the closet doorway. "Would you bring the first specimen, please?"

Binninger emerges from the dark of the closet with a large grocery bag, which she holds near the students. They have been instructed to use their sense of touch—to reach unseeing into the bag, feel the contents, and determine which of Mr. Brown's parts it contains. The effectiveness of the preparation is evident; no one wants to reach into the bag. Finally Willie dares Richard, who, after much cajoling, reaches into the bag, withdrawing his arm suddenly, as though snakebitten.

"Oh, how gross!" he exclaims. Curiosity overwhelms the others, and each in turn cautiously, tentatively explores the bag's contents.

"Yuck, yuck."

"Ooooooh . . ."

"Intestines! It's his intestines."

"No, his brains."

"Yeah, that was his brains."

Cleveland continues the reading, "—brains. Now here are his—" He pauses again. "We have another part," he says diabolically, leering at the students with cocked eyebrow.

"I *hate* these kinds of stories," Jennifer moans as she volunteers quickly to touch first this go-round.

"What images go through your mind? What part are you feeling? Use your mind's eye," Cleveland guides.

"Green slime."

"It's moist. What did you do about the decay?"

"Do I have to touch?"

Willie runs his hand down Richard's spine as he reaches into the bag, causing a minor uproar as Richard leaps into the air.

"You're trying to make us regurgitate."

"Good word!" Cleveland observes, all the while jotting notes on a pad of paper.

"I've lost my appetite."

They progress through the story to similar cries of "Gross!" "Ooh, this stuff is sick!" "I'm not touching it!" Richard is clever enough to use his sense of smell and taste together after finding one mystery part sweet in both regards. He abandons that strategy quickly when the next item is not nearly so rewarding.

The items are revealed at the end of the story, and the offensive sample proves to be uncooked calf's liver. Other items confirm or disprove the students' hypotheses. Cooked spaghetti, a rib bone, ketchup, a peeled grape, an apricot, and a cut-up tomato account for all of Mr. Brown's parts, from his intestines to his eyes to his brains. Richard volunteers for the next class's experience, "Mr. Cleveland, they have real cows' eyes in the science room. Want me to go get some?"

The students are surprised in a follow-up discussion when Cleveland writes down all the vocabulary they generated during the activity: regurgitate, appetite, radical, mind's eye, tongue, waxy, flesh, moist, decaying, werewolf, guillotine. . . . It is a varied and sophisticated list, hardly the kinds of words typically expected of students in corrective reading classes.

Before the bell rings, Cleveland explains that they will use some of the words to write their own horror story the next day. The class is dismissed after solemnly promising not to tell any of the other classes what is in the bags.

Such lessons are typical of the kinds of experiences that are central to reading and writing instruction in the Kenosha Model. The program serves more than 1,400 students in grades K–12 (500 to 600 in grades 7–9) who are in need of supplementary literacy instruction. Students qualify for services by scoring at or below the 23rd percentile on the Iowa Tests of Basic Skills and by attending a school that has a high concentration of low-income families.

The coordinator and creator of the program is Thomas Zuhlke, who wrote the original proposal in 1965 and has served as the sole director since the program's inception. His responsibilities have since widened to include coordinating all of the district's programs that are supported by federal funding. His assistant in the Chapter 1 program is Marybeth VanLanduyt, the curriculum consultant, who sees to the day-to-day maintenance of the program.

Kenosha, a city of 77,500, nestles in the southeastern corner of Wisconsin on the shore of Lake Michigan, some sixty miles north of Chicago and thirty miles south of Milwaukee. The county is home to several major industries, including AMC Chrysler, Jockey Underwear, and Ocean Spray Cranberry, and three colleges, Gateway Technical Institute, Carthage College, and the University of Wisconsin-Parkside. Kenoshans by birth include the well-known author Irving Wallace and the actors Orson Welles and Daniel Travante.

An area of considerable natural beauty, Kenosha also presents a study in contrasts. The town is firmly entrenched in the highly industrialized region known disparagingly as the Rust Belt. Kenosha's unemployment rate is currently the highest in the state, except for the Indian reservations.[2] Official estimates range from 10 to 15 percent, but the actual figure may be closer to 25 percent. The American Motors plant, which once employed nearly 16,000 workers, now provides work for barely 5,500. Much of the labor previously done manually has been relegated to robots, and hand-welding is no longer necessary. A bar across from the plant offers a 20-percent discount on drinks to unemployed workers, and another down the street has happy "hour" from noon until seven o'clock.

Kenosha's downtown is dwindling. Sears is the only large department store in the city limits (the school system's administrative offices are housed in the former Montgomery Ward store), and the largest shopping mall is not doing well. There is great wealth in the area, but also extreme poverty. Many middle- and upper-class families have bought property in Kenosha but work in Illinois.

Although there are three colleges in the area, less than half of the population of some Kenoshan neighborhoods even finishes high school.[3] The community is ethnically diverse, with substantial numbers of first- to third-generation Germans, Poles, and Italians. A current 20-percent minority population of blacks and Hispanics is projected to reach 50 percent in the next fifteen years.

Wisconsin is attractive to low-income families because of its generous welfare program, and Kenosha is particularly convenient in its nearness to the Illinois border. Large numbers of people are migrating to Kenosha from Chicago, many from the inner-city housing project Cabrini Green. Many Hispanics have also settled in the area, having traveled north from Texas and Mexico, as well as from Puerto Rico. Sizable numbers of migrant workers have chosen to settle out of the migrant stream in Kenosha because of the presence of the United Migrant Opportunity Service, an agency that assists them in their transition to residential status.

These demographic factors have combined to produce a highly mobile and challenging school population. Wilson Elementary School represents the extreme; a school of 500 students, it had 250 transfers in and out last year. Zuhlke tells of a student who, when asked of his plans for the following day, replied, "I'm either going to move to my aunt's house [in Kenosha] or New Jersey." With children transferring in and out of schools, placement becomes problematic. Approximately one-fourth of the students are older than average for their grade level. Thirteen- and fourteen-year-old 6th-graders are becoming the rule rather than the exception, particularly in remedial programs.

Despite the students' mobility and past academic failures, the Kenosha Model is a highly successful and prospering Chapter 1 program. The program recognizes students' needs to feel competent and to achieve and builds an approach to reading and writing that responds to those needs. As Zuhlke characterizes the program's goal: "We have kids who are in the buzzards' reading group. We want to make bluebirds out of them."

Philosophy and Methodology

As Zuhlke and VanLanduyt freely admit, language experience, the basis of the Kenosha Model, "is not new nor was it created in this community."[4] Indeed the use of student-dictated texts as beginning reading material was recommended as early as the 1890s.[5] Language-experience stories have been used for reading readiness and beginning reading materials, as comprehension builders in social studies, science, and other classes, as supplementary reading and/or writing in language arts classes, and as a remedial technique for older students with reading problems.

Language experience typically consists of student involvement in an experience, after which the teacher encourages discussion. The teacher writes down what the students say, and this transcript subsequently becomes the reading material. A variety of instructional sequences and activities can follow to reinforce skills and strategies.[6]

The central belief of the Kenosha Model is stated in a quotation on the first page of its training manual: "Observation more than books, experience rather than persons, are the prime educators."[7] In this belief, the program creates successful experiences to arouse student curiosity. As Zuhlke puts it, the idea is "to lead students to learning, not force them."

The Kenosha Model consists of four instructional components: anticipation, participation, exploitation, and variation. To heighten anticipation, teachers encourage preliminary thinking, discussion, and enthusiasm about a new unit. Participation refers to the students' actual involvement with the experience. When the students make ice cream, they are directly involved; when a live turkey visits their classroom, they learn by observing; and when they participate in follow-up activities such as reading, creative writing, and watching filmstrips, they learn vicariously. Exploitation is the teacher's job: capitalizing on children's interests to help them learn, generating vocabulary about the experience, and creating follow-up activities that build on that experience and vocabulary.

Variation refers both to the diversity of activities within each unit and to the range of the unit offerings. As Zuhlke puts it, "What can be a language experience? Yes." For example, a unit on pineapples includes comparing aspects of the pineapple in discussion and writing, making a pineapple-shaped book, writing to a pineapple company in Honolulu, and growing a pineapple from the crown. The varied unit themes in the current training manual include "Communicate by CB Radio," "Making a Woodland Terrarium," "Visit a Newspaper Publisher," "Use Science Fiction to Stimulate Language," and "Silkscreening a T-Shirt."

Because it does not rely on a single textbook, the Kenosha Model does not tie itself to specific, individual subject areas. Instead the units are thematically unified and designed to enable the students to practice their listening, speaking, writing, and reading skills with plenty of teacher assistance, thereby boosting the basic skills so vital to their success in school. "The particular content is immaterial," explains Marvin Kellerman, the Chapter 1 teacher at Bain Elementary School. "It's simply a vehicle for learning."

Each unit begins with an experience that generates thought. The rationale is straightforward: what you think about, you can talk about; what you talk about, you can write about; what you write about, you can read about. Teachers create language experiences around students' current interests, following their lead whenever it seems profitable.

Kellerman is exceptionally effective in taking his cues for instruction from his students. During a transportation unit last year, one of his students became interested in rockets. The boy purchased a model rocket, assembled it, and launched it near the school. Unfortunately a breeze caught it and blew it on top of the school, where it caught fire, eliminating the possibility of further flights but not harming the building. The youngster was taken to the police station to deter him from future launches.

The following day, Kellerman's lesson focused on the class's newly found law-enforcement expert. Students talked about fingerprinting, handcuffs, and police cars, and eventually took a field trip to the station. Then the class returned to the transportation unit, which was now a rocket unit. Kellerman himself became so interested that he applied for the space shuttle program, reached the runner-up level in Wisconsin, and met the late Christa McAuliffe in the process.

Zuhlke and VanLanduyt point out specific advantages they see in the Kenosha Model: cultural fairness, personalization, an integrated and varied curriculum, and flexible instruction that capitalizes on teacher and student strengths. These advantages particularly suit the developmental needs of young adolescents, an age-group characterized by its extreme diversity. Young adolescents display not only a wide variation of normal physical development but also greatly differing rates at which they master cognitive skills like reading and writing.

Zuhlke, a second-generation German, explains the program's view: "The United States is not a melting pot. Different people look and act differently. Language experience allows students to write in their own words about their own background. We don't force textbook language on students." As young adolescents question what it means to be black or white, Polish or Italian, male or female, the Kenosha Model implicitly tells them they are unique in each of those contexts because their words and experiences are valued. The program provides the foundation for students to build a positive sense of self-worth.

One 8th-grader's poem showed just how important that self-respect can be:

Kids

I feel sorry for kids
Who have dads that neglect them,
                    beat them,
And who are sad . . .

For, I have a dad
That makes me feel real bad . . .
He screams and yells at me
For I don't know what.

Deep down, (for if I was to die),
I know there would be
A tear in his eye.

Sometimes I feel
Like puttin' it all away
And having not to wake up
Another day . . .
But that's the coward's way
For I say . . .
I did not lose a dad—

> He just lost a son
> He could be proud of.
>
> FOR . . . I AM GLAD FOR THE KIDS
> WHO LOVE THEIR DAD.

The Kenosha Model nurtures students' existing strengths. Introductory discussions draw from students what they already know about the topic. Early activities aim at providing students with tangible experiences, so that they have something about which to generate language. Students know that their contributions are valued when the words they suggest are added to the class vocabulary chart, their interests become units of instruction, and their writings are published. Though teaching that remedies "deficits" may result in students' improving in areas of weakness, it can also result in dismal drudgery and failure as they labor unsuccessfully day after day. By appealing to strengths, teachers capture and hold students' interest. They foster daily success and an interest in language that carries over into broader language learning.

Teaching to young adolescents' strengths is especially appropriate because these students' self-esteem rests on uneasy ground as they adjust to the physical changes of their bodies, their new relationships with peers, and their self-conscious awareness of others' attitudes toward them. Doing something well and receiving recognition for it bolsters feelings of competence and confidence.

Zuhlke observes, "If all our kids did was feel good during the time that they're with us, that would be worth something." But the Kenosha Model does much more than that. It helps students take giant strides toward literacy.

Curriculum and Instruction

Middle-grades literacy programs must address the needs of a broad range of young adolescent learners, from those who are beginning readers and writers to those at more advanced levels of mastery. Many students achieve basic competency but falter when they are asked to contend with the more complex literacy demands of the middle grades: reading for science and social studies classes, making inferences and generalizations, or writing reports. The

Kenosha Model meets this challenge by teaching literacy skills and strategies in the context of learning new concepts and content.

Gloria Peterson, a Chapter 1 teacher at Wilson Elementary School, demonstrates the effectiveness of such an approach. She envisions her curriculum structure as a pyramid, built with a wide base of active student involvement supporting abstract and vicarious experiences in writing, reading, and skills instruction. For instance, for a unit on frogs, frog memorabilia and student work cover the classroom walls, bulletin boards, and partitions. Peterson, her aides, and the students have gathered materials and books, both fiction and nonfiction, on frogs and related themes. The classroom library provides interesting reading material of varying difficulty about frogs. Class assignments range from watching and reporting on developing tadpoles to researching and writing about frogs. Read-alouds, filmstrips, and class outings provide students with common experiences and a shared text and vocabulary. Special materials and activities appeal to a variety of young adolescents' interests and abilities.

The Kenosha Model staff has found that integrating skills instruction with the unit materials and activities is a successful way to teach middle-grades students. In Peterson's classes, vocabulary instruction is used to expand students' personal word stores and their conceptual understanding of the subject. For example, in a study on hands, students work in small groups to list words and expressions that include the word "hand": "handy," "hand-me-down," "I've got to hand it to you."

In another vocabulary exercise, individual students underline unfamiliar words in a group-generated list. Then, rather than copy the dictionary definition, they work with Peterson, their classmates, and the aides to create a personal definition. The task removes any fear of failure engendered by working alone. The structure of this simple activity allows young adolescents to interact with adults on a meaningful task, to contribute to the success of their peers, and to experience success with what could otherwise be a difficult task.

Researchers have noted how seldom middle-grades students are taught how to comprehend a text's meaning if they have difficulties.[8] Kenosha Model teachers are well aware of their students' lack of comprehension strategies. Lynn Rutter, a Chapter 1 teacher at Lincoln Junior High School, pairs each reading or writing activity with a comprehension strategy to be introduced or practiced. For example, in a language-experience unit on illiteracy, students practice skimming and scanning a *Milwaukee Journal* article on functional illiteracy, taking notes on a literacy videotape, and highlighting a *Woman's Day* article, "Illiteracy: Read All About It." The activities are even more effective developmentally and instructionally because the class uses typical adult reading materials.

Because Rutter is aware that good test-taking skills are essential to survival in the modern junior high school, she prepares her students carefully. In teaching test-taking skills, for example, she begins the lesson by asking students to role-play their test-day behaviors. Then, as a group, they list all the useful strategies they can recall. Working as a group distributes responsibility for the answer and prevents any one student from feeling inept. The students next scan a one-page handout of strategies for other ideas to add to the class list. By the end of the lesson the board is full of ideas, and the class has discussed when and how to employ each strategy. The lesson expands their repertoire of test-taking skills while implicitly telling them their own ideas are important and valued by the teacher. The students have been collectively responsible for the bulk of their learning.

Young adolescents in the middle grades begin to make many crucial schooling decisions that may greatly affect their future success. They may decide which school to attend, whether or not to skip certain classes, or whether to continue to take a reading class. Rutter recognizes her students' need and ability to participate in the decisions that affect their schooling. Consequently, in planning each year's work, she sits down with students individually, to discuss personal strengths and weaknesses, where the student stands in relation to peers, possible reasons for past performance, and how they can improve the situation together in the coming school year.

Kenosha Model teachers recognize that young adolescents with literacy needs are often unaware of resources in the school. Kellerman connects his students with a variety of other adults who can help them explore their own interests and grow intellectually. Mary Norris, the school librarian, is one such ally. She uses her talent as a professional storyteller to excite students about reading and add spice to language experiences. Book-sharing sessions are a regular part of visits to the library, and Norris makes a point to talk to the Chapter 1 students about her own reading interests and habits. She makes notes of the books the students choose and keeps in touch with Kellerman so she can recommend supplemental reading.

Reading and writing instruction are integrated in the Kenosha Model. Through writing about shared experiences and using that writing as the first reading text on a new subject, students are quickly involved in their own learning. The concepts and vocabulary that students have generated create a springboard for further exploration of the topic. From reading their own writing and the works of their friends, they progress to reading works written by others. In the Kenosha Model writing reinforces reading, and reading in turn reinforces writing.

This integrated approach is especially suited to students with literacy problems. Writing enables them to work at their own levels of ability. They choose words, syntax, and organization according to their understanding of those aspects of language. In the Kenosha Model students are not penalized for using colloquialisms or language particular to their cultural or regional backgrounds; moreover, they select their own writing topics within a given unit. The personal meaning of the activities often helps middle-grades students overcome their now all-too-common dislike of reading and writing.

Mary Swanson, a Chapter 1 teacher at Bullen Junior High School, involves her young adolescent students in demanding but exciting writing workshops. In these sessions students get both support and criticism from peers and adults because Swanson encourages them to question their own and others' work, and to ask for help from whomever will assist. The "upgrade technique" is one method she employs to help students rework their initial drafts. Students choose three or more words from their writing and replace them with better descriptions or more active verbs. "Left" might become "fled" or "slinked off."

Swanson has not found it difficult to motivate her students to write. In fact, her classes write five-chapter novels each autumn. Those who do not care for the quantity of writing still enjoy illustrating their novels and sewing cloth covers to protect them, and everyone seems to enjoy giving the novels to relatives as Christmas gifts.

Thanks to VanLanduyt's guidance, the variety and forms of student writing in the Kenosha Model are truly astounding. VanLanduyt, who has training in art, urban education, and curriculum and instruction, is quick to see the book possibilities in any subject or material. In the lobby of the Chapter 1 office stand greeting card racks filled to overflowing with student publications. Students have made books from cereal boxes, paper bags, paper plates, greeting cards, calendars, restaurant placemats, and old book covers. They have constructed their books with letter shapes when learning initial consonants, with a window in the cover to show a picture on the title page, with a pocket in every page, and with a hole to fit over a doorknob. The varied book forms have stimulated a wide range of writing by furnishing new angles to old assignments.

Poetry becomes a fresh experience for students when they can write about a personal mishap or illness and publish the piece in a Band-Aid container. A collection of short poems published in a Sucrets box has this label on the lid: "Dedicated to all who have ever had a LOUSY cold." Stacey submitted the following acrostic:

> I can't S ee
> I wa N t a Kleenex, please.
> Red E yes
> R E d nose
> Z - z - z - z - z - z
> Go to sl E ep please

Daryl contributed another:

> C over your mouth!
> O bey your mother.
> U nderstand the reasons.
> G etting the advice.
> H elping me get well.

"Often the idea is just to make books not look like books," VanLanduyt explains. "In a sense we've given permission for teachers to make writing fun."

Making books also serves as a powerful stimulus to motivate young adolescents to do research. One such project started when VanLanduyt returned from a trip with restaurant placemats decorated with a map of North Carolina. A group of students became interested in the state's tourist attractions—Old Salem, Kitty Hawk, Roanoke Island, and other historic sites—and she encouraged them to find out more on their own. The information they gained from their further research now fills books they have written; the placemats, folded, fit nicely as attractive covers.

Student-authored books, concrete examples of the value and productivity of the program, have served as a bridge between the Chapter 1 classroom and students' homes. The mother of one student who recently entered the program says, "Jeremy loves Chapter 1. He tells me about the book he's making all the time. He's so excited this year." Ernan, an 8th-grader in Swanson's class, wrote an autobiography last year. It still sits on the coffee table in his living room, where it is proudly displayed for visitors.

Staff Development

Adherence to a philosophy and methodology is what unifies the Kenosha Model. The program requires accountability to its central ideas:

1. All children can learn, even the ones currently having or causing difficulties.
2. Everyone needs to be actively involved in students' learning—parents, teachers, administrators, and the students themselves.
3. Language should be taught as it is used, as a form of communication.
4. Students can only write about what they know.
5. Students know best what they experience most directly and completely.

Zuhlke manages the hiring process and looks for creativity, enthusiasm, and commitment in new teachers. "They should not be committed to orthodoxy," he says. "We want people who are open to new ideas, people who are creative implementers." He also looks for people committed to the language-experience approach.

Much of creative instruction lies in the ability to make a new combination of old ideas or discover a different approach to a standard lesson. Creative instruction involves borrowing from multiple sources, rearranging, juxtaposing, experimenting. The

Kenosha Model fosters creativity by encouraging regular and frequent training and communication among its teachers.

The monthly Breakfast Club is one of the many ways the Kenosha Model keeps lines of communication open among staff in the various Chapter 1 resource rooms. Representatives elected by their peers from each phase of the program—kindergarten, elementary, secondary, math, and teachers of students from the migrant worker population, plus one aide from each of the elementary and secondary levels—attend these meetings to discuss how Chapter 1 is functioning. Each serves as a liaison, reporting back to the other Chapter 1 staff in the school.

"We hold all our Chapter 1 meetings in an open forum," Zuhlke explains. "People are free to speak their minds. Staffs will grow if they feel freedom. It's the best way to keep a lid on problems, which inevitably come up in a complicated business like teaching. If we can't defend something, we'd better revise it."

In addition to the Breakfast Club meetings of staff representatives, the Kenosha Model holds weekly leadership staff meetings and quarterly sectional (kindergarten, math, elementary, and secondary) meetings. The program also offers one-day orientations for new teachers, a "buddy system," support visits and demonstration lessons from VanLanduyt and Zuhlke, teacher and aide swaps, and an opportunity for each teacher to attend one state conference per year with financial support from the program. VanLanduyt publishes a monthly listing of resources, activities, and opportunities that she circulates to all teachers. She also edits the Chapter 1 newsletter *One-to-One* and sends "goodies in the mail," materials for teachers to try out in their classrooms as they see fit. Each teacher has a copy of the most recent *Kaleidoscope*, a collection of classroom-proven language-experience plans.[9]

VanLanduyt is the primary channel of support to teachers, offering in-classroom training, workshops, and materials. She would like to visit classrooms frequently, but she admits, "I can't be involved directly as often as I would like." One way she extends communication and support is through the Chapter 1 newsletter. Circulated to Chapter 1 teachers and their principals, the superintendent, the district parent representatives, and community leaders, the newsletter offers an avenue of publication for students, informs teachers about what is working in other classrooms, and keeps outsiders informed about the Kenosha Model.

Two particularly effective ways the Kenosha Model prevents teacher isolation are the buddy system and the swap program. The buddy system offers new teachers the wisdom and benefit of veterans' experiences, but the veterans seem to gain from the relationship as well. Kellerman often meets with his partner, Shirley Spence, after school for an hour or two. They meet more often in the fall term and before special occasions such as the Children's Fair. Kellerman enjoys being Spence's mentor: "With a program like this, it's overwhelming at first—grouping, testing, scheduling, planning themes, keeping up with the reading club, motivating students, understanding the rationale. Explaining to someone how you're doing it is neat. It's teaching." Rutter, who spent a year as Cleveland's buddy, speaks of mutual benefits: "Scott's typical of the new people: he's very bright, but implementation was initially difficult for him. I tried to share ideas and learn from him, too. We honor the knowledge of new people, and they honor our experience in return."

Teacher and aide swaps are encouraged by the program. Often new teachers choose to observe a veteran buddy, but any teacher is free to arrange a two-hour time block with another. The first hour of the visitation is designed for observation, the second for questions and answers. VanLanduyt also asks teachers having difficulties with some aspect of the program to visit the room of a teacher who is strong in that skill. By taking advantage of the twice-daily planning periods, the experienced aides (one or two per class), and VanLanduyt's substituting, the program gives teachers a simple, inexpensive, unthreatening opportunity for professional growth and problem solving.

Zuhlke believes the swap system benefits the program in other ways as well: "The idea is to walk in another person's moccasins. The high school teachers feel, 'No one's seen the trouble I've seen,' until they visit the extended-day kindergarten. It gives everyone a better understanding of the total program." The program itself benefits from this support and managerial system by involving several people in staff development and problem solving. VanLanduyt remains available as consultant to a staff of more than forty, but many issues are resolved by other experienced hands.

In the Kenosha Model, opportunities to learn from other teachers as well as outside professionals are not limited to the staff alone. BASICS, a Chapter 1 conference, and the Children's Fair involve staff and parents in learning about new methods and approaches in effective literacy practice. BASICS is a locally organized annual conference for Kenosha Chapter 1 staff and parents. The acronym stands for the ideals and goals of the conference:

B elieve in education
A ssist others in learning experiences
S timulate curiosity
I ncrease participation
C reate a positive environment
S hare dreams

Speakers present information on topics ranging from family wellness, job retraining, and active participation in parent-teacher conferences to language-experience demonstrations, the impact of technology in classrooms, and projections for state and federal funding. A keynote speaker gives the conference a focus each year; in 1984 the address was delivered by Dr. Emeral Crosby, principal of Detroit's Northern High School and a member of the National Commission on Excellence in Education.

At the Children's Fair, an annual Chapter 1 celebration attended by students, parents, teachers, and other local people involved in education, students' publications are on show, student volunteers read from their work, and teachers present awards such as the 100-Minute Reading Club certificates. Each Chapter 1 room has its own display booth, as do many of the community agencies involved in education. Cleveland notes, "It's a chance for us all to blow our own horns, and to see how others are managing the language experience. And we hear directly from parents and students what they think of the program."

Administration

Classroom teachers are the reason VanLanduyt prefers to call the Kenosha Model a "send-in, not a pull-out, program. We solicit classroom teachers' cooperation and referral, and then we keep up communication." Although the program operates from the first day of school, serving students of the previous year who still require supplemental instruction, Chapter 1 teachers spend much of their initial few weeks perusing cumulative records and talking with classroom teachers in order to locate new students.

The regular classroom teachers must give permission for students to attend the Kenosha Model's Chapter 1 resource room three to five times per week during their study halls or other class time. Requiring teachers' approval is rarely problematic. "Teachers by and large feel Chapter 1 is worthwhile enough to let students go to the resource room for the least intrusive amount of time," says Zuhlke.

Once classroom teachers have approved the placement, they are asked to complete an observation form, ranking the student's performance from 1 (low) to 6 (high) in ten different categories including social, reading, and writing skills. This procedure is repeated at the end of the school year, without reference to the first assessment, so classroom teachers can see for themselves the value of the program. (Sample statistics are given in the Evaluation section, below.)

During the course of the year, Kenosha Model teachers meet with the regular classroom teachers to discuss the students' progress reports. Junior-high students receive no grades in Chapter 1; instead, their resource teachers give them a written commentary on their work. Classroom teachers may choose to include Chapter 1 performance in their own grading schemes.

Chapter 1 teachers maintain ties with the regular classroom teachers in other ways as well. They negotiate and clarify class requirements for their students, assist them with homework and assignment difficulties during Chapter 1 study halls, coordinate instruction with other teachers when feasible, and even offer training sessions in the Kenosha Model methods for the classroom teachers at each school. "We don't see our teachers as aides to the content area teachers," Zuhlke concludes, "but they do work together. Our goal, after all, is regular classroom achievement."

Facilitative leadership undergirds the entire Kenosha Model support system. "You have to include people in the decisions that affect them," VanLanduyt explains. Open-forum meetings allow support staff, aides, and teachers to speak their minds and have an equal vote. Parents hold a majority vote in the program's guiding councils. Students can choose their topics and responses for writing. Classroom teachers permit placement in the program and suggest students' instructional needs. The result is universal, self-sustaining "ownership" of the program.

Parent Involvement

A noted researcher in education has recently remarked that "one of the main things public schools have done throughout this century has been to try to distance themselves from parents. They're only slowly coming to realize that parents and the relations between parents are strong resources that they can use."[10] In contrast, the Kenosha Model actively involves parents at the program level in the District Advisory Council, the school level in the School Advisory Councils, and the classroom level in a variety of ways, including volunteerism, observation, and participation in conferences. The program even provides leadership training for parents elected to the representative councils.

The School Advisory Councils (SACs) meet at least four times a year at each resource center. Each SAC elects eight parent leaders, who form the actual council. They identify school problems, suggest program improvements, assist in gathering other parents for meetings, and establish the agenda. Two of the parent leaders, elected by the parent group as a whole, represent the school at the monthly District Advisory Council (DAC) meetings. Parents form the majority voting membership on the DAC, which also includes district administrative staff and community members. DAC representatives serve on all needs-assessment and evaluation committees (as do SAC members), decide funding issues, and approve substantive program decisions. When funding was cut, a parent vote kept the high school Chapter 1 component.

Wilma Johnson, who has served a two-year appointment to chair the DAC, began her involvement as a classroom volunteer when her own children were in the program and has become one of the program's staunchest supporters. "If I had anything to do with it," she says, "I'd have all the children in Chapter 1. The kids get more attention. They don't get a spelling test; instead they use the words to write." Johnson has represented the parents at state meetings ("We usually carry a couple of busloads of parents"), helps plan BASICS, and works tirelessly at involving parents and showing them the voice they can have. She estimates that some 200 parents attend the BASICS conference, and about 20 gather for each DAC and SAC meeting.

Johnson says she is thankful for the ideas the program provides for parents to promote learning at home: taking children shopping, letting them help cook, reading the newspaper, reading aloud with children, discussing the news or what happened at school. "We're actually psyching them out," she says, "fooling them into learning."

Parents have been involved districtwide in volunteer projects. They helped plan the yellow school bus float for Chapter 1's entry in Kenosha's Fourth of July parade. When Dorothy Lewandoski, a Chapter 1 teacher at Durham Elementary School, obtained free tickets to the Milwaukee Ballet, parents chaperoned. For many it was their first trip to the performing arts center, and they were thrilled with a tour backstage afterwards to meet the performers. Parents help out with childcare during SAC and DAC meetings, help make materials for the resource rooms, perform clerical chores, and help plan and prepare parent workshops.

Parents can claim a large share of the responsibility for the success of the 100-Minute Reading Club, which has extended the Kenosha Model beyond classroom walls. Each afternoon students carry home cards, which parents sign and date after their children have read to them, or after they have read to their children, for five minutes or more. Teachers award a certificate to each child who has accumulated 100 minutes of reading, and for increments of 100 minutes after that.

Teachers also send home with students a seven-page handbook that includes tips for parents on being a good listener and reading well aloud. The handbooks explain how parents can help their children get a library card, teach their children to take care of books, and praise their children's reading efforts. The booklet ends with a bibliography of related books on helping children learn to read. All of the recommended books are available in the library for parents at the central office. In keeping with the program philosophy of guiding rather than limiting education, the booklet reminds parents that "student-authored language-experience books, comics, box tops, grocery labels, recipes, books, newspapers, and magazines could be used in addition to traditional texts."[11]

The importance of the 100-Minute Reading Club should not be underestimated despite its simple structure. A recent report from the National Institute of Education observes that "Most children will learn *how* to read. Whether they *will* read depends in part upon encouragement from their parents."[12] Research has identified a strong tie between the amount of reading children do outside school and their performance on standardized reading achievement tests. One study found that children who scored at or above the 90th percentile read five times as much daily as children at the 50th percentile, and 200 times as much as children at the 10th percentile. The amount of reading done correlates with growth in reading ability "as strongly as any variable in school effectiveness research. It is a moderately strong predictor, as strong a predictor as we know of."[13]

Much of Kenosha's parent involvement is a benefit of solid groundwork in previous years. Funding cuts over time have reduced the Community Outreach Aide position to half-time and eliminated three Community Liaison Teachers and one Evaluation and Parent Involvement Consultant—a serious setback in the staff that works most directly with parents. Within the constraints of budget, however, the Kenosha Model recognizes and values the worth of parents' contributions and participation in the program, and keeps the lines of communication open and available. The support and goodwill returned are evident.

"Chapter 1 teaches the kids how to do assignments. They explain," says one satisfied parent. "And the kids learn. They're not made to feel dumb, just that they need extra help."

History and Development

The Kenosha Model: Academic Improvement through Language Experience traces its roots to the passage of the Elementary and Secondary Education Act of 1965, Title I, and Title III funding for compensatory education. At that time Zuhlke, who was then an elementary school principal, suggested that the district submit a proposal for the available funds. He chaired the committee that worked on the project and later became the program's first and only coordinator.

The Kenosha Model began as a diagnostic-prescriptive program; that is, teachers diagnosed students' language proficiency with a battery of tests, and then prescribed instruction to correct the identified deficiencies. Kenosha used all the available technology to assist students individually: tachistoscopes;[14] controlled reading machines that present one line of text at a time at a set rate; programmed reading packets; reading textbooks with controlled vocabularies; visual, auditory, and motor training packages; and a vast array of workbooks.

Like many other remedial reading programs of the 1960s, Kenosha's relied on machinery because the machines supposedly could provide material of appropriate difficulty to all students, allow students to work at their own pace, provide immediate feedback to students as they worked, and free the teacher to assist individuals as needed. "None of it worked," Zuhlke candidly admits. Instead students often found themselves working page by page through machine-monitored practice activities, rarely reading text much longer than a few sentences, rarely discussing what they had read, and never writing. Teachers, rather than feeling free to teach, felt compelled to monitor and keep students busy. "It took years of constant evolving to get where we are today," Zuhlke says.

An event that played an important role in the transition of the Chapter 1 program into today's language-experience model was a summer camp experiment. Zuhlke recognized that the diagnostic-prescriptive approach differed little from what the students received in regular reading classes. After reviewing research, Zuhlke decided to test a language-experience approach in a six-week summer program. No outside experts were involved in the planning, because, he explains, "I felt Kenosha was unique, and I wanted to meet its special needs."

He and Frank Splitek, who was then curriculum administrator, considered options for improving the program and attempted "not to limit or narrow the focus of learning," Zuhlke says. "We tried to take the best of the old-fashioned, one-room schoolhouse approach because that encouraged real teaching. They didn't have materials for all the students, so they had to promote hands-on learning and language experience." The program was implemented that summer and the following school year, and, Zuhlke admits, "If it had flopped that summer, we would have dropped it."

According to Zuhlke, the staff's initially mixed feelings about the program were easily understandable: "In a language-experience program you don't just hand a teacher a text and say, 'This is it.' Language experience is not specific to any particular subject matter; instead it allows you to teach to your own strengths and interests." He developed a philosophy and a management system; then he gave the teachers wide latitude to be creative in content and process. "We freed teachers to teach."

This experiment set the stage for a program that today retains many of those early elements: awareness of the individual needs of students, recognition that many students require something far different from the regular classroom if they are to be successful, maintenance of smaller class sizes than the regular classroom, and solicitation of and respect for the contributions of the student's classroom teachers and parents.

Zuhlke has such firm beliefs in the strength and versatility of the language-experience model he has constructed that he willingly extends the range of its application at any opportunity. Through a national dissemination program, the Kenosha Model has been replicated in twenty-eight other states. Locally, too, Zuhlke has implemented the same language-experience model in each of the programs in his charge: Chapter 1 Math, Chapter 1 Migrant, Chapter 1 Extended-Day Kindergarten, Head Start, Bilingual, and At-Risk (a comprehensive plan for any Kenosha student in danger of dropping out). He is only half-joking when he says, "There are only two ways to teach. One of them is language experience and the other isn't." More seriously, he contends, "All our programs are interconnected. I just don't believe in fragmenting education. Good education is good education, whether it's for 4-year-olds or 18- to 20-year-olds."

Language experience has proven to be an especially appropriate technique for teaching bilingual students. Ruby Gemmell, Kenosha's bilingual consultant, explains, "Students can relate to the English language by experiencing the language. They have a picture they can see, or the actual object or experience. Abstract concepts presented in English are often incomprehensible. Words don't stay if they have no meaning. How do you explain Halloween to a child who has only been in this country six months? Once she goes trick-or-treating, though, she'll never forget."

The Kenosha bilingual program, serving 200 students in grades K–12, the majority of whom are Hispanic, places a heavy emphasis on oral language, repetition, and modeling before students write. The elementary bilingual program is designed to teach the students to read in their native language before they make the transition to English. All junior-high instruction is in English, though students can receive bilingual tutoring as needed. "Our goal is to teach English, but we use the vehicle of the native language," says Gemmell. "If you learn to read and write well in one language, the second language is easy. You don't have to learn all the skills all over again."

Evaluating and Documenting Program Success

Accolades for the Kenosha Model have come from the state and the nation. In 1978 the Joint Dissemination Review Panel of the U.S. Office of Education recognized the success of Kenosha's Chapter 1 students and validated the program as exemplary. In 1980 the Wisconsin Department of Public Instruction nominated the program for recognition in the National Diffusion Network (NDN), an arm of the U.S. Department of Education that disseminates exemplary program practices nationally. For the next four years, the Kenosha Model participated in the dissemination network until it simply became too difficult to respond to all the requests for consulting and training.

The Kenosha Model has been recognized in a variety of publications. Since 1978 it has been described in *Educational*

Programs That Work, the catalogue of NDN-funded and nonfunded programs.[15] It was nominated by the state of Wisconsin and accepted for inclusion in *Winners All!*, a U.S. Department of Health, Education, and Welfare publication describing forty-one of the best, most innovative Title I programs in the United States.[16] It has also been included in a National Council of Teachers of English publication, *Speaking and Writing, K–12: Classroom Strategies and the New Research.*[17]

Still, the program is not without problems, although today the worries are external rather than internal. Zuhlke is concerned about political problems, such as federal funding and local support, not about how to get teachers to accept the language-experience methodology.

Locally, the Kenosha Unified School District operates on an "effective schools" format that is widely different from the Kenosha Model's language-experience philosophy. Although the effective-schools design supports a common body of skills and knowledge for all students—a standardized curriculum—the superintendent and school administration appreciate the success of the Kenosha Model. They continue to support the program because Zuhlke and VanLanduyt know how to demonstrate its effectiveness not only to the administration but also to the school board, parents, teachers, and the students themselves.

According to Zuhlke, the Kenosha Model has "the most comprehensive evaluation in the district." This evaluation occurs informally in the open-forum staff meetings, looseleaf curriculum guide, and wide-ranging and thorough communication system, and formally in an annually published evaluation report of quantitative and qualitative data. The state's Department of Public Instruction requires only pre- and post-test scores on a standardized achievement test, but the Kenosha Model also supplies qualitative data, giving voice to everyone involved in the program.

The evaluation includes some seventy pages of information that begins with pre- and post-test results on the standardized tests, organized by grade level. Elementary and secondary classroom teacher pre- and post-observations are summarized next, followed by representative student writing samples with summaries of pre- and post-testing arranged by grade level. Next come a summary of the parent survey, a summary of elementary and secondary student surveys with representative comments, and similar summaries for the mathematics component (grades 4–9) and the extended-day kindergarten. The evaluation is thorough and provides tangible evidence of success from a number of viewpoints.

These local evaluation reports are consistent with the judgments of external evaluators. One independent study validated the program with an analysis of standardized test scores and found "average growth in excess of 1.5 months per month in the program."[18] The certification by the Joint Dissemination Review Panel required objective test information and a thorough series of interviews before the panel conferred the label "exemplary" in 1978. State Chapter 1 observers also labeled the Kenosha program "exemplary" after a visit in 1985.[19]

From kindergarten through 12th grade, the Kenosha Model earns positive results. The performance of the middle grades in 1985–86 is representative. Standardized test results for reading (see Table 1) reveal that students who previously had lost ground were gaining some of it back through language experience.[20]

Once in the fall and again in the spring, regular classroom teachers are asked to rate the Chapter 1 students on a six-point scale in ten categories.[21] They do not refer to their initial observation form when they complete the final form. Teachers' reading and language ratings for 275 7th- to 10th-graders (1985–86) are summarized in Table 2. The general pattern—students move out of the lowest category and into the upper two—is typical of each yearly evaluation. The results reflect classroom teachers' judgments that the Chapter 1 program effectively improves their students' language and reading abilities.

Table 1. Kenosha Model students' standard test scores (normal curve equivalents) in reading, 1985–86 school year (total 286 students).

Grade	Pre-test (fall)	Post-test (spring)	Difference
7th	33.0	37.3	+4.3
8th	35.6	41.2	+5.6
9th	33.0	41.3	+8.3

Note: 7th- and 8th-graders took the Iowa Test of Basic Skills, 9th-graders took Stanford Test of Academic Skills.

Table 2. Classroom teachers' ratings of Kenosha Model students in reading and language, 1985–86 school year (grades 7–10, percentage in each category; total 275 students).

	Below average	Average	Above average
Reading			
Fall	33	51	16
Spring	15	58	27
Language			
Fall	42	48	10
Spring	19	58	23

The Picture Story Language Assessment is another locally developed measure for evaluating the progress students make in their written language skills. The test presents students at each grade level with a different picture to prompt their writing. At 3rd-grade level and above, students write a story in response to the picture. The test is given in the fall and again in the spring. The papers are scored in eight objective categories. Results for grades 7–9 in 1985–86 are given in Table 3. In order to retain some of the personalization of the program and make the numbers come to life, the evaluation report is also filled with representative student writing samples from the picture story test.

The objective measures of student writing shown in Table 3 mean little in isolation, nor does their sum necessarily represent what good writing is; however, they do provide evidence of student improvement. On average, students are writing more (words, sentences, paragraphs) and increasing their use of writing conventions (correct spelling, use of punctuation, use of descriptive and action words). Krissy's sample provides specific examples of what the numbers represent. (Mistakes have been left uncorrected.)

Pre-test

This is a computer that got confused. The computer got so confused from doing all of my homework. Now, just, think, if I would have done all of that homework, I wouldn't have had to go to school any more. Because, I would be so confused. Ha! Ha! If only it would happen.

Table 3. Kenosha Model students' scores (average number per child) on the Picture Story Language Assessment, grades 7–9, 1985–86 school year.

	Pre-test	Post-test
Grade 7 (35 students)		
words written	56.1	138.7
descriptive words	4.0	9.7
action words	5.2	16.8
sentences	4.3	10.2
sentence length	17.8	17.2
paragraphs	1.0	1.6
words spelled correctly	51.6	131.0
punctuation marks	5.2	13.0
Grade 8 (51 students)		
words written	59.1	139.2
descriptive words	5.1	12.1
action words	5.4	14.1
sentences	4.5	10.0
sentence length	14.9	16.5
paragraphs	1.3	1.8
words spelled correctly	57.7	134.5
punctuation marks	5.2	14.3
Grade 9 (24 students)		
words written	62.6	180.7
descriptive words	6.2	14.3
action words	5.7	21.8
sentences	4.1	13.8
sentence length	16.6	13.9
paragraphs	1.1	1.8
words spelled correctly	56.5	175.4
punctuation marks	4.5	16.7

Post-test

One day in school, it was so funny! We had a computer in class, and the teacher gave us a lot of homework. My friend and I decided to use the computer to help us with the work. We stayed after school to do the work.

At around 4:30, our teacher left. So we told him that we would lock up the classroom for him. He said, "O.K." So we started on the computer. We got done with our homework, and then we decided to stay a little longer. We put a game in and we played and played. Finally it was our last game. Something was wrong. The game wouldn't work. We tried and tried, but it wouldn't work. So we took the disk out, waited about 10 to 15 minutes to put another game in. During that time, something happened. The computer lit up and said, "Hi! What's your name? I'd like to be friends." We ran out of the classroom and got a teacher. We told her everything. We even brought her back to the classroom to show her. But when we got there, the computer wouldn't do anything. She told us to stop trying to be funny and walked out! The computer said, "I told you not to tell anyone. You'll pay!" . . . and it blew up into a thousand pieces.

From that day on, we never told anybody what we knew. When someone told us something, they didn't want anyone to know, we didn't tell a soul!

Teachers send out parent surveys each spring, by way of the students, through the mail, or by distributing them at SAC meetings. Response is strictly voluntary, and in 1985–86 parents returned 331 surveys. The majority reported that their child's academic progress had improved as a result of participating in the program and that their child's attitude toward school and schoolwork had also improved. They believed that the individual attention, the focus on the child's strengths, and the making of books were significant factors in their child's success in the program.

The students themselves are also surveyed for their feelings about the program. At the end of the 1985–86 school year, 238 in grades 7–12 returned surveys. An overwhelming 221 responded that the program had helped them. They reported that the program was fun, that teachers cared about them, that they were respected, and that the Chapter 1 program really helped them to improve their reading and writing. Students, too, rated making books as a highlight of the year.

The gains that Chapter 1 students make in the program are sustained after they leave it. In a 1987 study Kenosha Model administrators traced the records of students from grades 3, 5, 7, and 10 who had received Chapter 1 help in the 1984–85 school year and then graduated from the program because their reading scores had increased. Their sustained gains after leaving the program were an average of 7.1 NCEs.[22]

Thorough and comprehensive, the Kenosha Model's evaluation system involves all the program's participants and responds effectively to the questions of outsiders. The central administration is pleased by the gains in standardized test scores, typically in the range of four to five NCEs. Classroom teachers and their principals are impressed by the visible gains they themselves document on the elementary and secondary observation forms. The school board is impressed by the range and depth of the evaluations, and by the breadth of lesson plans in their complimentary copies of *Kaleidoscope*. Since the inception of the language-experience model, the board has voted unanimously for the program. Parents remain supportive because of their involvement through the SACs and DAC and because of the publications and vocal support of their children.

Conclusions

From anticipation to participation, to exploitation and variation, the Kenosha Model motivates students to learn by capturing their interest and involving them in the study of new and exciting subjects. Absorbed in the content, they eagerly undertake projects that demand the mastery of new literacy strategies and skills. Once learned, this new knowledge stays with them because it was acquired in the pursuit of meaningful personal goals. The Kenosha Model is a powerful example of the very best in successful literacy programming for young adolescents.

Notes

1. In *Scary Stories to Tell in the Dark*, ed. A. Schwartz (New York: Harper & Row Junior Books, 1981), 54–55.

2. Kenosha Unified School District, "Children at Risk Program Plan," proposal submitted to the Wisconsin Department of Public Instruction, July 1986, 43.

3. "Kenosha's Neighborhoods," a series of feature articles in *Kenosha News*, 21 September–27 October 1986 (clippings on file at the Center for Early Adolescence).

4. M. VanLanduyt and T. Zuhlke, eds., *Kenosha Model Training Manual: Academic Improvement through Language Experience*, rev. ed. (Kenosha, Wis.: Kenosha Unified School District, 1982), 3.

5. A.J. Harris, "Progressive Education and Reading Instruction," *The Reading Teacher* 18 (1964): 128–38.

6. See, for example, R.G. Stauffer, *The Language Experience Approach to the Teaching of Reading* (New York: Harper & Row, 1980); R.V. Allen and C. Allen, *Language Experiences in Reading: Teacher's Resource Book* (Chicago: Encyclopaedia Britannica Press, 1966); M. Hall, *Teaching Reading as a Language Experience* (Columbus, Ohio: Charles E. Merrill, 1970); R. Gans, *Guiding Children's Reading through Experiences*, 2d ed. (New York: Teachers College Press, 1979) (1st ed. published 1941).

7. VanLanduyt and Zuhlke, *Kenosha Model Training Manual*; the quotation is from A.B. Alcott, *Table Talks* (1877).

8. See, for example, Dolores Durkin, "What Classroom Observations Reveal about Reading Comprehension Instruction," *Reading Research Quarterly* 14 (1978–79): 481–538; Richard L. Allington et al., "What Is Remedial Reading? A Descriptive Study," *Reading Research and Instruction* 26, no. 1 (1986): 15–30.

9. *The Kenosha Model Kaleidoscope: Language Experience Forum Participant Idea Exchange* is published periodically by the Kenosha Unified School District.

10. James Coleman, cited in L. Olson, "A Prominent 'Boat Rocker' Rejoins the Fray," *Education Week* (14 January 1987): 14–16.

11. *The 100 Minute Club Handbook* (Kenosha, Wis.: Kenosha Unified School District, n.d.), 2.

12. R.C. Anderson et al., *Becoming a Nation of Readers: The Report of the Commission on Reading* (Washington, D.C.: National Institute of Education, 1984), 26.

13. R.C. Anderson, "The Necessity of Promoting Voluntary Reading," presentation at the meeting of the International Reading Association, Philadelphia, April 1986.

14. A tachistoscope is a machine used to test word-recognition ability or to influence the rate of reading. It operates by flashing a word on a screen, usually for a set length of time less than a second.

15. *Educational Programs That Work: A Collection of Proven Exemplary Educational Programs and Practices*, 12th ed. (Longmont, Colo.: Sopris West, 1986).

16. *Winners, All! 41 Outstanding Education Projects That Help Disadvantaged Children*, ed. J.S. Park (Washington, D.C.: U.S. Government Printing Office, 1978).

17. See R.R. Allen and R.W. Kellner, "Integrating the Language Arts," in *Speaking and Writing, K–12: Classroom Strategies and the New Research*, ed. C.J. Thaiss and C. Suhor (Urbana, Ill.: National Council of Teachers of English, 1984), 208–36.

18. Allen and Kellner, "Integrating the Language Arts."

19. S.A. Bates-Watkins and T. Diener, "Kenosha ECIA Program Review, March 25–28, 1985," enclosed with letter to John Hosmanek, District Administrator, Kenosha Unified School District, 15 April 1985.

20. Normal curve equivalents (NCEs) are widely used for reporting standardized test results in Chapter 1 evaluations, because they are more sensitive to change in students' performance at the lower levels than are the more commonly used percentile ranks. Usual range of variance is 3.3–1.6 NCEs.

21. The categories are (1) follows directions, (2) comprehends content material, (3) spells correctly, (4) expresses in written form, (5) expresses ideas orally, (6) participates in class discussion, (7) relates with teachers, (8) relates with peers, (9) demonstrates interest in subject, (10) works independently.

22. *Chapter 1 Evaluation: Sustained Effects Study* (Kenosha, Wis.: Kenosha Unified School District, 1987), 2.

STAR: STRUCTURED TEACHING IN THE AREAS OF READING AND WRITING

The students of New York City's District 4 represent the myriad cultures and languages that thrive in the neighborhoods of East Harlem. In La Marqueta, the big country-style market tucked under the railroad tracks a few blocks from the school district office, one can purchase goat meat for a Caribbean curry, sugar cane, and Puerto Rican *chuchifritos,* as well as the ingredients for southern American specialties—black-eyed peas, pigs' feet, and okra. A few blocks east, on First Avenue, stands one of the few reminders of the area's once large Italian community: a pizza parlor favored years ago by the young Frank Sinatra and his friends.

District 4 is also home to STAR (Structured Teaching in the Areas of Reading and Writing), an innovative Chapter 1 program with a unique approach to helping students improve their literacy skills. Unlike many reading programs, which either emphasize skills at the expense of reading or promote enthusiasm for reading while sacrificing skills, STAR excites students' interest in reading and writing while showing them how to read and write more effectively.

STAR was created by the district and for the district as a result of public and staff dissatisfaction with the district's first Chapter 1 program (1973–78). In that program, purchased as a package from a large commercial publisher, students worked alone on self-paced skills activities that focused on remedying specific deficiencies rather than enriching their knowledge of literacy. When it was instituted in 1973, the year the district was created, only 15 percent of the 15,000 students (the total population was 52 percent black and 47 percent Hispanic) were reading at grade level. Under this first Chapter 1 program, students' reading scores rose to 26 percent reading at grade level but did not climb further.[1]

District 4 teachers and administrators groan when they recall those years. "After a while I didn't want to teach," remembers STAR coordinator Pat Piro, who was a classroom teacher at the time. "I just couldn't keep track of thirty-two kids doing thirty-two different things. There was little application of skills to reading. You couldn't talk to kids about books. You couldn't get students together for a discussion." The individualized instruction method also required a high teacher-to-student ratio. The classroom teacher, a reading teacher, and five aides were needed to serve a class of thirty students in the reading lab.

The continuing low test scores, difficulty in tracking students, and staff and student dissatisfaction with the program led the district's communication arts department to search for alternatives. The department formed a committee of teachers and administrative staff that worked with consultants to develop a plan for a new reading program. The plan combined a theoretical base with practical methodology for using new research findings in the classroom.

Developing the new Chapter 1 plan was an exciting and unforgettable experience for those who participated. "We felt like dreams could become real," recalls Camille Aromondo, director of the district's communication arts department and former supervisor of the STAR program. Aromondo's department is responsible for all reading instruction in the district's grades K–9.

There were many differences between the old program and what the staff wanted in the new program. The old system had been created by a commercial publisher, but the new system would be created by the district staff, incorporating their understanding of the research with their perceptions of their students' needs. The old program taught a discrete hierarchy of skills that were supposed to lead to reading; the new program taught that skills such as phonics and decoding are only one part of the reading process. The new program would teach students skills in the context of other reading tasks. The old method sought to correct the child's diagnosed reading deficiencies; the new program would build new skills on the child's assessed knowledge and strengths. In addition, the new program would emphasize instruction in reading comprehension strategies. "We tried to involve students in an interest in language, the fun of language. The new program stresses just plain good teaching, preparing students for what they couldn't get on their own," Aromondo explains.

Having enjoyed tremendous success in improving students' literacy skills, the STAR program has been expanded beyond the district's 2,509 Chapter 1 students; it is now also the teaching method for classroom reading instruction in 11 of District 4's elementary and junior high schools. Today, 63 percent of the students in the district are reading at grade level. District 4 now claims the highest reading scores of New York City's school districts with high minority student populations. STAR is one of the major reasons for this spectacular improvement in students' reading achievement.

Purpose and Goals

STAR focuses on the teaching of "strategies," the generic questions readers ask to help themselves decipher text. For example, capable readers use strategies to figure out unknown words, locate specific information in a textbook, anticipate the outcome of a mystery, or analyze an author's viewpoint. Many of the skills capable readers demonstrate are not acquired through direct instruction but are absorbed through watching and being around more experienced readers. For instance, when parents take small children to the library and help them select books, they are modeling how experienced readers make selections. According to one authority in the field, this modeling that experienced readers provide to less experienced readers is critical in developing literacy skills.[2]

Children who enter school with limited exposure to literacy need extra support to gain a knowledge of strategies. Without such support, they may acquire a growing sense of helplessness and hopelessness about their reading, increasing the inevitability of failure in school when they reach the middle grades. Through teacher modeling and direct instruction, STAR compensates for these students' early losses, making the strategies good readers employ explicit to older beginning readers.

The program's approach stresses that strategies and comprehension are central to language and that literacy is only one part of the continuum of language learning.[3] The processes involved in learning to read and write are similar to those involved in learning to speak. School-aged children who have learned to speak one or, in some cases, more languages should be considered highly efficient and successful language learners with a wide repertoire of existing strategies for continuing their language learning. By focusing on the strengths students bring to the classroom as successful language learners, and by showing teachers how to build on these strengths through teaching strategies for reading, STAR infuses the remedial classroom with a positive philosophy.

With its emphasis on students' capabilities rather than deficiencies, STAR is responsive to both the developmental and the instructional needs of students. By keeping the focus on students' strengths, the program builds self-esteem, and by developing each student's repertoire of reading strategies, it helps students improve their reading and writing skills.

STAR boldly contradicts many of the conventional myths about remedial readers. Program advisers urge teachers to use methods and practices for remedial students that in many schools are reserved exclusively for the highest achievers. These include teaching students strategies as well as skills, having students make their own reading selections, conducting class activities that focus on reading extended texts rather than only words or sentences, and, most important, insisting on the importance of comprehension.

The STAR method combines effective instructional techniques with a positive and caring classroom climate. In STAR classes, young adolescents feel comfortable in risking their thoughts and asking questions about things they do not understand. "This is no place to be afraid, which is a good thing. Reading is such a personal thing," explains Agnes Ennis, a thirty-year veteran teacher. Echoing her, Michelena, a 13-year-old STAR student, says, "Opinions are okay. We work as a family here. In other classes they yell at you if you're wrong, but there's no arguing here."

Expectations for students are high in STAR, and students respond positively. Ten-year-old Chenequa says her STAR teacher, Caryl Sterne, "[isn't] letting us down. She's forcing us to go on. She asks us—What is reading for? How does it help us?"

STAR students are acutely aware of the differences the program makes in their future. Michelena believes she is going to be a more successful adult worker because of the skills she is learning in her Chapter 1 class. "It's helping me. I want to graduate; this work helps so it won't be so hard in high school."

Experienced teachers and administrators have been attracted to STAR because they see that it gives students an understanding of the purpose of reading as well as the skills. Sterne says, "I've been a reading teacher for sixteen years. I taught in a mastery learning program in which everything was broken down into little parts. This program is better. It gives kids a handle on *how* to comprehend. Total communication is the emphasis."

By stressing new strengths rather than previous failures, STAR helps young adolescents to regain confidence in themselves as students. This attention to students' social and psychological needs, combined with instruction to promote cognitive skills, has made STAR a powerful approach for improving adolescent literacy.

Curriculum and Instruction

New STAR teachers start off their first year in the program with a week-long orientation to the program and the methods. The orientation gives them the building blocks for their curriculum units by teaching six basic lesson types:

1. Foundation lessons
2. Narrative reading lessons
3. Readership lessons
4. Strategy lessons
5. Skills reinforcement lessons
6. Writing lessons

The basic lessons are incorporated into each curriculum unit, and each curriculum unit has a reading or writing strategy as its objective.

Every new teacher's orientation also gives careful attention to pre-assessment techniques such as interest inventories, writing samples, standardized tests, and the reading miscue inventory to assess a reader's individual strengths and strategies (see Administration, below).

Foundation Lessons

The foundation lessons, a two-week set of introductory lessons to introduce students to the STAR methods, are divided into two sections: (1) the role of readers and writers and (2) the characteristics of narrative prose. From these lessons students learn the terms and philosophy of the program.

In the first section of the foundation lessons students learn that language is the tool of speakers, listeners, readers, and writers. They learn how one uses language differently in different roles. For example, a student who has to struggle with deciding on a setting, creating a mood, and plotting the action of a story may approach the reading of another's story with a deeper appreciation and understanding of the author's process. Piro, the STAR coordinator, explains that students are told, "You have a job to do when you come to the story." Students learn about the author's job, the listener's job, and the reader's job. Teachers make it clear to students that the first job of any speaker, listener, reader, or writer is to ask, "Does it make sense?"

In the second section of foundation lessons, on the characteristics of narrative prose, the STAR teachers introduce students to the tools of the trade: character, plot, setting, mood, theme, and genre. The vocabulary introduced here will be used again and again throughout the year, and these terms will become as familiar to students as "hall pass" or "cafeteria."

In a sample foundation lesson from the STAR manual, the characteristics of narrative prose are introduced by comparing the elements of a story to making a hamburger.[4] Students are asked to name the ingredients essential to a Big Mac: hamburger, bun, sauce, pickle, relish, and lettuce. As the students name them, the teacher lists the ingredients as spokes surrounding the central word, "hamburger." Then the teacher puts the word "story" on the board, explaining that stories, like Big Macs, are built and that all the ingredients are necessary to make the final product. The teacher elicits the ingredients of a story with questions like, "The people in a story are called—?" or "What do we call where a story takes place?" At the end of the lesson, there are two diagrams on the board (Figure 1).

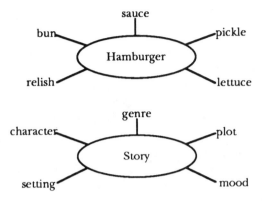

Figure 1

Like all STAR lessons, this one starts from the known—the vocabulary for hamburgers and the concrete experience of buying and eating a hamburger—and works toward the unknown, in this case the vocabulary for the story elements and the concept that stories, like hamburgers, are built from several ingredients. This approach fulfills young adolescents' need for competence in two ways. It encourages them by starting from something they know, and it also teaches them new skills and sophisticated vocabulary. STAR students boast about the vocabulary they learn in class. Almecca, a 5th-grader, reports that she likes learning the meaning of "big words" because it makes her sound "like an 8th-grader" when she talks to her friends. She has learned words like "obese" and "gaunt" in her STAR class.

Narrative Reading Lessons

In the STAR program, narrative reading lessons build on literature, poetry, and drama texts. They follow a predictable three-part pattern:

1. *Pre-reading.* Students discuss what they know about the subject. They make predictions about the text based on their expectations. The teacher helps the students set purposes for reading.

2. *Reading.* Students read silently. Reading aloud in turns is discouraged.

3. *Post-reading.* Students compare what happened with their predictions. They analyze the text in terms of the purposes they had set for reading.

This format helps students make the most of their information by modeling the ways that good readers ask questions and set goals when they read. The follow-up discussions help students to see the relationship between what they knew before reading the materials and what they have learned as a result of reading them.

By asking open-ended questions, praising the process of a student's thinking rather than the product alone, and modeling aloud their own processes and strategies for answering questions, teachers facilitate rather than lead the discussions, creating a positive atmosphere where meaningful interaction can occur, both among the students themselves and between students and adults. As Aromondo explains, "We say, 'Let me help you,' rather than 'That's wrong.'"

A class taught by Juan Martinez, in the bilingual program at Junior High School 45, illustrates the way STAR teachers help students approach new text. He bases his narrative reading lesson on "Child Missing," a story by Ellery Queen. He begins by drawing out the background knowledge of the subject from each of the eleven 9th-graders in his class.

"What are some of the reasons a child could be missing?" he asks. Students call out several answers.

"Kidnapped."

"Ran away."

"Got lost."

"Visiting."

Martinez lists the possibilities on the board.

"Have you ever had an experience like this?" he asks the class.

One student describes being lost, and another tells how he had been accidentally left behind at the Coney Island amusement park. This student says his father became hysterical when he was found. The class discusses how parents react in this situation and why. Young adolescents, with their growing ability to consider their own and others' motives from a broader perspective than that of a younger child, are concerned with understanding their relationships to those close to them. They put their parents' attitudes and behavior under close scrutiny in their own search for self-definition. Martinez's question appeals to the group's existing interest in examining these motives, while it brings the discussion into a literary context, building a bridge from personal knowledge to the impersonal world of the text.

He guides his students toward a discussion of the text with the next question: "Has anyone seen 'Murder, She Wrote'?" He compares the star of the television program to Ellery Queen's role as detective and writer in the story they are going to read.

He asks the students to read the first page of the story silently, keeping these items in mind. Although the students are already familiar with the terms from the foundation lessons, he quickly reviews their meanings.

After the students have read, they talk about the first page of the story and compare what happened in the story with what they discussed before they read it. They follow the same routine with each succeeding page of the story. From pre-reading to post-reading, Martinez follows a consistent format: tapping each student's knowledge and experience, connecting that knowledge with expectations from the text, and weaving the strands of old and new knowledge together.

Readership Lessons

Readership lessons help students expand their understanding of the functions of written text and encourage independent reading both in school and out of school. They encourage students to read for enjoyment. A teacher reading aloud to a class, a sustained silent reading period, echo reading (two readers reading the same text aloud, one after the other), choral reading (reading aloud as a group), and paired reading (reading to each other) are all examples of readership activities. Through readership lessons, students learn about new kinds of reading material and new ways to approach reading.

This exposure to reading is essential for older beginning readers and writers. Many have not realized that there are books written about subjects that interest them; they may have no idea of the range of information available to them through books or magazines. A young adolescent whose only experience with reading has been one of failure will be reluctant to explore written materials even if they are available. Often the first and most valuable lesson the STAR teacher imparts is to awaken the student's interest in books through readership lessons.

Ennis starts each of her classes by reading aloud a new episode from a continuing story. She uses the predictable format of the narrative reading lesson: pre-reading discussion, reading, and post-reading discussion. Before she begins reading, her students review what happened previously and make predictions about what might happen in the next part of the story. Then she reads, stopping periodically to ask questions: "What do you think will happen next? Why?" After the reading, the class discusses the continuing story in light of the day's new information. Ennis helps them prepare for the next day's reading by asking, "What questions do you have on your mind about what's going to happen in the story?" She wraps up the discussion by explaining that they will hear more of the story tomorrow to see how many of these questions they can answer.

Ennis uses readership activities to convey to her students her own love of reading. She tries to show students that reading is "a source for finding out anything and everything they'd like to know, or an escape, a vicarious adventure."

Access to books is fundamental to promoting reading and readership activities. Ennis possesses an ideal classroom library. Around the edge of her room and dividing the space are twenty-four three-foot-high bookshelves packed with books. More books are displayed on tables. The room is also stocked with magazines for different reading levels and interests. On Fridays her students spend half the period selecting and reading books of their own choice. "They don't have to check out any, but they all do," she says. "I don't guide them much in the beginning, but later I pick up on their interests and help out. They read the back blurb and guide each other. They seem to like the self-discovery. I try to read to them a lot and tell them about new books when I get them."

Students in STAR talk enthusiastically about the books they have read. Chenequa reports that her two favorite books are *I Wonder* (a description of how babies are born) and *Hansel and Gretel.* Her choices show the wide variability of interests that is typical of young adolescents. Thirteen-year-old William is enjoying *Then Again Maybe I Won't* by Judy Blume, a painfully accurate account of the trials and travails of a young adolescent boy. Promoting independent, self-selected reading is one way the STAR program responds to the diverse interests of its young adolescent students.

Strategy Lessons

"Is there anything in this room as red as this apple?" asks Pamela Mason, apple in hand.

The ten 5th-graders in Mason's STAR class glance around the colorful room. There are many places to find the color red. Bright posters and charts cover the walls. Some even hang from the light fixtures. There is red on the covers of the 500 or so volumes in the class library. It is a stimulating setting designed to appeal to young adolescents. Hands shoot up, and the answers start to flow.

"The red marker on the list of writing rules."

"The cover of my math book."

"You're very observant. Are you sure that the red you're pointing out is as red as this apple?" Mason prods them to make a closer comparison.

On the board behind her is a chart (Figure 2). The day's lesson is on similes. By learning what a simile is and how to recognize and use one, Mason's students will master an important strategy to help them in discussions, reading, and writing.

The Apple's			
color is	shape is	weight is	size is
as a	as a	as a	as a

Figure 2

Mason asks the students to pick up the objects they are using for comparison and pass them around the class. When they have explored color, the class moves on to shape.

"Round," says a student.

"Circle," says another.

"Sphere," someone calls out.

After Mason concludes the class discussion on the differences between these words, she passes around a bag filled with unknown objects. Each student reaches in and feels an object. Next, each has to use a string of similes to describe his or her object while the class tries to guess what it is. Everyone is excited and involved in the activity. The variety of formats Mason uses appeals to young adolescents' need for diversity. Talk, an activity many teachers expect students to leave in the hall during class, is actively incorporated into the lesson. By using students' natural desire to talk as a tool, Mason encourages collaboration and interaction.

These first two activities for the day use speaking and listening skills and build on each student's experience and personal observations. In the second part of the lesson, Mason helps her students to transfer their knowledge of similes to reading and writing. She makes the transition from talk to text by explaining to them that authors often use comparisons to make ideas more real to their readers.

She hands out a two-paragraph story:

Poor Me

I was as hungry as a wolf when I got home from school. I got up too late for breakfast. I didn't like what they had for lunch so I just had the bread and milk.

I ran home like lightning and dashed up the stairs like a speed racer. Quickly, I opened the refrigerator. Oh my gosh! It looked empty as a desert. Then I remembered, Mom was out shopping. Soon she would be home with her basket as full of good things as a Christmas stocking. I sat down to watch TV and wait. Every minute was like an hour.

The class reads the story twice silently—once for meaning, the second time to identify similes.

"Anyone see a simile?" asks Mason.

"'As hungry as a wolf,'" answers a student.

"Why is it a simile? What two objects are being compared?" Mason asks.

"'Me,' the writer, and a wolf," says a student.

"What's the clue word?"

"'As,'" several call out.

The fourth activity, written skill practice, is to complete a sheet of incomplete similes taken from a workbook.

Mason's lesson demonstrates the essential elements of a STAR strategy lesson. Like all STAR lessons, this one on how to recognize and use similes seeks to integrate all four communication areas: speaking, listening, reading, and writing. From making comparisons and using similes in conversation, Mason guides students to finding similes in text and, finally, to writing similes. She keeps her students focused on "getting the meaning," and uses students' experience and personal knowledge to build new vocabulary and concepts.

Mason's lesson is also well suited to young adolescents' need for competence, for interaction and collaboration with peers, for diversity, and for clear structure. For instance, the concepts she introduces are simple, but she gets and keeps the class's interest by having each student make his or her own observations. By bringing meaningful dialogue into the lesson, she makes learning about the variety and uses of language fun. In her classroom, students are actively involved in their learning; the discussions are animated and the mood is purposeful but enjoyable.

The teaching of reading strategies is woven throughout the STAR program, but strategies are also taught as separate lessons. These separate strategy lessons may focus on techniques for reading comprehension, such as how to recognize and use similes, how to use prefixes to help figure out an unknown word, how to tell where a story is taking place, or how to use headings when reading a social studies text. In strategy lessons, unlike narrative reading lessons that use complete texts, students practice their new learning on short passages of material first. After they have mastered the use of the strategy there, they apply it to a longer text.

Aromondo describes the importance of strategy teaching in the STAR program. "When kids learn strategies, they have ways to figure out what they read," she says. "Now they know characterization, and they can take it and apply it to the text. Kids have experiences, and we help them label the concepts they already know. We are *not* teaching that teachers know everything and students know nothing."

Ennis, who has taught for eight years in the STAR program, believes in the effectiveness of the strategy lessons, "especially vocabulary. They have a lot of trouble with word meaning. I teach them to look for clues, to use their own experiences, and to use context clues and antonyms." The STAR manual gives teachers a rationale and activities for teaching strategies in all areas of reading development. Under the heading "Vocabulary" there are sections on contextual, morphemic, classification, and dictionary strategies. Under "Comprehension" there is information on teaching structural, contextual, and literacy strategies.

Evidence that strategies are being taught appears in every STAR classroom. One poster on Ennis's wall asks:

1. What is the strategy?
2. Why is it useful?
3. When can we use it?
4. How do you do it?

Another poster states:

A good STAR pupil listens on four levels:

1. What happened?
   Where did it happen?
   Whom did it happen to?
   When did it happen?
2. Why did the person do this?
   How did what happened affect this person and others?
3. What does the author want us to understand?
   What is the central meaning?
4. How does this story affect me?
   Did I learn something I can use elsewhere?

STAR students feel they have benefited from learning strategies. Michelena, chosen for the STAR program because of her low reading scores, explains, "Last year I stumbled on every word I came to. I used to read a sentence, not understand, and go on anyway. She [the STAR teacher] told us to read it again, look for context clues, use the glossary, talk about it, and let other kids help you figure it out." Learning a variety of strategies for comprehending text helped Michelena to become a more flexible reader and, hence, a more proficient reader.

Skills Reinforcement Lessons

For readers and writers to function efficiently, they must have attained automatic control over the many discrete skills involved in each literacy task: decoding, spelling, handwriting, grammar, and punctuation. Researchers refer to this efficient control as "automaticity."

> An automatic activity is an activity that can be performed instantaneously and without conscious attention. At least some of the sub-processes that are part of the overall process of reading must be automatic if the reader is to get any meaning out of what he or she is reading.[5]

The STAR method values these discrete skills and values the development of automaticity in these areas but urges teachers to provide skills practice within the larger context of comprehension strategies. Program administrators try to discourage teachers from teaching skills for skills' sake. "We're aiming for a natural process. In public schools, teachers so often give students a list of isolated words to look up. We don't deal with vocabulary that way. We read words before and after, use context. We don't run to the dictionary as the first response," explains Aromondo.

The STAR manual provides a variety of suggestions for teaching skills within the context of strategies. For instance, a section on vocabulary strategies includes synonym clues, antonym clues, multi-meaning clues, experience clues, and graphic clues. All these skills are familiar to reading teachers, but the STAR system approaches them in a new way, as means to an end rather than as an end in themselves.

Writing Lessons

STAR students' writing abilities are developed both in conjunction with reading activities and in separate lessons focused specifically on writing.[6] STAR views writing, like reading, as part of a language continuum. Like the reading lessons, writing instruction stresses the teaching of strategies, learning skills in context, and teacher modeling as primary teaching techniques.

For example, to involve students in writing about their reading, as well as to give them a chance to interact with her on a one-to-one basis, Ennis has her students write literature journals. They write summaries and comments on their reading, and she reads each journal and writes back to the student about it; she does not correct errors in grammar and spelling, but focuses on the content of the writing. "I try to get them to react, not just summarize," she says. "I want a personal response." Michelena finds her journal helpful. "We read a chapter from books and write what we thought it was about. It helps improve the way I speak, how I think, the way I do in my classes."

Administration

Pre-assessment

Because STAR emphasizes students' existing literacy skills, pre-assessment is critical in its approach. The STAR manual devotes almost forty pages to the topic. Pre-assessment, it explains, helps teachers to learn what students know about reading and writing, how they feel about themselves as readers and writers, and what experiences or interests they have had that could be used to motivate them to read and write.

Pre-assessment starts in the fall, when each STAR teacher gets a list of eligible students and their reading scores from the standardized tests administered each spring. When classes start, STAR teachers distribute questionnaires to ask students about their reading habits: "What is the name of your favorite book?" "Do you have a library card?" "What types of comic books do you enjoy reading?" Students also respond to interest inventories that include questions about school activities, hobbies, collections, and travel experiences.

The Reading Miscue Inventory (RMI) is one of the most important pre-assessment tools. Teachers conduct this analysis of a child's reading and language skills when they feel they need more information than the standardized test results provide. In administering the RMI, the teacher listens to a student read a passage and notes the student's strategies for making sense of the text when confronted with an unknown word, structure, or concept. Then, after reading the passage, the student is asked to retell the story in his or her own words. Finally, the teacher asks the student questions about the story. Often the teacher tapes the session for further analysis.

The teacher analyzes the kinds of miscues the student made, and the ways the student tried to figure out unknown information. In addition, by eliciting personal responses from the student, the RMI enables the teacher to learn about the student's overall comprehension, including the ability to recall facts and the ability to make inferences from those facts. Most important, the RMI gives the teacher an understanding of the strategies the student uses to decipher text. For instance, some students breeze over unknown words, never stopping to figure out what would make sense; others refuse to continue reading if they come to an unfamiliar word. Many students try to sound out each unfamiliar word; others rely totally on context. As the teacher catalogues the miscues, a profile of the student's strategies, strengths, and needs gradually emerges.

Pre-assessment also includes taking a writing sample. The STAR teacher analyzes the sample and prepares a writing profile that rates the student in five areas: (1) understanding of the task, (2) organization, (3) sentence structure, (4) language, and (5) mechanics.

Throughout the year, pre-assessment is also a part of each lesson. Teachers begin their lessons by first finding out what students know about the subject they will be studying and what experiences they have had that relate to that subject. Older beginning readers and writers, humiliated by years of reading failure, often stop trying to connect what they know with what school is trying to teach them; past experience has shown them that it is hopeless to try. Pre-assessment gives teachers important information on students' strengths, experiences, and interests that can be used both to respond to students' needs and to excite them about reading.

Supervision

Pat Piro, the coordinator of District 4's STAR program, observes and supports STAR teachers in their classrooms. By visiting two schools every day to work with teachers, watching teachers deliver one or two lessons, talking to them about her observations, and discussing future plans, she helps teachers integrate the STAR theory and methodology with actual classroom practice. She reports to the principal and to Aromondo on the instruction she observes.

Piro and Aromondo plan monthly staff development meetings, combining an agenda that covers new initiatives from Aromondo as well as teacher needs Piro has observed in her classroom visits. The amount of time Piro and Aromondo have with teachers varies from month to month. They use the same techniques to teach teachers in the staff development sessions that they would like to see teachers using in their own classrooms: modeling, building upon participants' interests and experiences, and focusing on thinking processes as well as the product.

At the beginning of the sessions Aromondo and Piro explain to the teachers that they are to take the session information back to their schools. In some instances, teachers are even asked to make formal presentations to their colleagues on material from the training workshops.

Several district schools have elected to use STAR not only as their Chapter 1 program but also as the model for the schoolwide reading program. For those schools John McKeever, coordinator for the overall developmental reading program in all the elementary and junior high schools in the district, assumes a role similar to Piro's. A STAR trainer of teachers and administrators, as well as an experienced classroom teacher, McKeever believes that the classroom teacher's role is pivotal to creating new readers. "Learning to read isn't easy. It's slow. Students go at different rates, but society pushes for the same rate. It's a developmental process. I think the key is the teacher."

McKeever visits classrooms every morning between nine and eleven o'clock, the designated hours for reading instruction throughout the district. Like Piro, he watches lessons, consults on lesson plans, teaches demonstration lessons, and gives workshops. After observing a class, he discusses his observations with the teacher and, later, with the principal. In some cases he must report on undesirable findings in the classroom, but he emphasizes that his role is that of a support person.

His approach to staff development in the classroom is to tackle the problems one step at a time. He prefers to select two or three very specific objectives for the teacher to implement in the classroom, such as encouraging silent reading instead of oral round-robin reading, instituting a 100-minute reading club, or establishing a time when the teacher reads aloud to the class. He waits until he sees positive signs that these have been implemented before going on to the next set of objectives.

Organization

As the Chapter 1 program, STAR is an important part of District 4's reading program, which comprises several interlocking pieces. All students in grades 1–6 have one and one-half hours of daily reading instruction with their classroom teacher. In grades 7–9, students study literature and grammar five periods per week.

Students with special literacy needs get help from several different sources. Chapter 1 helps students with low reading scores who are from low-income families. All District 4's schools qualify for Chapter 1 help because of the poverty level of the neighborhood. Through Chapter 1, eligible students can receive an additional forty-five minutes per day of instruction in reading and writing. The District 4 Chapter 1 program has a $2.5 million budget and a staff of two administrators, one professional support person, thirty-six teachers, thirty-six paraprofessionals, and three family aides. Student-to-teacher ratios are set at a maximum of 15:1 in the elementary schools and 25:1 in the junior high schools.

Students receive Chapter 1 help on the basis of their scores on the reading tests administered throughout the district each spring. New York City used the California Achievement Test (CAT) to measure reading achievement until the 1985–86 school year, when it switched to the Degrees of Reading Power (DRP) test.[7] The district also administers a writing sample, devised to comply with criteria established by the state's Board of Regents.

Each fall Chapter 1 teachers rank the eligible students in their schools in priority order. The first priority are students scoring below the 25th percentile on the district reading test; second are those who score between the 26th and 30th percentile, and third, those who score between the 31st and 35th percentile. Students already in the program who have improved but need further support to continue a successful level of achievement may be continued on "maintenance" if space permits. Finally, students who have very low writing scores may be accepted in the Chapter 1 program on a space-available basis.

In the elementary schools, classes are divided during the Chapter 1 period. Those who are eligible for Chapter 1 go to the STAR classroom with the STAR teacher for their forty-five-minute period of instruction; the others stay with their classroom teacher for a reading enrichment period. In grades 7–9, Chapter 1 students receive each week an extra five periods of instruction in reading and writing from the STAR teacher. In the larger junior high schools, Chapter 1 students are assigned to a daily two-period language arts class that includes their Chapter 1 period and their English period, both taught by the same teacher. This system was instituted after numerous complaints from Chapter 1 and English teachers alike, who found it difficult to coordinate instruction for their Chapter 1 students within the framework of the large junior high school curriculum and schedule. Combining the two classes means that instruction for Chapter 1 students is less fragmented. In some smaller junior high programs in which teacher communication is a less complex issue, the English and the Chapter 1 classes are taught by different teachers.

Students in the district's many alternative schools are served by the Pupil's Special Education Needs (PSEN) program, similar to STAR. PSEN provides a combined reading and math lab in each of the alternative schools in the district, where reading and writing skills are presented in a style akin to STAR.

STAR as the Classroom Reading Program

In eleven schools in District 4, principals have elected to use STAR not only as the Chapter 1 program but also as the regular classroom reading program. In these schools all teachers (including those of science, social studies, and math) as well as administrators have received the teacher orientation to STAR, regular follow-up workshops, and supervision.

Mamie Johnson at P.S. 146, an elementary school, and Marvin Galina at the Search program, an alternative middle school, are two of the principals that have chosen STAR as their schoolwide reading program. Both their schools are characterized by high reading scores and good attendance, and both principals are dynamic and politically savvy leaders. They communicate to their respective staffs their strong commitment to creating a literate community. "Everything in the building has to center on literacy, so that when they leave here they're literate citizens. Literacy encompasses everything in one's life," says Johnson.

When Johnson arrived at P.S. 146 in 1981, STAR was already in place in the Chapter 1 lab. She made the decision to implement the program schoolwide and then spent two years working with the district's communication arts department to train her staff, who use STAR methods with the textbook reader system the school has chosen.

STAR is only one part of P.S. 146's literacy emphasis, which also includes such activities as weekly class visits to the school library, an annual book fair, and schoolwide essay contests for Black History Month and Puerto Rican Discovery Month with books as rewards. Johnson also encourages teachers to establish a daily sustained silent-reading period.

This schoolwide literacy approach, coupled with STAR, has been successful at Johnson's school. In 1981 only 34 percent of the students at P.S. 146 read at grade level. In 1985 55.5 percent of the students read at or above grade level on the CAT. In 1986, on the DRP test, 72 percent read at grade level.

Galina is both principal of Search, a middle-school program with 150 students, and building director of P.S. 109, a former elementary school that now houses five separate school programs, including Search. From 9:40 to 10:40 every morning, every Search student is in a reading class, every reading class is using STAR methods, and every Search teacher is engaged as a STAR reading teacher. Social studies, English, and science teachers too have all been trained in STAR, and all teach reading as well as their specialty.

The Search program responds to the diversity of early adolescent reading abilities by grouping students according to three criteria: reading scores, class performance, and teacher recommendation. Fifth-graders have reading class with their classroom teacher, but 6th-, 7th-, and 8th-graders are mixed together during this period. In this way, each teacher can use materials that every student in the class can understand.

Galina likes STAR because he believes it is responsive to the physical, intellectual, and socioemotional needs of his young adolescent students. To him, the typical junior high English class seems too fragmented for most students. In many junior high schools English classes are usually literature classes, and reading instruction is abandoned. Students are asked to write more frequently, but they receive almost no instruction in writing. Galena believes that STAR, on the other hand, addresses his students' varying needs by providing comprehensive literacy instruction for all students at any level.

Getting social studies, English, and science teachers to accept their role as reading teachers has not always been easy. "It sometimes takes years to train teachers to become comfortable with the different parts of the STAR technique," Galina explains. "You must start with those elements that are least artificial to the teachers." He relies heavily on Agnes Ennis, the STAR teacher in the Search program, who trains the Search teachers and works with them individually.

It is in the middle grades that students are first exposed to large doses of reading and writing in many subject areas, and it is there that many began to flounder. By providing all teachers with a strong grounding in how to encourage students to develop the literacy skills they need to complete their work successfully, STAR helps students to do better in all subject areas.

Parent Involvement

Johnson and Galina believe that good school-parent relations are essential to supporting their school literacy goals. Parent support for P.S. 146 and Search is strong because school-parent communication lines are good. Both Johnson and Galina keep an aide busy all day contacting parents by phone or mail about absences, school meetings, and children's progress—the good and the bad.

Johnson and Galina also facilitate parent-teacher conferences, sending home to parents each fall a list of teachers' preparation periods. Johnson says teachers have arranged parent meetings as early as 7:15 in the morning to accommodate parents' work schedules. She also has teachers who call parents at home or who give parents their telephone numbers. In the New York City schools, where many teachers are reported to punch in at 8:00 and punch out between 3:00 and 3:10, this disregard for the clock is unusual. Johnson says she never pressures her teachers to work overtime, but when they do bend their schedules to help parents, she lets them know she appreciates their consideration.

Galina and Johnson are sympathetic to the concerns parents face. Johnson explains, "It's not that parents don't care, but that they lack resources in the home. Middle-class kids come to school with so many skills. Our kids come with less knowledge, and less readiness."

Parent involvement is considered a vital part of STAR's special focus on "readership." The district employs a parent involvement coordinator, Minnie Bee, whose job is to provide workshops for parents on the school district's reading, writing, and math curricula and on ways parents can help their children to do better in school. Many school principals, like Galina and Johnson, support Bee's work by scheduling workshops and conveying to parents the importance of their role in promoting literacy in the home.

Bee finds that parents of middle-grades students come to workshops with different concerns than parents of younger children. Providing help with homework, in particular, becomes more difficult for some parents as their children move from the elementary to the middle grades and begin to assert independent thoughts and opinions. "He thinks he knows everything," is a lament Bee hears frequently.

Many parents of middle-grades students also seem intimidated by their children's skills. They want to help, but in some cases they do not have or may have forgotten literacy skills. Bee is especially moved by parents who, knowing their children's skills have passed their own, still want to find a way to help them achieve in school. She introduces these parents to the adult basic education programs in the area.

She encourages parents to "read with your child. Let the child see that you read." She urges parents to make sure the whole family has library cards. She also recommends that parents cut back on the amount of television the family watches in the evening and establish a time for reading, both aloud and privately.

Bee says it is not unusual for parents to protest some of the measures she advocates. "This would never work with my kid," they say, shaking their heads. However, when they do implement her suggestions, they often return to the next workshop elated and eager to tell her about the successful results.

Responding to Diversity

Sensitivity to parents is just one facet of STAR's responsiveness to the diverse individual and cultural backgrounds of the students in the program; attention to the needs of students who are not native speakers is another. Many of the children in the district are not native English speakers. Bilingual schools provided with STAR labs assist them in learning to speak, read, and write English. Although the teachers are bilingual, the instruction is the same as in all STAR classrooms: students in bilingual programs are placed in STAR when their teachers judge that they have made the transition to reading in English.

STAR urges teachers to use literacy experiences as a forum for students to explore questions of personal identity and cultural heritage. By integrating materials about a variety of people and cultures into their activities and discussions, STAR teachers respond to their students' needs for culturally appropriate role models. In Ennis's class, students read a biography of Mary Bethune, a black activist and educator. Young adolescents, says Ennis, admire Bethune's courage as they come to grips with their own race and gender. The issues and concerns that surfaced in Bethune's life— career decisions and the struggle to maintain personal integrity in the face of society's indifference—are also of interest to most young people, who often face similar situations as they mature.

Assessing Success

Standardized achievement tests are administered every spring in New York City schools. An air of nervous anticipation permeates classrooms and faculty lounges as testing week approaches. Classroom teachers often abandon the regular curriculum for the six weeks preceding the achievement tests in order to prepare students. Minnie Bee reports that her early spring parent workshops on improving children's comprehension are usually very well attended by parents who are concerned about helping their children get ready for the upcoming reading tests. The test results, listed by school and district, are printed in the *New York Times* and frequently spark hot debate in the education community. Local community boards demand explanations when scores are low; principals receive transfer papers, and staff members are reshuffled. Local politicians quote the statistics. Parents demand new reading initiatives.

STAR acknowledges the importance of gathering citywide data on student achievement; however, within the parameters of the program, staff members have attempted to use a broader assessment process to create a more comprehensive profile of each learner. Assessment starts before the student begins STAR and continues on a daily as well as cumulative basis. The emphasis on ongoing assessment puts the citywide spring testing in a more positive, less fearsome context for STAR staff and students.

Standardized test results for District 4 and STAR have shown that students in the program are making considerable progress. In the spring of 1985, the last year CAT was used as the standard achievement test, 75 percent of the students in STAR had improved their relative standing in reading by the end of the year, and 53 percent of the students in the district were reading at grade level. In 1986, using the DRP, 63 percent were reading at grade level. Comparisons of CAT and DRP results that are specially adjusted to overcome the differences in the scoring methods show that the district's performance on the two tests indicates consistent improvement.

The 1984–85 school year was the first year in which District 4 began to assess writing ability. Students each produce a writing sample, which is scored holistically; that is, the sample is given a single score that reflects its integral quality as a written text. For the elementary grades, the scoring system is based on criteria established by the New York State Department of Education. In the junior high schools, scoring conforms to standards established by New York State's minimum competency test. In the fall of 1984, only 35 percent of the district's STAR students passed the writing assessment test. By the spring of 1985 that figure had risen to 63 percent, and by the spring of 1986, to 77 percent.

STAR's success is also reflected in the respect it has earned from professionals outside the program. Teachers and administrators in New York City's GATES program (for 4th- and 7th-graders who read below grade level) can request special training in STAR, to replicate the program in their schools; to date, staff in ninety-seven elementary schools and forty-four junior high schools have been trained in STAR techniques. STAR is one of only three models that have been recommended by the New York City school Board for wider replication. The program also receives visitors from around the United States and from foreign countries. It has been invited to join the National Diffusion Network, an honor reserved for top-notch educational programs.[8]

Conclusions

The combination of effective reading instruction focused on the teaching of literacy strategies and responsiveness to the developmental characteristics of the student has made STAR successful. The program has had a significant positive effect in a district where reading failure was once the norm. STAR proves that good literacy programs can make a difference to young adolescents, giving them the support as well as the skills they need to lead full and productive adult lives.

Notes

1. M. Trika Smith-Burke and Lenore H. Ringler, "STAR: Teaching Reading and Writing," in *Reading Comprehension from Research to Practice*, ed. Judith Orasanu (Hillsdale, N.J.: Lawrence Erlbaum Associates, 1986), 215–34.

2. Shirley Brice Heath, *Ways with Words* (New York: Cambridge University Press, 1983).

3. Program staff cite several works as having influenced this rationale, including Kenneth Goodman, "A Linguistic Study of Cues and Miscues in Reading," in *Reading Research Revisited*, ed. Lance M. Gentile, Michael L. Kamil, and Jay S. Blanchard (Columbus, Ohio: Charles E. Merrill, 1983); Yetta Goodman and Carolyn Burke, *Reading Strategies: Focus on Comprehension* (New York: Holt, Rinehart & Winston, 1980); P. David Pearson and Dale D. Johnson, *Teaching Reading Comprehension* (New York: Holt, Rinehart & Winston, 1978); and Frank Smith, *Understanding Reading*, 3rd ed. (New York: Holt, Rinehart & Winston, 1971).

4. Communication Arts Department, Community School District 4, City of New York, *STAR*, vol. 1 (New York: District 4 Manhattan, 1981), 205–07.

5. Michael Graves, *The Classroom Teacher's Role in Reading Instruction in the Intermediate and Secondary Grades* (Minneapolis: University of Minnesota, 1982), 11.

6. Smith-Burke and Ringler, "STAR," 218. The STAR writing component, still in the implementation stages, draws heavily from the research of Donald Graves, Sondra Pearl, and the Weehawken Writing Project; see, for example, Donald Graves, *Writing: Teachers and Children at Work* (Portsmouth, N.H.: Heinemann Educational Books, 1986).

7. Up until the 1985–86 school year New York City used the California Achievement Test (CAT) to measure reading achievement. In the spring of 1985, the last year the CAT was used, 75 percent of the students in STAR improved their relative standing in reading by the end of the year. In the 1985–86 school year New York City switched to the Degrees of Reading Power test (DRP) because the Board of Education decided it measured reading ability more accurately than the CAT does. Experts may disagree on the relative merits of each test, but few would dispute that comparisons of the results yield little valuable information, because the two instruments measure reading in different ways that cannot be easily reconciled. The CAT has separate subtests to measure vocabulary and comprehension. The comprehension passages are followed by multiple-choice questions, which require students to demonstrate their understanding of specific facts as well as their ability to make inferences and generalizations. The DRP, on the other hand, consists of passages of text with key words left blank. Students must decide which word from a set of five possibilities would best fit each blank.

8. Thus far, STAR has been unable to participate in the Network because of an unforeseen hitch in eligibility: because all the district's

schools have Chapter 1 programs, there are no "control" groups (students from schools without Chapter 1 programs) from which to obtain the comparison statistics needed for some kinds of evaluation.

HILT: HIGH INTENSITY LANGUAGE TRAINING—
AN EFFECTIVE MODEL OF SECOND-LANGUAGE
LITERACY INSTRUCTION

El Paso, a sprawling and growing city set in a harsh landscape and beautiful climate, lies on the far southwestern edge of Texas. The Franklin Mountains come to a halt just at the edge of its downtown, driven like a wedge between two northward-stretching suburbs. The natural landscape is dusty gray, barren rocks punctuated by occasional scrub. The twenty-sixth largest city in the United States, with a population of more than half a million, El Paso might be even larger if not for an imaginary line and a very real chain-link fence topped with barbed wire. Just across the Rio Grande is the northern edge of Ciudad Juarez, the fourth largest city in Mexico, population 1 million.

El Paso's proximity to Mexico and especially Juarez has made it truly a city of two cultures. Spanish and Mexican flags flew over what is now El Paso long before any U.S. settlers arrived. El Paso has a population that is more than 50 percent Hispanic, supports a daily Spanish newspaper as well as two daily English ones, hosts an international airport where announcements are made first in Spanish and then in English, and is as much dependent on the value of the Mexican peso as on the U.S. dollar for its economic well-being. Residents of both El Paso and Juarez frequently travel across the border for business or pleasure.[1]

Because of this large and mobile Hispanic population, many of them newly arrived in the United States, the demand for English literacy instruction in El Paso is pressing. Educating non-English-speakers in the United States is as much a political as an educational issue, and the politics are evident in El Paso. In fact, developing an effective education program for students with limited English proficiency in El Paso was, if anything, even more complex than it might have been elsewhere because of the city's special characteristics. The magnitude of the need is felt not only because great numbers of Spanish-speaking students enter the schools but also because, proportionately, Hispanic students make up a majority of the school population.

The El Paso Independent School District is a large one, the larger of two serving the city. The district is responsible for forty elementary schools, four elementary/intermediate schools, one intermediate school, ten junior high schools, eight senior high schools, and seven schools with a variety of other classifications. More than 70 percent of the district's nearly 60,000 students are of Hispanic origin. A large number of these students require special educational services to learn to speak, read, and write in English. Twenty-eight schools in the district, serving 31,000 students, house Chapter 1 programs, and forty-nine provide English literacy training to approximately 13,000 students with limited English skills. These are startling numbers for a district that did not initiate a program for students with limited English proficiency until 1970, when the state made it a requirement.

It was in this large context that the El Paso Independent School District founded its High Intensity Language Training (HILT) Program in 1982. HILT provides English language and literacy instruction in eight school sites to approximately 1,600 students in grades 7–12. Its primary goal is to prepare students for a successful transition into the regular high-school curriculum. HILT's staff of more than fifty teachers serves a population that comes predominantly from Mexico, although there are also a few students from Asia and the Middle East.

Philosophy and Methods

The major purposes of the HILT program are to help students feel comfortable in their new environment and to provide them with the skills they need to be successful in mainstream high-school English classes and extracurricular activities, and beyond. Language is used to communicate, not just for structural correctness. "The more interesting and relevant a lesson is to the student," explains Rosita Apodaca, co-founder of the program and its first coordinator, "the better the chances are that the language will be acquired. The lesson should be so interesting that the student is focused on the content and *not* on the language form."[2]

Teachers explain and act out new English vocabulary, assist students to adjust to a new culture, surround students with books and paper and pencils, and provide frequent and multiple opportunities to listen, speak, read, and write.

As Apodaca designed a program to meet these goals, it soon became apparent to her that an effective program for learning English as a second language "had to go beyond the typical plan for teaching the students English, to a broad educational design that would encompass the total curriculum."[3] The resulting plan consisted of four levels of instruction—beginning, intermediate, advanced, transitional—all buttressed by a series of "sheltered" classes, as well as modifications designed to assist students who had little or no previous schooling.

English typically dominates HILT language lessons, but at times key concepts or specific directions are presented in Spanish. Students may use Spanish at any time, but teachers respond in whichever language seems appropriate to the situation, student, and question. Though language learning is the focus of instruction in HILT classrooms, the program expects and respects a transitional "period of silence" for most of the beginners. Judy Meyer, formerly a HILT teacher at Lincoln Junior High School and now a bilingual/English as a Second Language (ESL)[4] instructional specialist in the Dallas Independent School District, explains: "It's particularly important that beginners not be forced to talk. Much like a child learning a first language, they must go through a silent period absorbing language. They jump in and talk when they're ready. For some students, it may take six hours, for others six months. It's a matter of individual differences. In the middle school it seems to take longer. The students are not only learning language, but also who they are. They're very conscious of others and embarrassed at making errors in front of their peers. Boys and girls are checking each other out. None of it is directly language-related, but it is influential."

In her training manual Apodaca stresses the value of silence and the necessity of an understanding teacher: "Remember that speaking ability emerges on its own after enough competence has been developed through listening and understanding. We acquire spoken fluency *not* by practicing talking but by understanding input. It is, in fact, theoretically possible to acquire language without ever talking. Speaking makes an indirect contribution to language acquisition. That is, the more a student speaks, the more people will talk to him/her. In fact, speaking affects the quantity of input as well as the quality of the output. Speaking should be encouraged, but not to the detriment of the student."[5]

Allowing a period of silence is not only linguistically sound but also developmentally responsive. Young adolescents vary widely in their physical, emotional, and cognitive growth. Allowing these students to speak when they are ready lets them progress at their own individual rates.

At the same time the value of *encouraging* spoken English must not be forgotten. All HILT materials for students are in English, except for some of the magazines and books for free reading used in the beginning level. Beginning-level students are allowed to read in their native language, to encourage them to keep up their reading skills, but activities around their reading are conducted in English; for instance, they may switch to English to discuss what they have read. Teachers often act out unknown English words, thus helping the students to connect the concepts with familiar Spanish terms. Lessons are structured so that when responses are necessary, students can nod, point, imitate, or otherwise demonstrate understanding by their actions, even if they are not yet ready to speak. When students show they are having difficulty in responding, teachers can modify the instruction and model the correct behavior. "There's strong motivation to learn, especially in junior high," Meyer says. "Students want to learn English to be a part of the school."

Other activities build upon this solid foundation of listening comprehension. For example, silent reading in self-selected books and magazines is a part of at least one ESL class period per day. Because this activity is as important for motivation and enjoyment as for language development, students are encouraged to read materials in English but given the freedom to choose otherwise. A parallel writing activity involves interactive dialogue journals. Students write each day in their journals in either Spanish or English about topics they choose themselves. Periodically teachers collect the journals and write back to the students. Even though the journals often contain flaws in grammar and spelling, the teachers neither correct the journals nor grade them. Instead they respond in English to the content and feeling of the writing. Students wait eagerly to see the responses to the entries. "When I pass the journals back, they cluster in small groups," Meyer explains. "I hear, 'What's this say?' Or they confer with me. They're eager to understand."

The evolution of their writing is remarkable and makes a strong statement for the value of founding language instruction in communication. With no pressure to do so and with no repetitive grammar or vocabulary drill, students gradually begin writing more English, and more correctly. Beginning students' journal pages in September could come from any classroom in Juarez. Through October and November English words and phrases begin to blossom like daffodils. By December most students are writing predominantly in English. By January HILT teachers are hard pressed to find vestiges of Spanish in the journal entries. The aural/oral foundation, the communicative purpose, the encouragement of teachers, and the daily practice exert a powerful cumulative effect. This general pattern is kept, and augmented, throughout all levels of instruction.

Language experiences are frequently used in reading and composition classes. Students participate in an activity and discuss it as the teacher notes the key vocabulary they generate. Then the students write. These compositions, as well as other more formal assignments, are frequently published in a variety of ways: stapled to classroom bulletin boards for casual reading, given folder covers and placed in the classrooms for silent reading time, or given more permanent covers and placed in the school libraries for wider reading.

Sheltered courses offer HILT students the same math, science, and social studies content and materials as the English mainstream classes but are specially tailored to their linguistic needs.[6] The sheltering plan allows students to comprehend the subject matter, enables teachers to address the specific difficulties encountered as students learn through a second language, and reduces students' anxiety about trying out newly learned English skills. Teachers of sheltered courses are permitted to use Spanish when it becomes necessary, and the courses allow students to transfer the language skills they are learning in HILT English classes to a specific discipline. This special help is a particularly well-conceived aspect of the HILT program. Middle-grades education is a difficult transition for many students. Suddenly they face heavier learning demands from many teachers, increased expectations for independent reading and writing, and extensive homework assignments. Without the safety net that sheltered courses provide, many of the students with limited English who are trying to balance these demands on top of a new language would find the task impossible.

To prepare for the sheltered courses HILT students take prerequisite "English for" classes—English for Math, English for Social Studies, English for Science—that introduce them to the subject area terminology they will need to know.

Program Structure and Placement

Accurate placement of ESL students is a difficult task in El Paso schools. Some arrive with no previous exposure to English, others with several years of formal or informal instruction. Some have a history of little or no schooling, others advanced training in subjects like mathematics and physics. However difficult the task, it is essential to assess each student's English language fluency accurately if he or she is to progress efficiently in schooling in the United States.

Because HILT is a program for 7th- through 12th-graders, time is of the essence. Even if entered into the program at the earliest point of eligibility, the beginning of the 7th grade, the student has at most three years in which to master enough English to succeed in the mainstream. Entry any later than the 8th grade reduces ESL instruction to two years because of the many other requirements to be fulfilled before high-school graduation. (See Table 1.) Students who enter HILT in the 7th or 8th grade take both the beginning and intermediate levels of English instruction as year-long courses. Those who enter the program in the 9th grade or later complete the beginning and intermediate levels their first year, advanced and transitional their second.

Table 1. Progress through the four instructional levels (Beginning, Intermediate, Advanced, Transitional) of HILT language instruction, by grade level at entry in the program. One-semester courses are shown, for example, as A/ (fall), /T (spring), A/T (fall/spring).

Grade level at entry	Instructional level taken at grade level					
	7	8	9	10	11	12
7th	B	I	A/T			
	I	A	T			
	A					
8th		B	I/A	T/		
		I	A/T			
		A	T			
9th (enter fall)			B/I	A/T		
9th (enter spring)			/B	I/A	T/	
10th (enter fall)				B/I	A/T	
10th (enter spring)				/B	I/A	T/
11th (enter fall)					B/I	A/T

Note: 12th-graders may not enter the program at the beginning or intermediate levels, but may be accepted if testing at time of entry permits assignment to higher levels.

Grade level is assigned by the student's age. HILT recognizes that "self-esteem is significantly [negatively] affected when a student is placed with students who are considerably younger."[7] Young adolescents in particular benefit from this consideration because of their extreme self-consciousness: age-appropriate placement implicitly removes the stigma often attached to placement in special classes.

The first step of the placement process is completion of the Home Language Survey, a pair of questions regarding the dominant language spoken by the child and in the child's home. Parents are asked, "What language is spoken in your home most of the time?" and "What language does your child speak most of the time?" The form is printed in both English and Spanish, as are all communications between the HILT program and parents. If the answer to either question is a language other than English, more specific language testing is conducted with the student.

The initial screening test for potential HILT students is the listening comprehension subtest of the Comprehensive English Language Test (CELT). A student who scores below 30 (out of 50) is eligible for HILT placement. HILT must also administer the Language Assessment Schedules as required by the state, but staff find the CELT far more accurate in identifying candidates. In accordance with state guidelines HILT also administers the language arts and reading subtests of the Iowa Test of Basic Skills (ITBS), a standardized test written in English.

Final placement decisions are made by the Language Proficiency Assessment Committee (LPAC), consisting of the student's school principal or assistant principal, two ESL teachers, the student's parents, and often a counselor or other campus representative involved in coordinating the committee. The committee also meets to approve the student's specific class level assignment and subsequent reclassifications.

Once placed at a given level of instruction, the student is also asked to write a paragraph in Spanish, "Quien Soy Yo?" (Who Am I?), so that the teachers can approximately assess native language literacy. Borderline students at any level also go through an oral interview, beginning in present tense and progressing to more advanced constructions.

HILT staff and administrators are well aware of the arbitrary nature of test scores and cutoff points and the variability of student performance. They also know their own individual observations can be equally fallible. "Language proficiency tests are a rough estimate at best and, therefore, students are sometimes misplaced," Apodaca explains. "When the student's performance in the classroom contradicts the test results, the student's teachers must meet and agree on the correct placement for the student. An individual teacher may not change the placement of the student."[8]

Once appropriately placed, the student progresses to higher levels by successfully completing the preceding ones. The student may be promoted one or two levels at a time, retained, or placed at a lower level if and when performance warrants.

Curriculum and Instruction

Beginning Level

The beginning levels of instruction immerse students in the English language and help them adjust to American culture. Throughout the beginning level, teachers try to provide a learning environment that is lively yet secure. Beginning-level classes are designed for a maximum of fifteen students. They receive four class periods per day in English: (1) listening, understanding, speaking; (2) speaking and writing; (3) reading and composition; and (4) English for math. Beginning-level students are also enrolled in a sheltered math class. Except for physical education (and, for 7th- and 8th-graders, an additional elective), students are in classes with other bilingual peers throughout the day. "We expect that by the end of the beginning level students will score at least at the second grade level in reading texts, understand spoken English, and know the English they need to succeed in math classes," says Alicia Mier, HILT chairperson at Bowie High School.

Judy Meyer's 7th-grade class in reading and composition at Lincoln Junior High School exemplifies these high expectations in practice. On one Friday afternoon in January her students begin the period with ten minutes of writing in their journals. Meyer does not write with them, preferring instead to circulate among the students, answering questions.

"Miss, how do you say . . . ?"

"Please, Miss, how do you spell . . . ?"

Routines have been clearly established; most of the students are already writing before the bell rings to begin class. Like all HILT teachers, Meyer has class rules and consequences posted at the front of the room. Her personal twist is posting not only negative consequences for anyone who breaks the rules, but positive consequences for those who obey. The class earns points for their collective good behavior: 50 points qualify for a game day (students play language arts games instead of engaging in formal instruction); 75 are worth an "open" test (one day when a test is scheduled, they can opt out); 100 earn an in-class movie and popcorn; 140 rate a party. On this afternoon, most of the students are remarkably well-behaved for so late in the day on a Friday. The systematic rewards and consequences establish clear guidelines for the students, allowing them freedom and choice within limits.

Journals are put away as Meyer passes out the day's text to be read, a nonfiction selection about a large city and a small community. She explains that the students will read silently first, and then listen to the text read aloud as they follow the words on the page. Before the silent read-through she gives the students questions to focus their attention. When they have completed their silent reading, she repeats the questions. The students answer, some speaking in English and some in Spanish. Meyer is equally accepting of and responsive to both languages, but all of her own comments are delivered in English.

Two concepts in the vocabulary, "larger" and "frustrated," seem to have caused the entire class particular difficulty. Because they have previously studied about New York City, Meyer has them recount some of what they remember. Next she has them provide the same information about El Paso. She then elaborates on the meaning of "larger" with a series of comparisons: New York's larger population, larger buildings, larger number of buildings. In a similar way, she helps them grasp the meaning of "frustrated" by having them describe their feelings when they want to say something in English but cannot think of the word. In both cases she effectively capitalizes on the students' own interests and knowledge in making the unknown familiar.

Later, as the students prepare to listen to her read the story while following along in the text, she raises a new question to listen for. The lesson is effective, helping the students deal with the same text twice and making use of both an aural and a visual instructional method. Repetition provides necessary practice, and multiple purposes for reading and different methods of working with the text ward off boredom.

Meyer wraps up the lesson by reminding the students that just a few weeks before, they had been unable to complete this same task with the same text. She praises their progress.

Intermediate Level

Once students successfully complete the beginning level, they progress to the intermediate level.[9] Here the student-to-teacher ratio is increased to a maximum of twenty to one, still much less than mainstream classes, and the ESL speaking and writing class dropped. The English classes for intermediate students include (1) listening, understanding, and speaking; (2) reading and comprehension; (3) English for science; and (4) English for social studies. Each student also enrolls in physical education and a regular math class. Seventh- and 8th-graders may take an additional elective.

At this level HILT teachers continue to rely on the same methodology and focus on communicative competence, that is, using language to communicate orally or in writing. Subscribing to recent research findings and their own classroom experience, HILT teachers believe that "hands-on" language acquisition should precede learning about language; in other words, grammar and "correct" or specialized usage are built gradually on the fluency students have already achieved.[10] The English for math and English for science classes help students bridge the initial gap between their conversational English skills and the academic vocabulary and skills they need to progress in their sheltered math and science classes. In sum, says Apodaca, "We expect much more production, both oral and written, from students at the intermediate level. We begin introducing grammar, because that's required as they move into the sheltered and unsheltered courses. Our methodologies are the same as at the beginning level, but the expectations rise. The texts are more difficult, the assignments more complex. Students begin keeping reading logs and using their reading as a basis for other writing. We never tell them how much to produce; we're flexible to individual needs." Mier adds, "By the end of intermediate level, we don't expect to hear Spanish used in class anymore. Students should have oral language production firmly established and understand the English they need for math and science. Usually they're reading at a 4th- to 5th-grade level in English."

Alma Rodriguez teaches an intermediate-level reading and composition class at Bowie High School. As one typical morning opens, her twenty students, all about 15 years old, sit quietly reading from a variety of English and Spanish paperbacks, hardbacks, and magazines. At the side of the room Rodriguez reads to herself from a well-worn bestseller. Ten minutes into the period a kitchen timer rings, the students put their books away, and the lesson begins.

Rodriguez's presentation involves four poster-sized black-and-white pictures, which are turned face toward the chalkboard. To the left of the chalkboard a large chart-paper tablet is securely fastened to a standing easel. She explains to the class that their homework assignment will be to write a composition about the pictures. To prepare for this, they are going to talk about the pictures beforehand. She turns over one of the pictures and asks, "What do you see?"

"Two persons."

"People."

She writes the responses on the chart paper and continues: "What's another name for 'two persons'?"

"A couple."

She continues to have the students elaborate on their own and others' comments, often writing her questions on the board and their responses on the chart. "Sometimes we call a couple, a husband and—?"

Two girls confer in the front of the room. A series of whispers in Spanish is interrupted when one of them, beaming, calls out, "Wife!" HILT teachers actively encourage student collaboration, realizing that language is a social tool learned in a social context.

The lesson continues with much prompting from Rodriguez to draw out multiple responses to a single question, to generate a wide array of vocabulary, to draw out students' justifications for their responses, and to aid their speculations about the characters' motives and actions. She is animated, listening in on this pair's Spanish whispering, nodding at that student's attempt, smiling, pacing. She supports every attempted response but always probes for more from the student and class. No one individual is accountable, but rather the entire group.

"What do you see?"

"What are they talking about?"

"Why do you say that?"

"What would you do in the boy's place?"

The questions she asks are primarily open-ended; this is a lesson in close observation and reasoning, not in getting the right answer.

"What do you mean, 'The woman's leaving'? Prove it."

The student calls attention to the exit sign above the woman's head in the picture.

"That's a sharp observation."

Discussion is thorough, down to elaboration of the meaning of gestures, such as one character's scratching his head in puzzlement.

Some twenty-five minutes later, when all four pictures have been turned forward and discussed in elaborate detail, Rodriguez shifts gears.

"Do you think these four pictures are in the correct order? Is this the way the events happened?"

They are not, and for the next ten minutes students confer with one another, argue back and forth, and suggest many alternative sequences. The pictures have no captions, and quite a few arrangements are possible. The class becomes so involved in the task that hands cease to be raised and conversation is directed toward peers rather than the teacher. It has been a fast-paced, productive, exhilarating half-hour, and the students spend the last few minutes of class planning their papers. They have spent the period expanding their vocabulary (two persons, people, couple, husband and wife, boyfriend and girlfriend), practicing their language in meaningful conversation centered on a single topic, and preparing thoroughly for their writing assignment.

Many potential difficulties with the assignment have been prevented before they could occur because of the diligent preparation. The preparation has also taken advantage of the students' social and cognitive skills. They have been allowed to use their collective vocabulary to broaden each other's individual word stores. They have assisted each other in interpreting language, gestures, and facial expressions. Their interactions with peers have been positive, and their contributions praised. The students clearly recognize this classroom as a safe environment in which to take risks and try out their growing second-language skills.

Advanced and Transitional Levels

The pattern of reduced English instruction and increased emphasis on subject areas continues at the advanced level. Students now have just two English class periods per day: (1) grammar and literature and (2) English for social studies. Additional classes include sheltered math, science, and social studies, plus physical education and an elective. Advanced, but not transitional, classes are offered in the junior high schools. The English instruction has become fairly formal, emphasizing traditional grammar and literature lessons, the type of instruction they will engage in soon as mainstream students. "Advanced students focus a lot on vocabulary development," Mier says. "They are fluent in conversational English and can produce the English they need for most schoolwork. Their reading ability moves up to about 7th-grade level."

Sometime near the end of their semester of advanced instruction in English, students go to the Testing Center for standardized reading comprehension and language testing in English. On the basis of scores on the CELT and the ITBS, as well as teachers' recommendations and grades received, students may be placed next semester in mainstream language arts classes, or continue in "correlated" (remedial) sheltered language arts classes that are available to all students in the school who score below the 40th percentile on the ITBS. Teachers confer over individual cases for which scores hover near the cutoff.

Transitional classes are offered to 9th-graders in the high schools. In essence they are a sheltered freshman English class. Students assigned to this class are generally newly arrived immigrants who have sufficient English skills to survive in the mainstream curriculum but who need help adjusting to their new environment. Ninth-graders who have still not reached a level where they can succeed in the mainstream English curriculum are placed in the "correlated" language arts classes.

One of Mier's grammar and literature classes offers a good example of instruction at the advanced level. After an initial ten minutes of silent reading on their own, the students open their literature books. Mier explains that they are going to read a short story called "The Monkey's Paw."[11] She has already written two sets of vocabulary words on the chalkboard. The first consists of words the students will encounter in the story, words like "talisman," "peril," and "dread." She asks the class which words they already know the meaning of, and then elaborates as necessary to illustrate their particular meaning in this story. The only word for which the students cannot furnish even a starting point is "dread."

"How do you feel on Monday morning when you have a test first period?" she asks. Responses clarify the meaning quickly.

The second set of words are literary techniques found in the story: "foreshadowing," "suspense," "imaginative language." The class obviously has already learned these terms in relation to stories previously read. Their responses are prompt and correct. "Look for foreshadowing, suspense, and imaginative language as we read this story," Mier directs.

Purpose set, the class begins reading aloud in turns. Between readers, every few paragraphs, Mier interjects questions. Some of these call attention to pivotal events, some to use of vocabulary and literary devices, others to inferences about characters' motivations or plot resolution. As the story progresses, the students read longer sections of text between questions.

The period ends before the class reaches the climax of the story; the homework assignment is to complete the story and then describe three wishes the student would make if he or she had a talisman like the monkey's paw. The difficulty of the task lies in Mier's admonition to remember the trouble characters in the story encountered when they did not follow the former owner's advice. "What if you wish for a red car," she asks, "and you wake up tomorrow morning with a red jalopy that won't run sitting in your driveway?" The students leave the room, obviously eager to finish the story, discussing with friends what their own wishes will be.

The lesson has held the students' rapt attention for a number of reasons. It has enabled them to test their growing abilities to hypothesize and reason abstractly. The thorough presentation of difficult vocabulary and story elements, before the reading, facilitated better comprehension as they read and therefore led to a more successful experience. The step-by-step, careful discussion of events and structure will serve them well, both immediately as they complete their homework and later as they encounter sheltered and unsheltered literature classes.

Sheltered Courses

Sheltered courses in math, science, and social studies, together with the "English for" classes that present the special terminology for each subject area, have enabled HILT students to make a smooth transition into the wider academic demands of high school. The student-to-teacher ratio in sheltered classes is thirty to one, but all the students are HILT classmates and the curriculum is modified to their needs. Social studies in particular is effectively geared to the needs of immigrants. Even though the mainstream curriculum does not do so, instruction in sheltered classes begins with the colonization period in American history, because the students usually have not previously studied American history. Further, because the state-adopted social studies texts are extremely difficult, HILT has replaced them with easier texts covering the same content.[12]

Summary

The design of HILT is remarkably responsive to the cultural, academic, and developmental needs of young adolescents adjusting to a new country and school system and learning a new language. Beginning-level classes are kept small to facilitate the individual assistance many of the students require, and to promote a feeling of security. Many have come from classes in Mexico with as many as fifty to seventy students, where attendance is not mandatory as it is the United States. The curriculum in Mexico is also different, often emphasizing advanced math and science courses at earlier levels than in the United States. Geographically, most HILT students have moved only a short distance, to the other side of a river; culturally they have entered a different world.

David, an 8th-grader in advanced-level classes at Lincoln Junior High School, came to El Paso at the beginning of the 7th grade. He had lived in Juarez and attended school there from 8:30 in the morning until 1:30 in the afternoon. His school had no library and did not serve lunch, and he had only one teacher all day. He recalls his move to El Paso: "The first year was tough. I couldn't understand what the teachers were saying. I couldn't speak. There were too many new things." One of his classmates, Laura, remembers, "I was afraid to talk or someone might laugh at me. I couldn't think how to say things in English."

HILT surrounds students with the sights and sounds of spoken and written English. HILT teachers do not force students to use the new language verbally before they comprehend it. Instead they respond to students' questions, whether asked in English or in Spanish. HILT modifies the curriculum to meet students' English-language needs, tapering off the English instruction as students gain proficiency. The program sequences the introduction of subject area instruction from courses with the least verbal demands (math) to those with the highest (social studies). HILT provides specific English instruction in central terminology and concepts as students are first introduced to each discipline.

HILT allows students to speak when they are ready, respond as they are able, and write according to their capabilities. HILT provides the support students need throughout the program as they tackle each new task. Individual assistance helps students over the cultural hurdles, such as becoming used to the U.S. school system, and the lack of insistence on immediate language production allows students to form a firm comprehension base in the new language before venturing into speech and writing. Vocabulary instruction in the subject areas provides specific academic terminology when needed, and sheltered courses allow a successful transition into the mainstream.

"We provide a total systematic program," Apodaca explains. "As students gain proficiency, we add more English and less sheltering. Then the students can begin making their own choices, the choices a good education provides."

Staff Development and Training

Teachers in HILT receive in-service training in four areas:

1. Theory of second language acquisition and applied linguistics research
2. ESL methods and techniques
3. Young adolescent development and cultural sensitivity
4. Program administration

One or two in-service sessions are held each month, usually all day on a Saturday. Attendance is voluntary. Approximately 60 to 75 percent of the staff attend any given session, for which they are often paid or receive credit for advancement on the state's career ladder. As Apodaca describes them, "We start initial workshops talking about theories of first and second language acquisition, of learning theories from Piaget to behaviorism. Most teachers, especially those fresh from universities, have training but no philosophical base for their instructional methods. They have to know the basis of instructional practices, so that they can analyze materials and methods. Many programs make the mistake of approaching teaching like a recipe book. Teachers must have a philosophy in order to make choices." Later sessions focus on language learning as a meaning-centered activity. HILT believes that students should use language in order to communicate. "We try not to chain teachers to one textbook or methodology," Apodaca says. "A variety of instructional methods are appropriate if they focus on comprehension and meaning."

Sessions are conducted on different paradigms of reading instruction, on creative writing, and on approaches to teaching math, science, and social studies to second-language students. Staff instruction in aspects of Mexican culture is also important. "We don't want to change the students to be just like us," Apodaca observes. "We want to be more accepting of differences, to understand our own prejudices, to look at students from a broader perspective."

Awareness of cultural differences, such as different holidays and different family roles, is particularly vital to the success of a program like HILT, which encourages but does not force language production. Like all people, HILT students are most able to talk and write about what they know best. Instructional activities therefore center on what is significant to the students. For instance, religion plays a more central role in the lives of Mexican natives than it does in the U.S. population as a whole. A baptism or first communion is an occasion of great importance. Young adolescent Mexican girls greatly anticipate their *quince anera*, a religious ceremony and festive celebration in recognition of their coming of age on their fifteenth birthday.

Meyer tells a story that aptly illustrates the importance of cultural awareness in teaching. A well-meaning teacher during the first year of the program listened to an excited student tell about her older sister's receiving a *gallo* the previous evening. The teacher looked up the word in a pocket dictionary, found the primary meaning, "rooster," and was a little puzzled about the student's excitement. She didn't realize that *gallos*, or serenades of young women by men with a hired group of musicians, are another common cultural event that students from Mexico take delight in observing and discussing. "She lost an important opportunity to stimulate conversation," Meyer explains. "Many successful instructional activities arise from student interests of the moment. We miss out as teachers if we don't understand the importance of certain events in Mexican culture."

Program History and Development

Until HILT was created in 1982, middle-grades students with limited English proficiency in El Paso were offered a daily double period of English instruction that was best characterized as "very disorganized," according to Ken Thomas, now Assistant Superintendent for Curriculum for the El Paso Independent School District. It could be little else, because the state had appropriated no funding for the program, despite the requirement.

The imbalance of great need with lack of funding was not the sole obstacle. More daunting, and much tougher to grapple with, were prevailing attitudes toward both Mexican immigration and education for students with limited English proficiency. The weight of Texas history and local economic pressures, as El Paso's economy took a dive with the Mexican peso in the early 1980s, must have made many Hispanic newcomers question the meaning of the phrase "the land of opportunity."

Within the schools, the disarray of the secondary ESL program had caused many of the teachers and administrators to view the program as a dumping ground for "dummies" and students with behavioral problems. Apodaca, who was then the district's consultant for ESL education, summarized student and faculty attitudes toward the ESL program this way: "Teachers did not want to teach it; bright students did not want to take it; unmotivated students did not want to leave it."[13]

In December 1980 the district's deputy superintendent created a fourteen-member committee to examine the shortcomings of the existing ESL program. Apodaca, Thomas, Enrique Perez (the Director of Federal Programs), and Luis Cortez (principal at Bowie High School) were members of the committee who were to play key roles in the development of HILT. After just two half-day meetings in January 1981, the consensus of the committee was to implement a new secondary program for Hispanic students who needed English instruction.

As the initial coordinator of the project, Apodaca was responsible for developing HILT from ground zero to full operation. She began by consulting the research literature, speaking with experts, and visiting programs as far away as Alexandria, Virginia. Her next task was translating her discoveries into a usable curriculum. Borrowing an idea from the secondary science consultant, another of Thomas's staff, she hired a group of teachers, who would be involved in the pilot program, to write the curriculum during the summer of 1981. "The teachers were hired on contract to write the materials," says Thomas. "We didn't have to worry about organizing a summer workshop, or the time that is often wasted socializing. They were paid a flat fee at the end." The curriculum committee was hand-picked from ESL teachers who were well informed on issues related to second-language learning and known for their conscientious approach to their duties. The committee also included an English teacher to insure that the curriculum would prepare students for success in the regular classroom.

Patricia Multhauf, who helped Apodaca direct the curriculum committee, explains the process: "The first question we asked ourselves was what skills students *must* have to succeed in regular English classes, and those became the minimum objectives of our classes. Then we looked at the wide range of skills students entered the program with, the number of credits they would need for high school graduation, and we worked from there." The committee quickly recognized that the existing ESL curriculum was not suitably comprehensive. Through it students might gain sufficient competence to converse with other English speakers, but, as Apodaca observed, "Our students need to be prepared beyond the interpersonal communications skills level to the academic proficiency level."[14]

A second concern was that students were pushed into mainstream math, science, social studies, and other classes at the same time they were trying to master English. In these classes no distinction was made between Spanish- and English-speakers, or between Hispanics of varying academic backgrounds. Quite naturally this created frustrations for students and teachers alike.

Though Apodaca held preliminary discussions and visited other programs, no outside consultants assisted directly in creating HILT. Multhauf explains, "We thought a ready-made program would fit like a ready-made suit: it would need many alterations." The committee wanted instead to make the program specific to the needs of El Paso's students.

Apodaca chose Bowie High School, which had a large population of students with limited English language skills, as the pilot site. Bowie is located farthest south of all the El Paso schools; students and staff can see Mexico from the back windows of the building, beyond a pair of fences, a highway, and the river. Bowie's principal, Cortez, was extremely eager to take advantage of any program that would lend assistance to his many Spanish-speaking students. Multhauf, his assistant vice-principal, was the on-site liaison for the project.

In January 1982, with a staff of eight ESL teachers serving 184 students (128 in the 9th grade, 49 in the 10th, 7 in the 11th), the pilot program began. The first semester, teachers experimented with methods, materials, and grouping patterns and experienced the typical growing pains of new programs: insufficient materials, difficulties with a new philosophy and methodology, and cultural differences. "But the students and teachers found it exciting. And *still* do," emphasizes Multhauf. Some components were discarded, some were modified, and others were earmarked for further trial.

Because HILT planners recognized that strong community support would be essential if the program were to continue beyond the pilot stage, they invited community leaders and school board members to see the program in operation. Classroom visits, open houses, and luncheons provided firsthand opportunities to observe the teaching and, more important, the learning. Apodaca and Thomas made certain the visitors were introduced to students and teachers in order to personalize the experience and to demonstrate the students' growing competence in English. "Inevitably the visitors liked it, were impressed with the kids' English abilities, and would tell their friends," says Thomas. Apodaca adds, "It's very convincing to walk into an intermediate class, where students have only been learning English less than two semesters, and hear the class debating abolition of the state's Blue Laws. In *English!*"

Thomas and Apodaca also took the program to the rest of the community and parents with a ten-minute videotape they had produced. Civic clubs, parent-teacher groups, and various businesses learned of the program without having to take special pains to find out.

No formal assessment data were kept, but by the end of its first semester the program had received such overwhelming support from administrators, teachers, the public, and students that the district decided to expand HILT to ten campuses; four senior and six junior high schools, to be served by nearly sixty teachers. "We didn't do anything spectacular," states Thomas. "Our support grew by word of mouth. We had something that works, and we showed people."

Assessing Success

Much of the evidence of HILT's success has thus far been anecdotal. As HILT's status shifted in 1987 from pilot to regular program, the district planned to compile and analyze the statistical data collected over the pilot years. But even from the anecdotal information available and the limited studies that have been done, it is clear that the program has been successful in improving the literacy skills and the future life choices of many students in the district. HILT has been recognized at the local, state, and national levels. In 1985 HILT was cited as an example of a successful program for second-language learners in a *Time* magazine article, which reported that "until 1982, many of El Paso's Hispanic high schoolers either failed or dropped out. Today HILT students regularly appear on the honor roll; many are members of the National Honor Society and several have graduated at the top of their classes."[15]

Many of the achievements, as cited in the *Time* article, have been dramatic. For instance, Monica Joloma, a HILT graduate from Bowie, was co-winner of the first $1,000 college scholarship awarded by the Texas Teachers of English to Speakers of Other Languages in 1984. She also became a member of the National Honor Society that year, a year in which every high school in the district reported at least one HILT student among its honor society inductees, and every junior high reported at least two in its Junior National Honor Society.

Mier proudly remarks that in 1986 more than half of Bowie's honor society members were former HILT students, though HILT students have always comprised a much smaller proportion of the student body (in 1986 they numbered just 233 among the school's total enrollment of 1,750). In the regional Modern Languages Speech Tournament held each spring, HILT students regularly shine in the ESL division. In the spring of 1986 they dominated the four divisions of the higher levels, winning eleven out of twelve places. In the intermediate and advanced sections they captured five of the eight possible first-place wins.

On a more formal level, the El Paso Independent School District's Office for Research and Evaluation conducted a follow-up study in 1985 to examine how HILT students were performing in regular classrooms.[16] The study covered 464 students who were enrolled in HILT at the beginning or intermediate level in 1982–83, comparing their performance in the sheltered subject-area classes during 1982–83 and 1983–84 with that of non-HILT students during the 1983–84 school year. Both groups of students covered the same material in their subject-area classes, whether HILT or mainstream. The study found that HILT students in sheltered classes scored substantially higher than non-HILT students in mainstream classes in all areas except algebra. For instance, 95 percent of the students in sheltered classes passed English, as compared to only 80 percent of those in mainstream English classes. Furthermore, this high rate of success was apparent at all grade levels. In a grade-level comparison of HILT versus non-HILT students, the same study found that HILT students were scoring very close to their mainstream counterparts in most subject areas. This finding demonstrates how quickly the language gap can be closed for many students. In just two to three years of intensive language instruction emphasizing comprehension prior to production, HILT students perform nearly on a level with mainstream students.

In another study, which covered the pilot programs for second-language learners across in the state in 1985, researchers for the Texas Education Agency concluded that the most effective secondary-level models were those that provided additional English language instructional time and sheltered subject-area transition courses.[17] HILT, which offers both, was rated the most successful program in terms of student classroom achievement by the Agency's Director of Special Programs Division of Planning and Research.[18]

Perhaps the most convincing evidence of the program's effectiveness is the low school-dropout rate among HILT students, particularly those who complete the program. Nationwide the dropout rate for Hispanic students is alarming. A New York State study in November 1986 assessed the dropout rate of its Hispanic students past the 9th grade at 62 percent; the Illinois Board of Education placed that state's dropout rate for Hispanics at 47 percent, and the statewide rate for Texas in the fall of 1986 was 45 percent.[19] The overall dropout rate for students who participate in El Paso's HILT program, however, is 25 percent, decreasing to 15 percent among those who remain through the transitional level of instruction. Among HILT students the main reasons for dropping out are age and returning to Mexico. HILT has little control over either variable and clearly benefits those who participate in and complete training.

Conclusions

By 1986 HILT was firmly institutionalized in El Paso. "There's no longer any debate about how to do English language instruction," Thomas says. "We're going to do it the HILT way. The question is, how do we do HILT as well as possible?"

Two areas of concern are paramount: attracting quality staff and meeting the special needs of the student population. Although more than half of HILT's current staff has been in the program since 1983 or before, Thomas says there is a limited supply of quality trained staff. Luz Elena Nieto, Apodaca's successor, worries that HILT may have to absorb untrained tenured staff who might be assigned to the program by the central administration when their positions are cut elsewhere. Though HILT still offers extensive in-service training, it can be difficult to work with staff who do not choose to attend.

Thomas recognizes there is nothing the school district can do about the composition and mobility of the student population, but points out the difficulties: "In many ways El Paso is the Ellis Island of the 'eighties. Mexicans are immigrating, and they're going to continue to do so. Our population is always shifting. We never know from year to year what the student body will be like. Three years ago we had eighty-six students in HILT with less than five years of formal schooling in their home country, this year twenty-six. Next year, who knows?" Nieto adds, "One of the biggest problems is that the students just don't remain with us. Many move to El Paso, attend a school in southern El Paso, their parents make some money and get more firmly situated, and then they move away to another school district or city."

Adjustments to a new culture and school system are always difficult. "They come to El Paso," Nieto explains, "and find the population where they live so similar to Mexico, they think school will be the same. The children are often here only because their parents wanted them to come. They can communicate with everyone in their neighborhood in Spanish, and they don't see why they should learn English."

HILT continues to modify approaches and fine-tune the program to respond to these challenges. In 1986 three itinerant teachers were hired to work with each of the low-schooled (less than five years of prior schooling) students. They meet one-to-one for four hours twice each week, and the rest of their students' time is spent in beginning-level classes. Because there were at the time only twenty-six such students, spread through seven different schools, there was no other cost-effective way to teach them all.

An important future goal is to hire community liaison staff to work directly with families and students, to assist with cultural and school transitions. "So many of the students and their families seem to go through culture shock," Thomas observes. "It's almost beyond the scope of the program. We hope community liaisons will help with the adjustments, and show families the importance of schooling in the United States."

Plans are also being made to add a pilot summer program, provide additional reading and writing emphasis for advanced-level students, and offer a separate advanced Spanish-language track for students who are native speakers of Spanish. This will help students who are literate in Spanish to retain and improve those skills. Because they have also gained similar literacy skills in English, these students can be said to be truly bilingual.

The most fitting praise of HILT comes from the students themselves. Jose Marrufo, a 9th-grader in the HILT program, composed this speech, which he delivered at the Modern Language Association's Speech Tournament:

> It doesn't matter if we say things wrong. We have to learn from our mistakes. There are many people who judge others by how the people speak. They might make fun, laugh at us. But there are people who want to help us. Many people want to help us by not making fun of our speech, and by correcting us in our vocabulary. Many of the people that want to help us are the teachers. They are always trying to make us understand that we must do every assignment, and all the work that they tell us to do. By doing all the things that the teachers tell us to do and by taking school seriously, we can have better opportunities in life. We can have better opportunities to get a better job.
>
> I ask you, fellow students remember always that what counts when we talk to each other is that we communicate not how we communicate. Keep learning and trying your best. You will obtain your education for a good job and become what you and your parents want you to be.

HILT demonstrates that successful programs for new English-speakers cannot be conducted as a "quick fix," but when done correctly can be a "sure fix." HILT gives its students intensive, almost full-day support for their first couple of years in the school system, and this approach pays off. In a relatively short time these students acquire the skills they need to be successful in the mainstream, monolingual English classroom.

Notes

1. An "In-Bond Program" established by the Mexican government allows foreign investors 100 percent ownership of manufacturing facilities in Mexico. More than 160 such companies are found in Juarez, the majority of them U.S.-owned.

2. *High Intensity Language Training: Program Information, 1983–84* (El Paso: El Paso Independent School District, 1983), 17.

3. R. Apodaca, "How We Educate Non-English Speaking Students Successfully," paper presented at the meeting of the National School

Boards Association, Anaheim, California, March 1985 (copy on file at the Center for Early Adolescence), 6.

4. Also called ESOL: English for Speakers of Other Languages.

5. Apodaca, "How We Educate Non-English Speaking Students Successfully," 9.

6. On sheltered courses see S.D. Krashen, *Principles and Practices in Second Language Acquisition* (New York: Pergamon Press, 1982).

7. *High Intensity Language Training,* 4.

8. Apodaca, "How We Educate Non-English Speaking Students Successfully," 7.

9. Patricia Mulhauf, assistant principal at Bowie High School, reports that as many as 75 percent of the students repeat the beginning level of HILT instruction. District policy allows students to be retained only once in grades 1–8. Students who arrive in midyear can be given an "incomplete," which is subsequently removed when they complete the same course successfully the following semester.

10. See Krashen, *Principles and Practices in Second Language Acquisition.*

11. W.W. Jacobs, *The Monkey's Paw* (Makato, Minn.: Creative Education, Inc., 1986).

12. Apodaca, "How We Educate Non-English Speaking Students Successfully," notes that the state-adopted social studies text is written at a 12th-grade level that even many native English-speakers find difficult.

13. Apodaca, "How We Educate Non-English Speaking Students Successfully," 3.

14. Apodaca, "How We Educate Non-English Speaking Students Successfully," 5.

15. E. Bowen, "For Learning or Ethnic Pride?" *Time,* 8 July 1985, 80–81.

16. S. Schneider, *HILT Follow-Up Study* (El Paso: El Paso Independent School District).

17. *Bilingual Education Pilot Programs: Interim Study Report,* staff report to the Texas State Board of Education (Austin: Texas Education Agency, 1985).

18. Cited in Apodaca, "How We Educate Non-English Speaking Students Successfully."

19. See P. Applebome, "Educators Alarmed by Growing Rate of Dropouts among Hispanic Youth," *New York Times,* 15 March 1987, 13.

AFTER-SCHOOL LITERACY PROGRAMS
FOR YOUNG ADOLESCENTS

Schools are central to efforts to solve the problem of adolescent illiteracy, but they need not have the monopoly on literacy instruction. Community-based organizations and their after-school literacy programs have an important role to play.

In early adolescence, young people begin to explore the world beyond their family, school, and most immediate network of connections. Although they are still deeply concerned with the feelings and beliefs of their families, relationships with peers and a variety of adults take on a new and deep significance in their lives. Consequently, they experience a new awareness of community and an eagerness to participate in community affairs. Using their newly discovered cognitive abilities—the ability to compare several elements, create a hypothesis, and project the answer into the future—young adolescents assess their own strengths and weaknesses, assess their likes and dislikes, and make decisions about their future possibilities.

Good after-school programs act as a bridge for young adolescents between the tight-knit world of family and school and the larger world of the community and the future. In 1982 researchers at the Center for Early Adolescence conducted an exhaustive search for successful after-school programs for young adolescents, ultimately visiting fifty programs in twenty-four states. Although the demand for such programs far surpasses the number available, programs do exist that offer young people a variety of stimulating opportunities, such as academic and cultural enrichment, recreation, career exploration, and religious activities.[1] Building upon this research into general after-school programming for young adolescents, the Center's Project on Adolescent Literacy (PAL) addressed a specific issue: Are there community-based programs that provide literacy instruction for young adolescents, and how do young adolescents respond to these programs?

There are indeed several after-school literacy programs that are greatly changing the lives of the young adolescents that attend them—programs where students who were not reading before now rush for new books, where young adolescents who once would become angry and sullen when asked to read are now eager to read to friends or younger children. These programs are sponsored by a variety of community agencies including churches, business volunteers, and comprehensive social-service agencies. The range of sponsors that can aid adolescent literacy seems very flexible.

Despite this good news, if there are too few good after-school programs of any kind for young adolescents, there are even fewer after-school literacy resources for the age-group. In the majority of programs PAL staff located, young adolescents are included at the upper end of programs that focus on elementary-school children. These programs can only serve a small proportion of the young adolescents who need help with literacy. Moreover, many young adolescents with literacy needs may be reluctant to attend a program with younger children, and yet they are generally ineligible for evening community literacy programs that focus on older adolescents and adults.

The three programs described in this chapter are a selection from the after-school literacy programs studied.

- *The Friendly Place,* a community literacy center serving all ages and levels through a combination library-bookstore and special programming, is located in New York City's East Harlem. The Friendly Place emphasizes enrichment, surrounding people with books and good literacy experiences, as its approach to literacy.

- *The Montgomery Ward-Cabrini Green Tutoring Program* is a partnership between business and community. Business volunteers provide one-to-one tutoring one night a week to children from Chicago's Cabrini Green Housing Project. This program could be called an academic encouragement model.

- *The Highline Indian Tutoring Program,* located in Seattle, Washington, is a cross-age tutoring program that employs high-school and college students to tutor young Native Americans. The program focuses specifically on aiding students who are in danger of academic failure because of low reading achievement.

These three programs exemplify the types of programs that predominate in after-school literacy programming: enrichment, encouragement, and remediation. They could serve as models to imitate, as suggestions for improving current programs, or as a starting point for planning new kinds of programs.

These programs are representative of the diversity, the potential, and the problems that after-school programs confront. Their success verifies PAL researchers' initial assumption that after-school programs can recapture the hopes of young adolescents who are drifting away from school because of academic failure.

The Friendly Place: Literacy for All Ages and All Levels of Ability

One of the first things one notices upon walking into The Friendly Place is the light flooding in through the full-length windows. In New York City's East Harlem, where grates, grilles, and bars protect most of the windows, unencumbered picture windows are an unusual sight. Walkers hurrying by glance up with surprise at another unusual sight: the people browsing over books inside. It is an odd activity in this neighborhood, where there are no other bookstores.

Tucked into a storefront on the ground floor of one of the huge low-income housing projects that line the East River, The Friendly Place is a place where everyone has the right to read. Because many of the neighborhood residents are Hispanic, the center is also known as El Sitio Simpatico. Billing itself as an "informal, for pleasure, library-bookstore," The Friendly Place has reached out since 1981 to expand the literacy skills of all ages and all levels of readers living in the neighborhood.

The Friendly Place has the feel of a den in the kind of home that is "lived in." The space is clearly organized but not intimidating. Couches are mixed with tables and chairs of various sizes, so that people of all ages can find a comfortable spot to read. Local artists display their work near the big picture windows.

Also located near the entry are the "for sale" books. Best-selling books for children and young adults, parenting information, and other books patrons frequently request are attractively displayed. A large number of inexpensive quality paperbacks are kept in stock for the school classes that visit. Many students purchase books as part of the field trip. The stock also includes good secondhand copies at very low prices.

The rest of the space is books "for loan." Unlike most libraries, but similar to bookstores, The Friendly Place displays its books with their colorful covers facing outward, to catch the eyes of browsers. Paperbacks outnumber hardback books, because they are easily replaceable and less intimidating to users, who are likely to be concerned about the cost of lost books. Users' ID library cards are filed at the front desk, as in some small-town and rural libraries, rather than carried home by the individual borrower. This system eliminates the problem of lost cards and is especially helpful to children, whose parents often view library cards as akin to credit cards, encumbrances to be approached with fear and caution.

The Friendly Place is a community literacy center serving all ages and all levels of readers. Books are not arranged by the Dewey Decimal system or the Library of Congress system. Instead the program uses its own system, one that models its philosophy of equality among readers. Books are organized more in bookshop style, by broad interest areas (for example, black history, Puerto Rico, poetry, romance, plays). In each section the most difficult to read are at the top of the shelves; the easiest to read are near floor level. Only books for very young children are shelved separately, across the back wall. Near them are the smallest tables and chairs. This system of arranging books by subject area and other visual cues helps readers find books in their areas of interest and ability, without feeling stigmatized for their level of reading skill.

Several mornings a week a toddler-and-parent group meets. The 2-year-olds meander from picture books to games, then back to their parents and a snack. Their parents meet new friends as they watch and, with the guidance of a staff person, learn how they can use the resources of The Friendly Place. In the afternoon a scattering of neighborhood users wander in to browse and borrow. Classes from local elementary schools are frequently scheduled for visits during the day. After school the tables fill with elementary-school students doing their homework. Program staff, adult volunteers, and the adolescent junior staff aid them. Many of these young people do not have someone at home able to help them, or they may lack a quiet place to work. Homework help is an essential service if they are to succeed in school.

After they have completed their homework, the young people join one of the Book and Game Club activities. According to the Book and Game Club manual, "A Book and Game Club consists of two parts: reading books and playing games in small groups."[2] As with homework, a staff member, volunteer, or teenage aide assists the young people, by reading aloud a story and then helping group members to play a game. "We feel that the games are an important method of improving basic skills and problem solving in a pleasurable, nonthreatening way," explains a staff member. "The games can and should be used in a progression so that the child, over time, goes from a game that requires little reading and strategy, like Sorry!, to Clue and Careers, or from hearts and 'take five' through Othello and Monopoly to chess." More importantly, perhaps, than promoting literacy and math skills, the games encourage young people to relax and have fun in a book-filled environment.

Special-interest groups also give young people the chance to use their literacy skills as they mix with their friends. After-school clubs that feature creative writing, arts, crafts, and comic books were among the 1986–87 offerings at The Friendly Place. Group leaders incorporate reading and writing into the experience. In the Comics Club, students may create their own comics, but they will also have the chance to compare their work with a variety of professional comic strips. Like the Book and Game Club groups, each of these special-interest groups is called a club, rather than a class, thus avoiding connotations of "school."

As the younger school children head home, the Rap Club, a group of junior- and senior-high students, meets to talk about matters that concern its members—family relationships, sexuality, teen pregnancy, drug abuse. Stephanie Robinson, the leader of the group and director of The Friendly Place, weaves literacy into the topics the group chooses to discuss. For teens, as for other Friendly Place users, the message is clear: "There are books written about your interests. You can find out more about those interests in books."

On Saturdays and during the summer The Friendly Place sponsors clubs for young people in a variety of interest areas from cooking to dance or drama. The clubs introduce young people to new books, new literacy skills, and new vocabulary.

In 1985 3,500 young people used the services of The Friendly Place, and almost half of these were young adolescents. They had many reasons to participate: to obtain help with schoolwork, to find a good book, to have a good time with friends or as junior staff members, to help others learn. At The Friendly Place, no one is stigmatized for a lack of reading skills, and there is support for anyone who would like to improve and use those skills.

The Friendly Place is only one of several literacy demonstration projects sponsored by the American Reading Council, founded in 1976. All of the Council's projects are closely intertwined with its three purposes: demonstration, dissemination, and advocacy. "Everything we do has to do with reading. All of our programs are aimed at community literacy. We want to see literacy become functional rather than stagnant," states Sara Schwabacher, assistant director of the Council.

Besides The Friendly Place, the Council operates The First Reading Program/Open Sesame, a literacy program for K-1 students that bases its literacy teaching on children's direct experiences with language.[3] The program is designed to improve the reading skills of children from impoverished backgrounds. In Open Sesame classrooms children are surrounded by books and book experiences. They dictate stories to their teachers, and talk about and read their stories to each other. Teachers also read aloud to them frequently, selecting from a wide variety of good children's literature. The program began in 1984 at the Brownsville Child Development Center in New York City and has now spread to the public schools. During the 1986–87 school year twenty 1st-grade teachers were trained in the methods.

The Mother's Reading Program in East Harlem, also sponsored by the American Reading Council, is an adult literacy program that develops its curriculum from the needs and life concerns of the participants.[4] The program works with low-income mothers, most of whom are on welfare and all of whom read at a 0- to 3rd-grade level. Like Open Sesame, the Mother's Reading Program helps participants create texts from their own language. These texts become their first readers.

The Intergenerational Program uses graduates of the Mother's Reading Program as mentors to parents in a Head Start program. Young parents learn about childcare and develop their literacy skills with the support of a strong combination of teachers: the Council's literacy professionals, the Head Start teachers, and the mentors.

The Friendly Place has also played an important role in the Council's dissemination work. *How to Start and Run a Book and Game Club* is a manual that grew out of the program.[5] New York City School District 6 is using methods from this manual in its services for "latchkey children" as a part of the Early Adolescent Helper Program, which provides meaningful work experience for young adolescents in a variety of community settings; in this case the young adolescent helpers are trained to lead Book and Game Clubs in after-school programs for younger children. The Council has created pamphlets, articles, and videotapes from its other demonstration projects as well. It also disseminates information on effective literacy practices that may not yet be widely known to professionals. *How to Start and Run a School Paperback Bookstore,* for instance, is a manual drawn from the Council's research on school bookstores in Great Britain and the United States.[6]

School libraries have received special attention from the Council's advocacy efforts. It was in part through the Council's work that school library allocations in New York State and New York City were recently resumed or increased. The Council also joined the battle for school library services in East Harlem's District 4, where The Friendly Place has long served as the sole library to several local schools. New York City elementary-school libraries got no state or city funding from 1975 to 1985. The district superintendent has now promised to provide library services in every school in the district.

The Council has supported the ideals of the Year of the Reader campaign to promote reading. Julia Palmer, the executive director of the American Reading Council, remarks that in modern society, "We've spent millions to market blue jeans. We haven't ever marketed reading." She is hoping that someday the doctor on a soap opera will say, "Gosh, I'm bleary-eyed. I couldn't put that book down last night." She envisions a scene in "Dallas" in which J.R. would be interrupted while reading a book.

Palmer has championed the cause of literacy for more than twenty-five years. Starting out as a school volunteer in East Harlem, she discovered that reading was presented to poor children as a bitter pill, a nasty necessity, rather than as an exciting and magical world that expands one's own experience. Teachers taught from reading textbooks to children who had never had the chance to hear stories read aloud. There were no books to choose from in the public schools where she volunteered, and few students had books at home. She quickly realized that access to books was part of the huge divide between the "haves" and the "have nots." Since that time she has done everything in her power to get books into the hands of adults and children from neighborhoods like East Harlem who, in her opinion, have been denied the right to read. She has organized classroom libraries, school book fairs, and school bookstores. She even ran her own bookmobile in Brooklyn.

As she explains to inner-city parents, "Common sense tells us that kids who come from homes where they're read to every day learn to read. Your children are just as bright. Your kids just didn't have the luck to be read to, have books surrounding them. They've got to have terrific school libraries and teachers who read to them daily."

Palmer has a special place in her heart for young adolescents. In the many literacy projects she has sponsored over the years, she has given adolescents jobs that were socially fulfilling as well as helpful in improving their literacy skills. In her Buttercup Project, the bookmobile she ran in the Bedford-Stuyvesant neighborhood in the mid-1970s, she employed young adolescents, many of whom had only rudimentary reading skills. They helped in all jobs, from directing traffic in front of the school where the bookmobile was parked, to organizing and checking out books. Palmer included her student aides in the book selection process, too. They were required to read the books under consideration for the bookmobile shelves and take part in the discussion about each book. As a result Palmer noticed a tremendous increase in the aides' reading skills.

The Friendly Place employs several 14- to 16-year-olds from New York City's youth corps. Most of these young people have limited reading skills, and some are dropouts. One of Palmer's favorite successes was one of these workers—a hard-boiled, surly young woman who was a beginning reader. The teenager began reading simple picture books to a handicapped child who used the center, over time forming a close relationship with her listener. By the end of her semester of service with The Friendly Place this young woman had read fifty-four books—more than any of the other workers.

The Friendly Place is a living illustration of the American Reading Council's and Julia Palmer's dream: a world where everyone can exercise the right to read, where everyone has books, where preschool and school children are read aloud to every day, and where young people can explore their future and their past through the written word. The Friendly Place has made that dream become real for many young people in East Harlem.

The Montgomery Ward-Cabrini Green Tutoring Program: A Corporate-Community Partnership

The Montgomery Ward corporate headquarters are on Chicago's north side, bordering the Cabrini Green Housing Project. Most of the area's residents have low incomes and struggle daily with the problems of surviving on limited resources. The housing project tends to receive more publicity for its problems than its strengths. Local newspapers periodically report on the gang warfare that plagues it, and it is this image of violence that sticks in the minds of most local citizens. The project is, however, home to many families with hopes and dreams for a brighter future for themselves and their community.

In 1965, concerned with the problems children in this community faced and believing they could make a difference to young lives, a group of Ward's employees decided to stay after work one night a week and share their skills and knowledge with the young people of Cabrini Green. The Montgomery Ward-Cabrini Green Tutoring Program, which achieved its twenty-first year of service in 1986–87, is the result of this unusual partnership between a corporation and a community. Founded, directed, and staffed by volunteers, it is an efficient and effective program.

The program's tutors work with all neighborhood children on a first-come, first-served basis, regardless of reading level. Because of the makeup of the neighborhood, many of the children are at great risk of failing in school unless they receive some outside encouragement. One of the attractions of the program to both parents and students is that it is not considered a remedial program, although many of the participating students need extra help in basic skills.

The program is far larger and more complex today than it was in 1965. One evening a week, some on Tuesdays and others on Wednesdays, 200 children from the nearby housing project and 200 tutors from Montgomery Ward, as well as several other corporations, come to the old Ward's catalogue warehouse to learn, share, and grow. In the cavernous hall where shoppers used to place orders for merchandise, the students, ranging in years from 2nd to 6th grade, each spend an hour and a half with a tutor. Almost half of the students are in the 5th and 6th grades.

The purpose of the program is to build children's self-esteem so that they will be able to break out of the cycle of failure that is the future of so many of the residents of Cabrini Green. The tutors want to get the children to believe they can be successful. "If I tell you long enough that you can, you'll believe and do better," says Betty Stanford, a nine-year veteran tutor. The program considers itself one of the many interacting pieces in children's lives that can have an important effect on their success.

The program director, Daniel Bassill, an executive in Ward's advertising division, has been with the program more than fourteen years. His leadership is characterized by thoughtfulness and attention to good management principles. Working with Bassill to direct the program is a cadre of experienced tutors; the majority of the leader/tutors hold management positions at Montgomery Ward or other companies.

Good management is the first thought one has upon entering the tutoring area. "We try to run a tight ship here," says Bassill. The two large tutoring spaces are filled with tables, chairs, and several study carrels that provide special privacy for student-and-tutor pairs. The large library of reading books, skills workbooks, tutors' reference books, and educational games is neatly arranged on bookshelves in an easily accessible area. One bulletin board gives information about the upcoming 6th-grade graduation essay contest; another displays beautifully matted photographs of tutors and students.

As students enter the building, volunteers at the attendance desk check them in and supervise them until their tutors arrive. On Tuesday evenings the site is overseen by Pat Wilkerson, a mechanical engineer in his fifth year with the program. He roves the floor, giving support where needed.

"Attendance is very important," says Wilkerson. Because the program is voluntary, attendance is an important indication of effectiveness, and attendance records are scrupulously maintained. Bassill keeps cumulative attendance records that are figured weekly on his office IBM-PC, then posted. Weekly attendance of students averages 90 percent, and tutors 75 to 80 percent. The program's computer-tallied statistics have also shown that 90 percent of the students return the next year, as do 60 percent of the tutors. This is an excellent example of the ways computers can be used to track mundane but very important details.

Because tutor attendance is lower than student attendance, the program employs substitute tutors, volunteers who are unable to make a firm commitment for the full school year but can participate frequently. When a student's regular tutor cannot attend, a substitute is assigned. Tutors who are consistent "no-shows" are soon dropped from the program. Hoping to avoid the unpleasantness of asking a volunteer to leave, as well as the effects on a student paired with such a volunteer, recruiters stress the importance of the commitment involved in tutoring when they interview prospective volunteers.

The friendly but clearly defined work environment reflects the spirit of the tutoring sessions. At each table, student-tutor pairs are closely engaged in their work. At one, a tutor reads a story aloud to a child; at another, a pair pores over the *Tutor Tattler* newsletter and makes plans for upcoming events, perhaps an essay contest or a field trip; still another pair plays an educational game from the many on the games shelf.

In another section of the room a tutor helps an older student with his handwriting. She has him write a single letter in the air, using his whole arm, before he writes it on paper. She praises him frequently. The student is focused, concentrating with all his power, trying to do his best on a task that is difficult for him.

Chrissha, an 11-year-old, is working with Annette Skaggs, a substitute tutor. Chrissha knows and likes books. Some of her favorites are *Ramona Quimby*, *The Littles*, and *How to Eat Fried Worms*. She believes the program has helped her improve her reading and writing skills. For the Halloween essay contest, she wrote a story about a lighthouse.

In most cases instructional activities center on sharing a good book, working on specific skills, or finishing homework. The program directors particularly stress developing a positive and consistent relationship between tutor and student, more than a particular method of instruction.

Doris, a round-faced 10-year-old with an infectious smile, is deeply engaged in weaving a potholder on a little metal frame. This is Doris's first year in the program and the first time she has ever tried weaving. As she puts it, she "crashed" one of the program's parties last year and liked it so much she was determined to get into the program this year. "I like my tutor. I like the people who work here."

Doris's favorite activity is using the computers. The computer area, like all of the tutoring area, is well organized, clean, and neat. It contains workspaces around five PC Commodore 64s. Ken Cartossa and Don Bohling, the volunteers in charge, spent one summer reviewing the software and planning their eight-week class in basic programming. By the end of the course, each student should be able to write a ten-line program. Some have already passed that goal.

Later in the evening Doris plays a computer math game. "I did it! I did it! I did it!" she squeals with delight, smiling widely as she answers another question correctly.

Students attend because they want to. "I like the tutors. They care. It's fun. At first I hated math, but not anymore," says Octavio, a former student and now a "milk kid," one of the junior assistants the program employs to pass out snacks.

The program has a long waiting list. Young people hear about the program from family, friends, or school. On admission, each student's parents must sign a permission slip allowing the program access to their child's school records and giving the tutor the right to confer with teachers at school. A volunteer takes the permission slip to the school and collects it when the school records have been copied. This information goes into the student's cumulative record in the program's files. The student's tutor is allowed to review the material but must sign and return the folder to the program staff.

Because the program's cutoff is at 6th-grade level, the young adolescents who attend are usually 10 or 11 or, occasionally, 12 years old. Sixth-graders receive royal treatment and a special graduation. Parents would like the program to work with their children through junior high and high school, but the program leaders have been reluctant to take on that responsibility. "We would like to extend beyond the 6th grade, but don't feel competent to provide the extra services we think adolescents need," says Bassill.

Though students wait eagerly to join the program, tutors must be recruited. Each fall Vanessa Lowery, who is in charge of recruitment, sets up booths in the three Montgomery Ward buildings, at the Quaker Oats Corporation, and at the Moody Bible Institute. There is no formal screening process. Lowery's team of recruiters, looking for people with sincere interest, try to impress potential tutors with the responsibility of the commitment they are making when they decide to join the program, but they are also enthusiastic about the benefits of tutoring. Tutoring is a good place to meet new people with similar commitments to improving the quality of young people's lives. One good example is Alan Tyson, a tutor in the program for eighteen years, who works in textiles. He joined the program because he was new to Chicago and wanted to get involved in the community. He has since introduced many friends to tutoring.

The program makes use of tutors' professional skills and special interests whenever possible. When they join the program, tutors are asked to fill out a skills and interests inventory. Program leaders use the information to get special help, such as a pianist for the 6th-grade graduation, or a textile artist to design a banner.

Karen Glazer is in charge of tutor support. She finds that the best training comes from pairing experienced tutors with beginners. She does this through monthly meetings where tutors can get together in a relaxed atmosphere to discuss their concerns. Other support includes a tutor guidebook, a yearly tutoring calendar, and a tutor newsletter. The newsletter is distributed through the work file that the program keeps on each student, which is picked up by the tutor at the beginning of every session.

In 1985–86 the Montgomery Ward-Cabrini Green program teamed with the Fourth Presbyterian Church tutoring program to

reinstitute an annual workshop on the teaching of reading and
writing. Reading professionals led the workshop, which was aimed
specifically at the volunteer tutor and held on a Saturday so
volunteers could easily participate. Forty Montgomery Ward-Cabrini
Green tutors attended. At the workshop Glazer learned about Jim
Trelease's *Read Aloud Handbook.*[7] Now she includes reading aloud in
her sessions with her student.

The volunteers' companies provide more than personnel.
Montgomery Ward is the major funder of the program, providing
the space and utilities free. Also, Ward's United Way Fund pays for
two part-time secretaries from Moody Bible College. Quaker Oats
makes an annual donation that pays for transportation of its
volunteers to and from the program, as well as field-trip
transportation for volunteers and students.

One especially valuable feature of the program is the strong
parent support group that Stanford has developed. In her position
as a project leader, and also as a systems analyst for Montgomery
Ward, she is a professional staff trainer. She uses the same
techniques to run parent workshops that she uses for her Ward's
training sessions. "Our parent workshop was one of the biggest eye-
openers we had," she stated. "They worked as well as any business
leaders I've known."

At their first meeting she had the parents form groups of five,
choose a leader, and discuss and choose three topics to work on.
She asked them: What do you expect out of the program? How
could you help this program? What would you like to see changed?
The parents agreed on four tasks they could perform to help the
program:

1. Collect materials to use in tutoring.
2. Collect and distribute clothing for children in need.
3. Assist in calling parents about tutoring.
4. Set up escort teams to bring children to and from tutoring.

They quickly began work on their tasks and implemented their
suggestions.

The parents likewise asked Stanford to organize workshops
on topics of interest to them. Topics for one recent year were stress
management, drug abuse, and parents and teens. The parents are
also planning a roller-skating field trip for themselves. Nine parents

have been working on a parent newsletter. This has brought them into contact with NYACK, a local political-action group, which supplies the newsletter with information on many upcoming events of interest to Cabrini Green residents.

The Montgomery Ward-Cabrini Green program has found its parenting group to be a remarkably successful source of support. Initially, staff members were skeptical about attempting to organize parents, because of reports in the press of failed attempts to engage parents from this kind of neighborhood, as well as discussions with staff of similar programs. Their success may be attributable to the way in which they approached parents: as capable fellow adults.

Youth workers and educators can learn some important lessons from the innovations the Montgomery Ward-Cabrini Green Tutoring Program has adopted from the world of business management. For example, using computers to keep track of program records is efficient. The records are always up-to-date, accurate, and useful in ongoing program evaluation. Stanford's parent group is also a successful application of management principles.

The Montgomery Ward-Cabrini Green Tutoring program stands out from the rank and file of volunteer tutoring programs. For more than twenty years these business volunteers have worked to shape an effective program that does make a difference in the lives of the children who live in Cabrini Green. They have been successful in many cases. For instance, one of Bassill's former students has graduated from Memphis State University. The success of this one student exemplifies the goal of the program. As Paula Fergeson, the program treasurer, says, "If one person believes you are special, it can break the cycle of failure."

The Highline Indian Tutoring Program: A Cross-Age Tutoring Program Serving Native Americans

In the 1950s the federal government established Seattle as an urban relocation center for Native Americans who wished to leave their reservations, thereby attracting members of many different tribes to the Pacific Northwest. By the mid-1980s the Highline School District in Seattle, Washington, was serving nearly 700 Native American students from sixty different tribes. In the district the

Native American high-school dropout rate is 30 percent, but the total dropout rate may be much higher, because some students drop out before high school.

The Highline Indian Tutoring Program works with students from this group who are at high risk of failure in school. "We try to hold children up in the water while we teach them to swim," explains its director, Cathy Ross. Teenage tutors from local high schools and colleges are trained to work with Native American students in an after-school tutoring program that builds students' self-esteem while helping them to improve their academic skills.

For many Native American children in the Seattle area, the Highline program may well be a critical factor that weights the balance towards future success. The 1986–87 after-school program, for example, included three new 9th-grade tutors who had once been students in the program. The positive experiences they had had in the tutoring program not only helped them to increase their academic achievement but helped them to see themselves as competent enough to lend a helping hand to others in the same position.

Ross believes that many of her students have trouble with classroom instruction, not because they are disadvantaged, but because their cultural backgrounds and learning styles are not compatible with the way they are taught in school. When teachers and students have been brought up in cultures with contrasting values and learning styles, misunderstandings can occur. A study of Navaho children has drawn thoughtful conclusions about this issue:

> It is difficult to assess how a growing child conceptualizes his world, but it is likely that in every classroom there are some children to whom visual imagery is a powerful tool of fantasy and thought, while other children in the same room may be primarily verbal in their ways of imagining and discovery. Cultural conditions may affect the distribution of the number of children for whom inner vision or inner speech is of primary importance, but too little is known at present to argue definitively for such a relationship.
>
> It is critical, however, to allow for the development of varied ways of thought in school. Nowhere is this injunction of greater importance than in the classrooms of Indian children, who bring with them a rich oral and visual tradition,

an asset seldom understood or developed in their school years.[8]

The program Ross has developed recognizes differences in individual learning styles. Staff are trained to appreciate these differences and to use teaching methods appropriate to the learner's style. For example, Ross points out that in the classroom, Native American children often refuse to answer questions or to read aloud in front of the whole group. They may avoid eye contact with the teacher. The teacher may interpret these actions as negative behavior; however, these children may have been taught at home that it is polite to respond to adults in this way. Ross urges her tutors to be sensitive to their students' feelings, watching for and responding to the cues they give in the tutoring sessions.

Students appreciate the differences between school and the tutoring program. "The program is good, because tutoring isn't like school. At first, we didn't want to go, but then we found out this was good," students say. "The tutors teach you tricks the teachers don't know."

Founded by Ross in 1975, the program is actually composed of two parts: an in-school tutoring program, which works with students in grades 1–12, and the after-school program, which provides help to 1st- through 6th-graders. In the after-school program Ross has a staff of two certified teachers (tutor-advisers) who provide supervision and support to the young tutors. Total enrollment in the after-school program is about seventy-five students, two-thirds of whom are young adolescents in the 5th and 6th grades. Students in the 4th through 6th grades are accepted into the after-school program if they are scoring at least four months below grade level on the California Achievement Test (CAT).

Tutoring is done at two centers. At the north end of the district, where the Native American population is heaviest, the program obtained space in an elementary school. The other site, centrally located in the district, is in a rented space in a former school building. At both centers the atmosphere is purposeful and orderly, yet loose and relaxed. The space is colorfully decorated with achievement charts, posters, and Native American crafts. Students can sprawl on chairs, sit on the floor, or play games in the corner. One of the centers has small rooms; the other—a single large, open area—is subdivided by bookcases and other dividers.

Student recruitment starts in the fall, when the program sends district principals a list of the Native American children attending their schools. They in turn consult with counselors, teachers, and parents to produce a list of eligible children. There are four criteria for eligibility:

1. The student wants to be in the tutoring program.
2. The student is recommended by a counselor, teacher, or parent.
3. The student has parental approval to participate in the program.
4. The student meets the test-score criteria for the program.

The program is popular, and students have spread the word to brothers, sisters, and friends. "I told my mom to get my sister in as early as she could, so she could do well in school," says one satisfied student. Occasionally a Caucasian student will try to claim Native American status in order to meet the eligibility requirements. (To be considered Native American, a student must meet the definition of Title IV(a) of the Indian Education Act, which requires that at least one grandparent be an enrolled member of a tribal group.)

Tutoring is divided into eight-week sessions with fourteen hours of instruction per session—one hour, two days per week. Academic progress is carefully monitored and closely tied to program evaluation. Students are pre- and post-tested on the CAT, and their scores are tied to program evaluation. The Highline program relates its objectives to academic achievement and provides testing data to support its claims of success.[9]

The value of the tutoring depends upon the quality of the tutors and the quality of their training. Ross devotes considerable time to obtaining good tutors and providing them with good training. Tutors are recruited from local high schools, community colleges, and universities. Ross looks for three special characteristics: (1) skill in instruction; (2) kindness mixed with firmness; and (3) the ability to set limits. She wants an individual who is both committed and reliable. She emphasizes the tutor's importance as a role model in the student's life, and the importance of following through with the commitment to tutor once it has been made. She tells potential tutors, "You'll be dealing with a human being on this job. You can't start and then stop so easily."

One of the most important lessons Ross has learned from her many years with the program is that "it is possible for high-school students to be outstanding teachers. I know this flies in the face of many university and college training programs, but some people have an innate ability." These young people "make wise decisions minute by minute as they tutor. They are constantly aware of what is going on in their sessions. They are always poised to move in whatever direction the student needs to go."

New tutors must take eight hours of preliminary training, during which they learn about the program's procedures, their responsibilities as tutors, methods for teaching reading and math, and the materials available to them. All receive the program's seventy-six-page manual that includes forms, procedures, and teaching tips. They must also take a two-hour training session on Native American culture, in which Ross provides instruction on recognizing individual learning styles and on varying teaching methods to fit the learner's style. They must successfully pass a test on each training unit before they are eligible to tutor. Once in the program, some tutors are paid, and others receive compensation in the form of school credits.

The after-school program runs two afternoons a week at each center. Students and tutors come on a Monday-Wednesday or Tuesday-Thursday schedule. The tutors arrive thirty minutes before each tutoring session, to write their lesson plans and prepare their materials. Ross stresses being well-prepared and having more than enough activities for each session. The adult tutor-advisers must check over each lesson plan and initial it before the individual sessions begin. At 3:30 the students arrive for their one-hour tutoring sessions. From 4:30 to 4:45 the tutors review their lesson plans, write notes, and put away their equipment.

Highly structured requirements for each lesson simplify planning, especially for the inexperienced. There are three parts to each tutoring session. First the tutor teaches a skill on the SARI hierarchy (SARI, Systematic Approach to Reading Instruction, is a commercially distributed reading skills package),[10] tests for competency by using a SARI worksheet, and notes the student's progress on a complex "bubble" chart provided with the kit. Next comes an exercise with the DOLCH words (a list of the 220 most common words in reading materials), to build sight-word vocabulary; tutors design their own games, drills, and tests based on the word list. Finally, the tutor and the student share a good book; the tutor reads to the student, or the student reads to the tutor.

Tutors are encouraged to use copious praise, rewards, and learning games to keep their students involved and excited about learning. The tutor handbook has a one-page insert called "60 Ways to Praise." Rewards vary from scratch-and-sniff stickers to a movie or a snack at a restaurant. Each tutor-and-student pair works together to design an imaginative progress chart that reflects the number of books read or other achievements. Each quarter, tutors also design homemade learning games for their students. Ross finds that these are especially enjoyed by the 5th- and 6th-graders, who "like competing only against themselves."

The program also takes part in the Reading Is Fundamental (RIF) program, through which each student receives up to six books a year. A girl who received copies of *Tales of a Fourth Grade Nothing* and *Freckle Juice* was overjoyed. Another says, "My tutor got me to read good books by reading to me. Now I even started liking books."

Although they are not central to the program, computers are seen as another aid to learning. The program has two Apple II computers, one at each center. Tutors and students use the computer to vary the daily pace. A variety of educational software, including story-completion drills, is available.

The close relationships that develop through tutoring benefit tutors and students alike. As an example, Ross describes a tutor who worked in the program in the late 1970s. Her student was trying to cope with a disastrous family situation. The two worked together for two years, and after that they kept in contact through letters. When the tutor got married, her former student, who was serving punch at the wedding, said to Ross, "You know, I was a rotten little kid—if it weren't for her, I'd have turned out bad, but she believed in me." On the opposite end of the spectrum was a tutor whose family life was in a state of upheaval. She had lost her home, dropped out of high school, and moved a long distance away from the tutoring site. "She should have been a basket case," recounted her tutor-adviser. Instead the tutor spent hours on buses getting to the program, because her relationship to the program and her student were "holding her life together."

The Highline program involves parents on three levels: acknowledgement, information, and involvement. Parents must give permission for their children to participate. They are also consulted on their children's assessments and individual plans of study. And they receive the results of testing and regular progress reports. As partners with the program staff, parents are encouraged to take an active role in the program, whose Indian Parent Committee functions like the PTA. This group sponsors an open house every year, at which parents can meet the tutors and see the tutoring rooms. In 1986 the committee sponsored a potluck supper and an ethnic program for parents and children. The committee also conducts phone surveys and sends out a questionnaire every spring to determine parents' satisfaction with the program.

Because it is part of the Highline Indian Education Office, the tutoring program functions as a component of a comprehensive service agency that also provides counseling, cultural activities, and curriculum support. Considered a school-district program, the tutoring program has a strong and productive relationship with the Highline school system. It is housed on school property. School personnel help the program staff to identify prospective students and assess their needs. Each tutoring quarter, tutors meet individually with their students' classroom teachers to discuss the students' progress and needs.

Before their conferences with teachers, Ross carefully trains tutors in appropriate professional behavior. The program provides a form to help the tutor guide the conference, and the tutor uses the same form to report back to program staff. The teacher conference serves as further training for the tutor, as well as providing the program with necessary information about each student's progress. The conference is carefully structured to make sure that the teacher's time is not wasted and that the tutor gains new learning and job skills from the experience.

Ross asks tutors to go through each part of the form, taking notes and asking questions. "If a teacher throws up her hands and says, 'He needs help in everything,' I tell the tutors—'Don't stand for that. Ask the teacher to prioritize the areas of concern. Tell the teacher that you only have a limited time with the student, and ask the teacher to decide what is most important for you to work on.'"

Teachers usually describe specific skills areas they would like the tutor to work on. Ross quotes teachers as saying, "She doesn't understand borrowing," or "It's lack of motivation. He doesn't want to work; if you could just get him excited about learning." The teacher may lend the tutor a copy of the textbook the student is working in, or give the tutor samples of the work the student is expected to do. For middle-grades students, the teacher often gives the tutor the long-term assignments so that the student can get help before the last minute.

Early adolescence is a time for considering and making critical decisions. Native Americans have an added dilemma: learning how to balance the two sometimes contradictory cultures they live in. Ross believes that the extent to which students resolve this dilemma determines whether they will go on and succeed in school. Dennis Cruchon, a guidance counselor at one of the schools that Highline's tutoring program's students attend, agrees. Students who cannot resolve the cultural dilemma, he says, are the most likely to make the decision to drop out of school in the middle grades if they do not experience success at school. The Highline program's combined emphasis on tutoring in academic skills and appreciation of Native American cultures seems well designed to attack the dual problems its students confront.

Conclusions: The Potential of After-School Programs

The after-school literacy programs reviewed here focus successfully on two goals. First, they seek to improve their participants' self-esteem, by involving young people who have been alienated from schools and reading in new patterns of success. Second, they encourage learning by trying to make it interesting and meaningful to these students. They introduce forms of literacy that their students may not have encountered in traditional schools, such as reading games, storytelling, and access to many different kinds of magazines and books.

The climate in these programs reflects the deep sense of caring and importance that the staff attaches to their work. Staffing patterns in these programs are as diverse as the types of programs.

Most common is a professional director who works with a crew of nonprofessionals, volunteer or not, who provide the majority of instruction. The Montgomery Ward-Cabrini Green Tutoring Program, founded, directed, and staffed by volunteers, is a wonderful example of the ways in which business initiative and management training can adapt to educational needs. Cross-age tutoring programs are a common way of providing for staffing needs in these programs, and when properly trained and supported, these young tutors do an excellent job.

All of these programs have similar standards for staff, whether volunteer or paid. They look first for individuals who are committed. They want personnel who like young people and who can be flexible but firm in setting goals and boundaries for their work with youth. People who are willing to take the "extra step" for their students are highly valued.

"Role model" is a term that frequently surfaces in discussion with after-school program directors. They stress the importance to young adolescents of positive personal interactions with older teenagers and adults. (Similarly, effective in-school literacy programs also emphasize the importance of students' and teachers' relationships to students' successful achievement.)

Training goals, duration, and methods vary from program to program. But program staff say that what is learned in training workshops transfers to teaching. Role playing and having experienced volunteers share "what works" with beginners were both mentioned as effective training methods by tutors and trainers alike.

Staff members cite several researchers whose work influenced the development and design of their programs. Translating this research into practice is usually the job of the more highly trained professional staff. At Highline, Director Cathy Ross conducts an extensive training workshop where tutors learn methods for teaching reading. Volunteer tutors at Montgomery Ward receive information on new approaches at a specially designed workshop taught by reading professionals. Generally, tutors are not as interested in the experts' names and theories as they are in practical suggestions they can use immediately.

Staffing is a serious concern for community-based programs. Finding trained and experienced staff who can work part-time in the afternoon or weekend hours is very difficult. Further, it is not easy to elicit full-fledged professional commitment on a half-time budget. Successful programs respond in creative and varied ways to this problem. Cross-age tutoring programs structure the learning for both tutor and student; tutors receive training in professional job skills and basic skills. Tutors in this kind of program are usually young, little older than the students. There is clear evidence from observations as well as a review of the research that tutors' skill levels and self-confidence improve in these programs.[11] Students benefit, too, from the close contact with slightly older role models who take their responsibilities seriously. And as anecdotes from the Highline program show, the experience can have positive lifelong consequences for the participants.

However, there are drawbacks to the cross-age approach. It requires a double commitment on the part of the professional staff, who must train and supervise the tutors and also encourage both the students' and the tutors' achievements. Tutors who have minimal skills levels themselves may reinforce incorrect information, or unwittingly mislead beginning readers because of their own lack of information on a subject. At its worst, cross-age tutoring perpetuates the cycle of failure that the students experience in school; at its best, it generates a warm and caring atmosphere that nurtures accomplishment.

After-school literacy programs are an ideal setting for cross-age tutoring programs. As a supervised learning experience, tutoring gives adolescents a chance for meaningful participation in their community and a place to learn new skills and explore new careers. Some activities seem particularly well suited to this kind of program: reading aloud to students, listening to a child read aloud, reading together in companionable silence, or working together on projects that make reading fun, such as games, dramatics, crafts, and field trips. These programs only work when the screening, training, supervision, and support of tutors is given as much consideration as that of students.

After-school literacy programs are very good at attracting young people who have been alienated from school and reading and helping them to reengage in learning. Staff in these programs look at each student individually, set goals that reflect the student's interests as well as needs, and encourage the student at each step of progress.

Successful after-school literacy programs expose their participants to rich and varied literacy experiences. Students at risk for failure in reading and schoolwork are often those most lacking in these kinds of experiences. Many have not had chances to hear stories, nor have they had chances to select books to read. Often they have no idea that there are books written about the matters that concern them.

The successful programs described here stress independent reading and the enjoyment of books as the mark of real readers: helping students to have a good experience with a book is a primary goal. The program directors urge their staff to read aloud books that the students themselves help select. Each of the programs has a good library of interesting materials that includes both educational games and books. The Friendly Place, as a combination library-bookstore, has the widest selection. Highline has an exceptionally good collection of books on Native American culture, as well as many homemade games to improve reading skills.

Instructional methods vary, from the use of the highly structured SARI[9] worksheets in the Highline program to the relaxed atmosphere of the Book and Game Club at The Friendly Place.

Staff from the programs report that young adolescents are especially concerned about getting help with homework. Homework assignments, totaling two and three hours of work an evening for an average middle-grades student, are even more onerous for students who can barely read. Tutors at this level spend more time helping with homework than do those who work with younger students. Julia Palmer, the executive director of the American Reading Council, which sponsors The Friendly Place, adds that "at The Friendly Place and throughout the city in after-school programs, we are being hit by a very unfortunate by-product of the campaign for educational excellence. Everywhere, children are being given twice as much homework, most of which, to say the least, is completely counterproductive—rote or drill work. This volume of mindless work is resulting in their having little or no time to hear a story, read independently, or play problem-solving games."

One of the most important strengths of good after-school literacy programs is their ability to lend support not only to the student but also to the student's family. The parents of a student who faces academic failure share in their child's sense of helplessness. In many schools the parents are considered at fault when a child does not read. Teachers and administrators may hold parents accountable for not preparing their children to learn, for being unable to help their children with homework, or for not having money to provide supplementary learning experiences. Whole families come to believe that there is no chance for any of their members to participate successfully in school, and thus the cycle of failure and withdrawal from school is perpetuated.

Staff in good after-school literacy programs are particularly sensitive to the needs of the parents of their students. They understand these parents' desire to be better educational advocates for their children. Program staff often help with communication between school and family—keeping parents informed of a student's progress, alerting parents to available school services, and helping them get the information they need. Students who attend programs that are part of a comprehensive social-service agency can also take part in recreation, counseling, or community service programs, and their parents also get support for their own needs, from medical referrals and parenting advice to job training and legal aid.

How successful are these programs? How do they measure their effectiveness? Evaluation has long been a difficult question for after-school programs of all types. As one observer explains it, "Working with extremely tight budgets, service providers choose increased service over program evaluation, trusting to their day-to-day experiences with youngsters to shape program and administrative decisions." Moreover, it is not only lack of staff and time that makes evaluation difficult, but also the kind of achievement that one is trying to assess: "Very little is known about the contribution that nonformal education makes to young people's school achievement, future employment, skills, attitudes, or behavior."[12]

The measures of effectiveness for after-school programs are "soft" as opposed to the "hard" measures schools employ, but program directors are remarkably consistent in ranking the assessment measures they use:

1. *Attendance.* This is the primary measure of success. It is axiomatic that young adolescents will not attend a program they do not like. The Montgomery Ward-Cabrini Green volunteers, with their business acumen, use computers to keep track of attendance data.

2. *Anecdotal evidence.* How do students talk about themselves and the program? What are they excited about, and why? Good directors have their fingers on the pulse of the lives that surround them. They are aware of and concerned about the daily events that touch each of their participants.

3. *In-house records of individual progress.* To augment anecdotal information, programs keep records of students' cumulative work. Library check-out records also provide staff with information on who is reading what and how much. Of the three reviewed here, the Highline program has the most structured assessment system. At each session the student is tested on specific skills, and progress is charted. Pre- and post-testing data for each student are carefully analyzed and reported each school year.

4. *Standardized testing.* Some after-school programs do use standardized tests to measure effectiveness, even though results may not be reliable. Standardized tests are generally designed to measure reading progress that results from in-school classroom reading programs, that is, progress after receiving daily reading instruction over a long interval of time. Hence, these tests may not accurately gauge the kind and amount of growth a student makes in the less structured, less frequent instruction offered in after-school programs.

Definitions as well as measures of effectiveness in after-school literacy programs are different than those employed in school programs. Schools must attend to group objectives and standards, but after-school programs are free to focus intensively on individual goals. After-school programs deem themselves successful when they can engage a young person on a continuing basis, promote success in some area of learning, excite interest in some aspect of reading or writing, and help the individual to see that literacy does have a place in his or her future.

Measurement methods that after-school programs could develop into a multi-layered and meaningful formal evaluation process include accurate attendance records, formal observations of instruction, structured interviews or questionnaires, and collections or displays of student work (journals, reading logs, writing samples, and other products). A more qualitative, rather than a quantitative, definition of and measurement of success is appropriate for these programs.

Observing the bright, positive atmosphere in these programs and the enthusiasm of their participants, it is hard to believe that many of these students have spent the earlier part of the day in school, where they have endured hours of failure. The contrast between the way they face literacy tasks in school and the way they face these same tasks in the after-school program illustrates an important finding: *for students who have failed in school and reading, school may not be the best place to start afresh.* In fact nonschool literacy agencies may be the place instead.

Students in successful programs report that they enjoy these programs because they are not like school. When pressed as to what they mean by this, they reply that the program staff know what help they need and can show them how to do the things they find difficult. "They show me a lot of things over here," says Ari, a 7th-grader, of his after-school program. "They write words I don't know on pieces of paper. They tell me how to pronounce. Nothing is hard here. They know what I need. They help if I can't do it. We don't read much in school. I read to myself and answer questions. Here I get a chance to read more. When I read in school, I don't always understand." These words are ringing testimony to the value of good after-school literacy programming.

Though teaching students to read is a primary function of schools, they need not have a monopoly on literacy instruction. When students have built up reservoirs of frustration and anger at their failure in school, school may not be the best place for them to begin anew. Research shows that for some learners, schools may actually be a deterrent to acquiring literacy skills. One study of literacy learning in in-school and out-of-school settings in three communities concluded:

> Reading and writing need not be taught exclusively in the schools. In fact, a strict adherence to formal methods of teaching and valuing literacy learning may limit potential opportunities for literacy learning and maintenance in homes

and communities, by alienating parents and creating feelings of inadequacy about their own competencies.[13]

The importance of community literacy programs for adults has been well documented. The Business Council on Effective Literacy reported in 1984 that the rate of completion in community-based literacy programs for adults is 65 to 70 percent, as compared to just 25 to 50 percent in traditional adult basic education and general equivalency diploma classes that resemble formal school settings.[14] But educators have thus far been less attentive to the potential benefits of community literacy programs for young people.

The programs described here represent only a few of the possibilities for sponsorship. After-school literacy programs could be expanded to many sites such as settlement houses, religious organizations, YMCAs, YWCAs, Boys and Girls Clubs, neighborhood associations, and schools. Various models for staffing and organization have been explored, but others need to be developed.

For instance, libraries, with their ready supply of reading matter, would be the logical hosts for community literacy programs for young people. However, a search for library-based adolescent literacy programs, conducted by PAL staff in 1985 with the aid of the American Library Association, uncovered no such programs. This is in part due to the overall lack of young-adult services in public libraries. Most public libraries combine young-adult services with children's services. In systems where there are librarians in charge of young-adult materials, those staff members have their hands full providing the traditional range of programs and services; they lack the time and the training to develop literacy services for teenagers. Strong young-adult collections and young-adult programming are important supports for both in-school and after-school literacy programs, but public libraries would also be appropriate sponsors or co-sponsors for such programs.

In the nationwide effort to combat illiteracy, partnerships between business and community have garnered much attention. The Montgomery Ward-Cabrini Green Tutoring Program in Chicago has successfully applied business-management procedures in an educational setting. The program has paid careful attention to setting goals and evaluating progress; it uses computers to track student and tutor data and has developed an active parent group.

This program has an advantage over many similar business-sponsored volunteer programs in that it is located so close to the population it serves. The site is convenient for both tutors and students. "Lack of transportation" has been identified as a fundamental barrier to young adolescents who seek after-school services.[15] Ease of access is a critical necessity in volunteer programs and youth programs.

In sum, after-school programs can successfully attract students who have been alienated from reading and school, and help them to feel good about themselves and to believe they can learn to read and write. In the relaxed atmosphere of after-school programs, students feel free to take risks and experiment. After-school programs also provide important support to parents by offering a variety of services families need, such as recreation programs for all ages, childcare, and medical and housing help. After-school programs may also serve as an advocate for the child and the child's family at the school.

After-school or summer literacy programs are weakest in providing large time blocks of structured instruction in reading and writing. For this reason they can neither replace nor compensate for in-school programs. To attain the literacy levels necessary to participate fully in our society—to vote, to fill out tax forms, or to read the newspaper—students with severe literacy problems must have more time and structured teaching than after-school or summer programs are currently able to provide. A 13-year-old reading at the 2nd-grade level is unlikely to bring his or her reading skills up to the expected 8th-grade level by attending an after-school literacy program. But through the help and support of that program, the student may reconnect to school and reading.

Successful after-school programs can combine literacy instruction with programming that appeals to a diverse set of young adolescent interests and needs, creating a context in which there is a need to be literate. Skills are then acquired, not in and for themselves, but as an aid to achieving more comprehensive personal goals.

Young adolescents, concerned with the many new biological, social, and intellectual changes occurring in their lives, need opportunities to explore these changes through interaction with peers and adults. After-school or summer programs can provide them with opportunities for meaningful participation in their communities, building skills at good citizenship in exciting and nonthreatening environments.

The findings of the Project on Adolescent Literacy indicate that program directors and youth workers in after-school literacy programs need training in two areas. First is the need for training in the area of good adolescent programming. Staff need to know what the characteristics of young adolescents are and how these characteristics should shape the design of their program. Second is the need for training in the area of literacy. Staff should consider at least three basic questions: What are the characteristics of effective literacy programs? What are the best techniques for teaching older beginning readers and writers? What are the best techniques for teaching students the many functions and uses of literacy?

Successful schools and good after-school programs are essential partners in the effort to solve adolescent literacy problems. Both have distinct roles to play in creating solutions. Together, schools and after-school literacy programs can create a community literacy net that will catch young adolescents before they cross into the adult illiteracy statistics.

Notes

1. Leah Lefstein, "Effective After-School Programs for Young Adolescents," in *3:00 to 6:00 P.M.: Young Adolescents at Home and in the Community,* ed. Leah Lefstein and Joan Lipsitz (Carrboro, N.C.: Center for Early Adolescence, University of North Carolina, 1982), 62.

2. Julia Reed Palmer and Sara Schwabacher, *How to Start and Run a Book and Game Club* (New York: American Reading Council, 1985), 6.

3. For background information see Sylvia Ashton-Warner, *Teacher* (New York: Simon & Schuster, 1963); and Frank Smith, *Understanding Reading,* 3rd ed. (New York: Holt, Rinehart & Winston, 1971).

4. For background information see Paulo Freire, *Pedagogy of the Oppressed* (New York: Herder & Herder, 1970).

5. See note 2 above.

6. *How to Start and Run a School Paperback Bookstore* (New York: American Reading Council, 1977).

7. Jim Trelease, *The Read-Aloud Handbook* (New York: Penguin Books, 1982).

8. Vera P. John, "Styles of Learning—Styles of Teaching: Reflections on the Education of Navajo Children," in *Functions of Language in the Classroom*, ed. Courtney B. Cazden, Vera P. John, and Dell Hymes (Prospect Heights, Ill.: Waveland Press, 1972), 341.

9. According to the 1984–85 evaluation summary, 63 students received 28 hours or more of individual tutoring in reading and had both pre- and post-test scores on the CAT. Their scores showed an unusually high gain of 17.67 NCEs. The evaluation report states that students' gains ranged from six months to four and a half years. But evaluation results could be skewed by even one student's showing a gain of four and one-half years. Also students were enrolled in school during the time they were being tutored; the gains reported cannot be solely attributed to tutoring. Overall gains, while still substantial, may actually be much more modest. In-house records on session-by-session progress, appropriately summarized, would be a more reliable measure for evaluation reportage.

10. *SARI, Systematic Approach to Reading Instruction* (Bloomington, Ind.: Phi Delta Kappa, Inc., 1973).

11. On cross-age tutoring see Eileen Foley, *Peer Tutoring: A Step-by-Step Guide* (New York: Public Education Association, 1983); Peggy Lippitt, Ronald Lippitt, and Jeffrey Eiseman, *Cross-Age Helping Program: Orientation, Training, and Related Materials* (Ann Arbor: University of Michigan, 1971); Annemarie Sullivan Palinscar and Ann L. Brown, "Reciprocal Teaching of Comprehension-Fostering and Comprehension-Monitoring Activities, *Cognition and Instruction* 1 (1984): 117–75; and Diana Pritchard Paolitto, "The Effect of Cross-Age Tutoring on Adolescence: An Inquiry into Theoretical Assumptions," *Review of Educational Research* 46, no. 2 (Spring 1976): 215–37.

12. Joan Lipsitz, *After School: Young Adolescents on Their Own* (Carrboro, N.C.: Center for Early Adolescence, University of North Carolina, 1986), 44–45.

13. Shirley Brice Heath, "The Functions and Uses of Literacy," *Journal of Communication* 30 (1980): 132.

14. "The Main Basic Skills Programs: An Introduction," *Business Council for Effective Literacy: A Newsletter for the Business Community* 1 (September 1984): 6.

15. Joan Lipsitz, *After School*, 21–23.

SUMMER LITERACY PROGRAMS
FOR YOUNG ADOLESCENTS

Educators have long been aware of the loss in skills that students experience over the summer months while school is not in session. Students from low socioeconomic backgrounds, who are most likely to have lower skills levels as well, suffer the greatest loss.[1] Summer is thus an exceptionally good time to help students with literacy needs. On this premise Title I, the federal government's compensatory education program that preceded today's Chapter 1, funded a number of summer literacy programs for students who were both economically and educationally deprived. This was the largest single attempt by the federal government to improve school learning by providing remedial programs during the summer.

Follow-up information on how well these programs succeeded has been scattered and ambiguous. Some of the programs fell under the more general heading of "compensatory education"; that is, they were designed to remediate other problems that interfere with learning, such as a student's lack of experience with community resources or need for growth in interpersonal skills, in addition to literacy; literacy skills themselves might receive little direct attention. Other programs, although they claim to aim specifically at literacy needs, allotted very little time for specific help with reading and writing skills. The Sustaining Effects Study, a report on Title I achievements from 1976 through 1979, found no evidence that summer programs bolstered the lagging fall test scores of students with poor literacy skills. The authors carefully pointed out, however, that "at the typical summer school, there is less than one hour of reading instruction per day for only four or five weeks. Thus, there is little opportunity to learn."[2] In short, they believed that good summer literacy programs could aid students, but that the programs they had studied did not offer enough instruction in literacy skills. They left untouched the question of what kinds of instruction might prove most effective.

Considering this unexplored potential, surprisingly few communities have yet offered any type of summer literacy program. When PAL researchers sent out their preliminary call for recommendations of good adolescent literacy programs, responses that named summer programs were fewest in number, far behind both in-school and after-school programs. PAL's database search for summer literacy opportunities netted almost nothing but programs for gifted students. And neither the National Coalition of Advocates for Students (NCAS) nor the Education Commission of the States (ECS), agencies that are concerned with monitoring schools, had any information on literacy-oriented summer schooling. One of the most complete reviews of summer compensatory education programs concludes:

> There is virtually no information on existing summer school programs, even those that are partially funded by the federal government. The content, structure, enrollment, duration and costs are not known. Moreover, anecdotal information and impressions suggest these programs are considerably more diverse and difficult to classify than regular school year programs, even when nominally devoted to comparable tasks such as compensatory programs.[3]

With the adoption of minimum competency requirements in recent years, many school districts in several states have initiated mandatory summer literacy programs for students who do not meet the minimum standards for their grades. Even for these programs, however, follow-up information exists only in bits and pieces; no comprehensive study has yet been done.

The advent of required summer school programs patterned on the regular school-year classroom has worried some educators. They see a danger in providing more of the same fare to students who have already failed in programs that employ traditional teaching methods. Rather than encouraging learning, a summer literacy program that is a carbon copy of the current school experience may simply accelerate the student's exit from school.

The two summer literacy programs described here—the New Orleans Effective Schools Project, a school-based program, and the Cross-Age Tutoring Program of the Literacy Council of Alaska, a community-based program located in Fairbanks—provide models of effective summer literacy programs that put these fears to rest by offering alternative solutions. Neither is mandatory, but both draw high attendance; both, in fact, have had to turn students away for lack of space. They achieve this by offering literacy instruction that appeals to their young constituents' interests and encourages them to make lasting gains in skills.

In these two programs, sound instructional techniques that focus on doing, not drilling, are combined in an exciting and warm atmosphere where young adolescents' interests form the basis of the curriculum and where their concerns are taken seriously. Strong staff development plays a central role in both programs. In addition, both were created as a response to their communities' specific literacy needs, and both have involved many segments of their communities in planning and development. The program administrators recognize the importance of unifying community literacy policies and making sure that alternatives exist for all ages.

Both the Fairbanks and the New Orleans programs have clearly defined goals. Like the after-school programs reviewed in an earlier chapter, they emphasize the "affective" side of reading: they want their students to *believe* they really are readers and writers, to feel excited about reading and writing, and to see the connection between literacy and their life goals. At the same time, both programs work hard to build the specific literacy skills so valued by school—spelling, decoding, and grammar among others—thus enabling their students to be more successful at school in the future.

Both of these summer literacy programs are literate enclaves. From the moment the student steps over the threshold, he or she is transported into a special world where books and stories are enjoyed in many ways. The shelves are packed with books, tables are strewn with books and magazines, and the walls are covered with posters describing books and extolling reading. In both programs, the amount of time spent on drilling skills is in inverse proportion to what one would find in many classrooms. The majority of instructional time is spent on reading or writing meaningful texts—texts created not as an exercise, but as a communication between an author and a reader. Conventional reading textbooks and skills workbooks are hidden away for most of the session. These two programs show that teaching reading by reading is a highly effective instructional method. Most important, students credit this way of teaching for turning them into successful readers.

The young adolescents who participate in these two programs also say they appreciate the respect they are shown by the teachers. The teachers demonstrate this respect in many ways: by involving students in discussions about meaningful matters, allowing them to select their own books, and giving them part of the teaching responsibility. For many, this is the first time in their educational experience that their opinions and capabilities have been valued. Sadly, they see this demonstration of basic respect and trust as being different from what they receive in school.

The New Orleans program employs certified teachers; Fairbanks uses teenage tutors. Both programs have developed equally strong staff development components. Key features are modeling as an instructional technique for staff as well as students, staff involvement and "ownership" in the program, and clear goals for staff behavior and staff mastery of instructional techniques. Staff in both programs are pleased with the support they receive.

Evaluation of the effectiveness of summer literacy programs is a complex issue, because there is no consensus about the amount and kind of learning that should take place in such programs, as there is for in-school programs. Unfortunately, the measurement tools these programs use—standardized tests for grade-level literacy achievement—are not sensitive to the kinds and amount of growth one would expect to see in a six-week program. More appropriate measures for the effectiveness of these short-term programs are the "happiness quotient" of the participants and anecdotal evidence of their involvement in real literacy activities. Viewed in these terms, both of these programs are very effective.

Every community has a "literacy profile," a unique spectrum of its members' strengths and needs. As their attendance patterns show, these two programs have answered a great need in their communities. Their success helps point the way for future developments in community literacy planning. The New Orleans program shows how one community built a partnership between schools, parents, and community agencies. The Fairbanks program shows how literacy councils can play an important role in community literacy planning for all ages.

Adventures in Excellence:
The New Orleans Effective Schools Project

It is just after 9:00 on a weekday morning. The class sits on a red shag carpet in the middle of a large, brightly lit, high-ceilinged room. The students are clustered in a rough circle around their teacher. Four fans whir busily but fail to stir the densely humid, rapidly warming air. The students seem oblivious to the heat; they are absorbed in reading and discussing "The Zodiacs" by Jay Neugeboren.[4]

The class—part of 165 rising 6th-, 7th-, and 8th-graders at Martin Behrman Middle School—is participating in a five-week summer program entitled Adventures in Excellence. The program is part of the New Orleans Effective Schools Project, a highly successful partnership venture of the Southern Coalition for Educational Equity (SCEE), the New Orleans school district, the local teachers' union, and the community. The students, who attend the program voluntarily, spend the three-hour morning session improving their reading and writing and then choose a pair of afternoon elective courses such as music or art.

On this mid-July morning the class has already gone through the text, circling any words or phrases that seem problematic. Now the students begin to ask questions.

"What's a 'skull session'?"

"What's 'thumbing through'?"

"What's 'phony up'?"

The teacher allows their fellow class members to respond first, and only elaborates when a response seems inappropriate. Then she takes a turn, asking, "What's 'whimpering'?"

Brian, a 7th-grader, demonstrates, complete with pouting lower lip, batting eyelashes, and breath catching in his throat. The room fills with laughter. The teacher smiles widely and praises the interpretation.

Though they often read silently, today the students volunteer to read a page at a time aloud. The teacher is interested in monitoring their fluency, and now is a good moment; she has only nine students for this half-hour, because half the class has gone to the computer lab for one of their twice-weekly lessons in computer literacy. As each student finishes a page, the teacher follows with general questions: "Did everyone turn in the raffle money? How do you know? What was Darryl doing? Why?" When a dispute arises or students are unsure, they return to the text as authority. The teacher has made it clear this is not an oral test, but rather a review of important details and the underlying motivations of characters.

At 9:30 the other classmates come back, and the group that has been reading departs in turn for the computer lab. It has been a productive beginning of the day, and for the rest of the morning, teaching and learning will continue in a similar vein. At Adventures in Excellence, students read orally and silently, write, discuss their reading and writing, and actively participate in the instructional process with hardly a pause over the three-hour session.

Brian explains why he and the 164 other students—all voluntarily enrolled—work so intently through the summer: "It's better than being at home. It keeps your mind occupied. It's different from school, too. We have more privileges. We can go to the bathroom when we want and talk quietly while we work. And we read more books."

Enrollment is up 65 students this summer over that of the first summer program, two years ago. "We could have enrolled even more students if we offered child care," says Barbara Campbell MacPhee, director of the New Orleans Effective Schools Project and its summer program. "Many of these kids are responsible for brothers and sisters in the summer." Acceptance is first-come, first-served, but the students must be current students at Behrman or entering 6th-graders. Class size is intentionally kept small, with a student-to-teacher ratio of 18 to 1 or less. Students are randomly assigned, so that all classes are heterogeneously mixed without regard to level of skill, to avoid the stigma many students in the lower reading groups often have felt during the school year.

Curriculum and Instruction

The program's summer camp atmosphere undergirds its success with poor readers, who have just completed thirty-six almost uninterrupted weeks in school. The action-packed scheduling, appealing electives, and use of high-school and college students as teacher aides make the program enjoyable as well as educational. The teacher aides assist in the classrooms during the morning session. They increase the amount of individual attention the students can receive, provide role models close to the young adolescents in age, and gain, as one aide put it, "far more valuable experience than working in a fast-food restaurant." Two of the college students teach the half-hour morning classes in creative writing and computer use, each attended twice a week by all the students.

In the afternoon the aides take full responsibility for the electives: art, music, drama, dance, more creative writing, and swimming. Many are hired from the New Orleans Center for Creative Arts and are highly qualified to teach such electives. The electives provide outlets for creative expression, physical activity, and achievement and are strong drawing cards for the program.

Each morning the schedule of events begins informally at about 8:45 in Behrman's basement cafeteria, after students have finished breakfast (90 percent qualify for federally funded breakfast and lunch during the program). The students gather en masse for announcements, sitting on the floor or on cafeteria benches around the director. Three times each summer during these morning meetings, program staff distribute free T-shirts bearing the program logo to all the students. The resulting sea of yellow, or red, or blue shirts enhances the relaxed mood of staff and students and promotes a sense of cohesion.

On one typical morning Anthony Recasner, MacPhee's associate director, stands before the group and tells them a story. MacPhee then reads the completion of a Roald Dahl short story begun the previous day. She precedes the reading with questions about the beginning of the story and elicits some guesses as to how the story may end. The students' thoughts are now focused on the events leading up to today's reading, and they are eager to learn the outcome. As they listen intently, one small girl suddenly blurts out, "I told you so," when her guess proves close to the mark. Recasner concludes by leading the group in a rhythmical chant. Energized by the activity, the students depart one class at a time with their teachers.

At 9:00 the students begin their three-hour daily concentration on reading and writing. Every teacher's agenda includes daily reading aloud to students, word-of-the-day instruction, sustained silent reading, journal writing, and a reciprocal teaching lesson in which individual students take the role of teacher for a portion of the lesson. As MacPhee explains, "We think you often learn more by having to teach something." Each student has a weekly book conference with the teacher, to discuss personal reading; these conferences are worked into the morning schedule, a few students per day.

A typical day's schedule might look like this:

9:00	read aloud
9:30	reciprocal teaching
10:00	word for the day
10:15	journal writing
10:30	snack
10:35	reading groups and individual conferences
11:00	reading and writing workshop
11:45	silent reading
12:00	lunch
1:00	first elective
2:00	second elective

Throughout the morning the students are surrounded by a literate and purposeful environment. Books and conversations about books predominate. Paperbacks and magazines fill shelves and cover tables in each room. Cheerful posters on the walls echo the theme: "Reading stirs the imagination!" "Plan ahead; it wasn't raining when Noah built the ark." "We are free to make mistakes while learning." "It takes courage to be willing to risk." Students' creative writing hangs on bulletin boards and walls for all to read.

One teacher keeps a space on the class bulletin board labeled "FYI": For Your Information. Every day or two she posts a new newspaper or magazine article there in order to hook students into reading—yesterday, a story about the world's heaviest turkey, today an article about a man with triple teeth. FYI is easily managed and clearly an attention-getter: a crowd of students can always be found reading and discussing the latest item between morning activities.

Noticeably absent from the classrooms are conventional reading textbooks, instructional kits, and workbooks. At the beginning of the summer MacPhee gives each teacher a $50 budget "for anything but worksheets or workbooks." Also noticeably absent are public address announcements, school bells, and students bearing messages from door to door. "Instructional time is sacred," MacPhee says with finality.

Almost all the teachers post the daily class schedule on the chalkboard in order to keep themselves and the students on track. But this is only a guideline, and activities often carry over a few minutes or wrap up a little earlier than scheduled.

The teachers appreciate the difference. "Kids are learning here, because they don't have to rush. We don't have to cut them off in the middle of a sentence because of the bell," says one. In contrast, during the regular school year teachers at Behrman are pressed to teach fifty "expected learner outcomes" each semester as required by the New Orleans school board. They must also prepare students for quarterly competency testing in basic skills, administer quarterly pre-tests at the principal's request, and ready students for the end-of-year California Achievement Test (CAT) and state competency testing. Because they are working with many students who have reading and learning problems, teachers often find during the school year that they have little time left over for leading the students to read and write longer passages, to apply their literacy skills in their work, or to read and write for pleasure.

During the summer program, on the other hand, all teachers must include the same basic elements in their language instruction, but they are otherwise free in their choice of content and use of instructional time. A look at several classrooms reveals that most of the teachers use their freedom to involve students in reading children's literature, writing their own stories and poems, and discussing the reading and writing as a class.

In one classroom the teacher passes out a picture of two men looking up at a woman, who is floating placidly over their heads in a chair. The teacher explains to the students that this is one of seven magic chairs from a tale of fantasy, and that each chair is capable of a different kind of magic. She tells them a brief story about one of the chairs that disappears each time a pompous person sits upon it. The students laugh and cannot wait to begin when she asks them to write their own stories about one of the chairs.

Ten minutes later volunteers are reading what they have written aloud to the class. The class sits in a circle to facilitate discussion following each reading. Eventually all but two students read; the two decline despite coaxing and praise for their previous stories. One student, who has already read, is inspired by another's story and delivers an impromptu tale featuring the teacher's aide. Many of the stories are vibrant with imagination, and all the students read confidently, even those who have written only a few sentences. The teacher praises specific aspects of each story—the central idea, colorful language, a clever opening sentence—and asks a variety of questions: "What happened next? Why did the main character do that?"

The lesson is a grand success: the students' imaginations have been tapped, the teacher has modeled the kind of behavior she was expecting, and the students have read to a highly appreciative audience. The lesson is particularly appropriate for middle-schoolers, providing them with many opportunities for meaningful participation. They create their own tales of fantasy, they contribute to the discussion about the original story and their own writing, and they share their work with the class if they wish. Because the teacher responds to the content of each with useful feedback, rather than sitting in judgment on the work, the students begin to see themselves as capable writers and they adopt the attitudes of a writer—no meager accomplishment for young people who have not often been successful in their past school experiences.

In another class the students freely choose among a variety of workshop activities. When they complete one, they move on to a new one. Desks are clustered around the room to encourage the students to help each other with directions or problems, and to allow the teacher and aide to assist small groups who have encountered a particular difficulty. The students work on vocabulary, read from the newspaper, search for synonyms of key vocabulary in a passage, work on simplifying the message of convoluted sentences, take turns reading aloud with a friend, or complete the endings of stories from given beginnings. Though each of these is a practice activity, the choice is broad. Young adolescents need to take part in their own education. They gain a sense of responsibility for their own learning when they can choose instructional activities and experience the results of those choices.

The computer instructor picks up students at their classroom door, a simple and efficient management strategy. He takes them to an air-conditioned lab—a treat in itself in New Orleans' summer heat—where each is given exclusive use, for the entire instruction period, of an IBM or Atari computer fitted with a color monitor. The computers are placed in paired rows, so that student partners can troubleshoot easily together. As instructional partners, the students not only learn about the computers but also learn to teach others. It is an important opportunity for young adolescents to practice their growing social and intellectual skills. Working with computers is a special bonus for the 6th-graders, because they do not have access to Behrman's handful of computers during the regular school year.

Computer lessons are not tied directly to the regular reading and writing program, but the students do use word-processing programs to write letters, poems, and short stories. The lessons simply serve as an introduction to computers for most of the students and extend their notions of literacy to technology. They learn of a powerful tool to assist their learning.

The computer instructor is positively buoyant with energy, circulating about the room as the students type friendly letters they will print out in their next class meeting. "Which finger do you use to type a *d?* Are you sure?" he quizzes one student. "How would I type a capital *g?*" he asks another. "Which shift key?" He is encouraging basic touch-typing methods, which promote speed at the keyboard.

"Hey, everybody," he calls out. "I notice some of you are using poor posture. Look up here. Can everyone see me? Get a straight back, left fingers over *a, s, d, f,* right over *j, k, l,* semicolon. Put your thumbs over the space bar. Raise your wrists, not your elbows. You're not flying south for the winter."

His playful manner, ever-present smile, and ready assistance put students at ease as they try this new and often confusing technology. He demonstrates a tolerance for error that allows them to experiment: "If you make a mistake, just leave it. I'll show you some of the edit functions next time."

He concludes the lesson by literally taking a floppy disk apart before the students' eyes. In earlier sessions he has sensed their bewilderment about this magical object. Today he shows them that a disk looks much like a phonograph record, and he makes an analogy about how the two systems store information. Then he points out differences, explaining how the disk is divided up into sections, which can be arrived at by naming and saving a file. A part of the computer mystery suddenly dissolves.

Just before noon a reading class sits in a U-shaped arrangement around a large roll of newsprint unfurled about ten feet along the floor like a runway. A large red balloon floats from a disk near the top of the roll. The class is reviewing a story, *The Red Balloon*, which they have been reading this week.[5] The teacher directs the class to recall the details and then focuses their attention on the ending of the story, asking several students to present and defend their opinions of the ending.

Next, as the students dictate, the teacher writes in large script on the newsprint the first line of an alternative ending for the story. The students then take turns adding a sentence or two to continue the story line. Each uses a different-colored magic marker. As the ending unfolds, the paper unrolls. It is an effective culminating activity, interweaving reading, writing, and purposeful verbal exchange in the collaborative effort. The multicolored story is hung from ceiling to floor by lunchtime.

Assessing Success

The success of Adventures in Excellence is evident. Students enrolled in the program gained seven Degrees of Reading Power (DRP) units the first summer and four the second. (Usual expected gains for an entire school year are three to five DRP units.)[6] Though it is not practical to compare the gains of 165 voluntary summer students with those of 750 students compelled to attend regular school, it is apparent that this summer program has a positive effect on reading achievement. Skills that once were apt to become dull over a summer of disuse are now honed through extensive practice.

The eagerness with which the students participate and the annually increasing attendance demonstrate the need for the program as well as its attractiveness. Shannon, a 7th-grader, attended last summer because her mother found out about the program and "*she* wanted me to attend. I came back this summer because *I* wanted to." She says she likes meeting new friends over the summer and not having to do homework. She also enjoys receiving no grades and "having a chance to make my papers better after the teacher sees them." She has noticed that "the more I read, the better I get," and recommends two books she has read this summer, *The Freedom Side* and a book of poetry, *Honey Love.*

Another 6th-grader remarks that he has read five books in three weeks of the program. "I used to see a big, thick book and think, 'Oh, I want to read this, but it's so big,'" he says. "Now I just start reading and get more and more into it." He says that so far *Am I Normal?* is his favorite book of the summer.

MacPhee has $3,000 to spend on paperback books each summer. "I know we lose many of them," she admits, "but you've got to let students handle books." She manages the book selection herself, on the basis of ideas from staff, students, and her own school-year observations in classrooms. She often tries to pick out books that feature children as heroes. At the end of the summer the books are left in the classrooms for teachers and students to use during the following school year.

One student believes the program is so popular because many of his summer classmates "have their minds on the camping trip at the end." MacPhee has offered an overnight camping trip reward this summer for good attendance and behavior and completion of a book project. Last year's reward was a field trip to the art museum. Despite teachers' "prior misgivings" about whether students would work for such a reward, "the kids loved it," says MacPhee. She explains that most "live very isolated lives." Two-thirds of the students last summer had perfect attendance records. This summer the camping trip is a hot topic of conversations in the halls, at breakfast, and at lunch. Who is still eligible? Who has already completed the book project? Will taking time off for a family vacation trip disqualify a student?

Discipline is seldom an issue and is handled very differently in the summer program than during the regular school year. Because the students choose to attend and are happy to be there, they seldom "act up." The aides function as counselors in each class and often dispel trouble by talking to students individually. When a fight does break out, participants earn a one-day suspension. Most misbehavior, however, is treated with a Glasser-like response: the student acknowledges the wrongdoing and, with the teacher's assistance, makes a plan to avoid the problem in the future.[7] The system implicitly acknowledges the students' growing capabilities to frame their own rules and limits and to participate in the planning that directly affects them, and makes them responsible for the consequences of their actions. One teacher analyzed the absence of discipline problems this way: "It's the interesting activities that make the kids want to be here and behave; too much time is wasted on discipline during the school year."[8]

Staff Development

Though the summer program was designed primarily to help students maintain and improve their reading comprehension skills, it has also proven to be a highly effective model for professional staff development. MacPhee reports that this aspect of the program, along with the lower pressure of summer instruction, has made the task of hiring teachers relatively easy. "Many of them find it's the kind of teaching they'd like to do all year," she says. "They like the program personally, because the aim is *strengthening* their teaching, not *evaluating* it. My goal is to function as a colleague rather than a supervisor."

There are three parts to this professional training: intensive pre-service training, regular in-service meetings, and frequent classroom observation and assistance from the director. Teachers' contracts begin four days before the start of classes. Three of those days are devoted to pre-service training and the fourth to classroom preparation. Because the program is very different from what many of New Orleans' teachers are accustomed to during the school year, this pre-service training is essential in providing teachers with important information about instruction, discipline, and other summer school matters.

The first day of pre-service training focuses on the value of reciprocal teaching and its methodology.[9] Reciprocal teaching in the summer program consists of four activities related to any single reading passage: clarifying vocabulary, asking questions, predicting story action, and summarizing the plot. Each selection may be guided by the teacher or one of the students, thus giving the technique its reciprocal nature.

The second day teachers focus on discipline. A full day is devoted to the topic because the teachers must learn to be more self-reliant in dealing with difficulties. MacPhee has found that if she provides teachers with more effective discipline strategies to use in the classroom, they make fewer demands on her limited time. She has also learned that her teachers continue to use these strategies during the school year, thereby reducing the amount of assistance requested from the central office to solve classroom discipline problems. With smaller classes and an in-class assistant most teachers are easily able to resolve the few problems that may occur. The summer class structure further cuts down on disciplinary headaches. Except for the computer lab and creative writing, the students spend the entire morning with the same class and teacher. They are able to develop deeper and stronger relationships with their peers and the teacher; the disconnected feeling engendered by class changes every forty-five minutes is absent. They spend the time reading stories they are interested in, writing stories of their own choosing, and talking with each other about their understanding of both. With a teacher and an aide providing consistent attention during the three-hour block—often one-to-one—there is little need for the attention-getting misbehavior prevalent in larger, less interesting classes.

The final day of pre-service training centers on a model of instruction based on the Junior Great Books Program.[10] The Junior Great Books Program consists of a core of recommended literature for students and emphasizes interpretive rather than surface-level responses to the reading of that literature. Rather than asking students to recount details of a story, teachers might, for instance, ask them to infer causality. After a reading of "Jack and the Beanstalk" a literal question, such as "How many times did Jack go up the beanstalk?" would likely be ignored. A preferable question, requiring deeper thinking, might be, "Why did Jack go up the beanstalk a third time, when he already had the gold?"

MacPhee conducts hour-long staff in-service meetings once a week during the summer. The teachers meet in one of the two air-conditioned classrooms and sit in a circle, thus emphasizing the collegial nature of the meetings and instructional discussions. Generally MacPhee initiates the meetings with a brief review of an instructional technique (for instance, the four elements of reciprocal teaching). On the basis of her observations over that week, she asks teachers who have been particularly innovative to tell the others what they have done.

MacPhee guides the meetings much as she would like the teachers to manage their own classrooms. An active, responsive listener, she elaborates as she deems necessary, praising teachers' efforts and drawing on their questions and observations. Most of the teachers contribute comments regarding the nuances of implementing the in-service ideas in their individual classes. MacPhee sees that every teacher has an opportunity to be heard, prompting the silent with such comments as, "You had an interesting arrangement yesterday when I visited. Why don't you tell the group about it?"

At one in-service meeting MacPhee passes out a seven-page handout on teaching analogies. She regularly provides the staff with such information. She explains succinctly how useful drawing analogies can be in reading comprehension, points out how poorly Behrman's students have done on such tasks on standardized achievement tests, and suggests that the teachers try out some of the activities over the coming week, so that the group can discuss them at the next meeting. She highlights some potential trouble spots in the activities. By the end of her presentation, the teachers have been introduced to a new technique, informed of its strengths and flaws, and given an incentive to experiment with it in their classrooms.

In-service meetings are often the time when the staff clarifies procedures and policies. MacPhee may bring up an issue like technical points of eligibility for the camping trip. Should fighting disqualify a student? Should a student who had perfect attendance except for a family vacation trip remain eligible? The staff discusses these problems, reaches a consensus, and draws up general guidelines for future cases.

MacPhee also uses the in-service sessions to remind teachers of aspects of the program that she thinks need renewed emphasis. For instance, she often reiterates the value of reading aloud to the class and the necessity of choosing one or two books to read aloud from beginning to end. "Many of these students start books, and never finish," she emphasizes. "We want them to experience whole books, extended texts."

The in-service meetings always wrap up with individual concerns: this instructional difficulty or that discipline problem. By the end of the hour the group has efficiently considered a variety of instructional matters, administrative issues of import, and their own individual concerns. Everyone has been heard, and most have received praise. Consensus has been reached on all decisions. MacPhee has gotten her message across, but the teachers have maintained "ownership," and no one has been alienated with imposed sanctions. The teachers leave for the afternoon with a feeling of accomplishment in what they are doing and a renewed perspective on the value of the program.

Like any program, Adventures in Excellence functions best in the hands of the best teachers. However, the training program fosters improvements among all staff. Intensive and regular training and follow-up classroom visits establish a structure that allows teachers the freedom to teach in ways that best suit them, the benefit of others' suggestions, and the incentives and means to improve.

History and Development

The Southern Coalition for Educational Equity (SCEE), a nonprofit organization that focuses its advocacy efforts on school improvement in the southeastern United States, conceived the New Orleans Effective Schools Project in 1980 as a model for improving schools. Its staff settled on the middle-school level for this demonstration project for two reasons: the middle grades have been generally ignored by school reform efforts, and yet they serve as a "last chance" to reach failing students before they begin to drop out of school. "We're in a race with adulthood in middle schools," explains MacPhee. "The chance of teaching a nonreading 8th-grader is slim. Teen pregnancy is a great problem in this city. Nearly half of the kids never finish high school. And transience often interrupts our instruction. But if we can reach that same child in 6th grade, then we have a fighting chance."

After securing funding,[11] SCEE formed the effective schools partnership with the New Orleans School Board and the United Teachers of New Orleans in 1981, and by 1982 Behrman Middle School had been selected from among twelve applicant schools that qualified on the basis of having large numbers of students at risk for dropping out. Located near one of New Orleans' poorest housing projects, Behrman has a 99 percent minority student population.

Once selected, Behrman created a Site Council composed of teachers, students, and administrators. With the assistance of MacPhee and Recasner they formulated a school improvement plan during meetings throughout the 1982–83 school year. The plan was designed to improve students' reading comprehension primarily by increasing the quantity and quality of instructional time.

Recognizing that many teachers lacked training in reading instruction, the Site Council and SCEE made staff development an important element of the plan. Behrman's teachers generally had received either the broad preparation in many subject areas that is typical of elementary-school teacher training or the specialization in a single subject area that is typical of high-school teacher training. The unique demands of middle-grades teaching—blending skills instruction, subject-area instruction, and the responsiveness that is so necessary for success with young adolescents—had not been a part of their previous preparation.

The program's administrative staff bring strong backgrounds to the task. MacPhee is a former middle-school teacher and now is also an education writer and consultant. She holds a master's degree in teaching from Harvard University. Recasner is a doctoral candidate in school psychology at nearby Tulane University. He is particularly interested in the problems black children experience in learning to read.

Appropriate teacher training has been the focus of much of MacPhee's efforts. She prefers a collegial approach, first sharing information and then following up with suggestions as the teacher implements the idea in the classroom. She explains, "I have the power of *not* being in a position of evaluation." The teachers respond well to the respect she gives them and, in return, respect the knowledge she has to share.

Recasner's emphasis has been on gaining parental support for the teachers' in-class efforts. One of his first successes was to initiate the Behrman Parents for Reading Power contract. Parents who sign up promise to read to their child for fifteen minutes a day, three days a week. If they cannot read themselves, they pledge to find someone else to read to their child for the same amount of time. Parents in fifty households participated the first time the contract system was attempted, and the numbers have since increased. "Parents are not apathetic," Recasner argues. "They just don't always know what they can do."

As a step toward further improving the reading and general achievement gains students made during the school year, the summer program, Adventures in Excellence, was started in 1984. Its impact has been greater than teachers, administrators, parents, students, or SCEE could have hoped.

Conclusion

On the second floor of Behrman Middle School is a classroom that MacPhee, Recasner, and the aides share as an office during the summer. Books clutter every work space, and reading motivation posters and related quotations cover the walls. Above the chalkboard behind MacPhee's desk hangs a small, well-worn poster with a proverb: "Tell me, I forget. Show me, I remember. Involve me, I understand." Adventures in Excellence involves students daily during five enjoyable summer weeks, with the result that they "read more books," choose to return a second year "because I wanted to," and not only maintain reading skills over the usually dormant summer learning season, but also actually improve their reading and writing.

The program's emphasis on an active schedule and a broad range of appealing learning choices within a structured environment seems to suit both students and teachers. Older adolescent and young adult teachers' aides make a positive contribution in several ways. Careful attention to staff development and efforts at involving parents in students' reading at home have led to support from the adults most immediately involved. The results of this tightly knit program are paying off in growth and increased community support. The school board has acknowledged the success of the program and plans to assume its expenses at Behrman, as well as expand and fund it in four new upper elementary and three additional middle schools.

The Cross-Age Tutoring Program
of the Literacy Council of Alaska

For six weeks during the short far-northern summer, the Cross-Age Tutoring Program of the Literacy Council of Alaska meets in two cheerful classrooms at the Denali Community School in Fairbanks. Young people aged 14 to 21, who have themselves faced reading and school problems, are trained and supported to tutor 5- to 19-year-olds with similar problems.

The two classrooms reflect the interests of their young users. Posters, many of rock musicians and television personalities, decorate the walls. The bulletin boards in both rooms are covered with the "passports" made by tutors and students, one of the first activities they do together. Each passport has a photo of the bearer and lists his or her name, address, birthday, favorite color, and hobbies.

The classrooms also reflect the philosophy of the program directors, Joanne Healy and Christine McMahon, who believe that the best way to improve reading skills is to read. They have scraped together an impressive library from garage sales, donations, and purchases. Paperback books are lined up on the window sills in each room, and magazines are displayed on two large semicircular tables; shelves and racks are also filled with books and magazines. Students can choose from Judy Blume, Beverly Cleary, and Lloyd Alexander as well as Dr. Seuss, Shel Silverstein, and *The Empire Strikes Back.* *STARS* (a movie magazine for teens), *Ranger Rick* (the National Wildlife Federation's magazine for young people), and *People* are also part of the collection, along with plenty of comic books.

Eight tutors and 96 students are enrolled in the program. Each tutor works with four students per day. Students come Tuesday and Thursday or Monday, Wednesday, and Friday. There are two seventy-five-minute tutoring sessions in the morning and two more sessions in the afternoon.

Each tutoring session follows a set schedule. The first five minutes are devoted to the "circle activity," which focuses on a different theme each week. Today the theme is music, and the activity is a variation of the game "I packed my grandmother's trunk." All the tutors and students gather in a circle in one room.

One of the tutors begins the activity by saying, "My name is John and my favorite band is Van Halen." Then each student and tutor in turn, around the circle, tries to repeat what has been said up to that point and adds his or her own name and favorite band to the list.

An alarm clock rings at the end of five minutes to announce the end of the circle activity and the beginning of sustained silent reading for the next ten minutes. Everyone—the program administrators, the tutors, and the students—reads a personally chosen book during the time.

After ten minutes the alarm goes off again. Journal writing is the next ten-minute activity. Tutors and students all write in their journals. Topics are up to the writer; journals are not considered an appropriate place for teacher-assigned topics.

Again the bell signals the end of the activity. Now the group splits up, most of them leaving the room where they had gathered for the circle activity. Some go to the school cafeteria, others claim a section of the hall. Favorite corners are the recessed niches that mark the doorways to the classrooms. For the next five minutes, it is the tutor's turn to read to the student, one-to-one. The tutor chooses the book to read aloud, keeping the student's interests in mind.

None of the tutor-student pairs has gone so far off that they cannot hear the bell telling them to switch activities. For the next ten minutes the tables are turned, and the student reads to the tutor. This time it is the student who chooses the book, with the tutor's help.

The tutors and students also enjoy reciprocal reading, in which they take turns reading aloud to each other from books of their own choice. The tutors read with much emotion and drama, and the students are deeply interested in the stories. Many urge their tutors to "read one more page." The students also enjoy trading places and reading to the tutors. The tutor lets the student read uninterrupted, unless the student makes an error that interferes with meaning; in that case, the tutor waits until the student finishes the sentence and then asks a question to make sure the student understands what has just been read. As much as possible, focus is kept on meaning rather than pronunciation. When the reading is done, the tutor asks the student questions about the passage.

For the remaining half hour of the session, the tutor and student work together on specific skills or special activities. Learning games are very popular. Games and other literacy activities are organized in folders and filed in baskets according to the skill involved.

Tutors and students alike enjoy coming to the program, and all feel they are improving their reading and writing ability, learning about new capabilities, and making new friends. "It makes you feel so good when they learn something," says Mika, a 15-year-old tutor. One of Mika's students, Lenny, drags his feet at the door when the session ends. "I don't want to go home," he says.

Meeting the Literacy Needs of the Community

The cross-age program was founded in 1985 in response to requests received by the Literacy Council of Alaska for a free school-age summer remedial program. The local school district did not provide summer remedial help, and the alternative—private tutoring—is prohibitively expensive for most parents.

For students, the purpose of the program is to help improve basic skills and academic progress and, by doing so, to improve attitudes towards school. For tutors, the purposes are the same, but with an added item: job training. The majority of the program's funding, a grant from the Private Industry Council, is for this job training. This money comes through the Summer Youth Employment and Training Program funds, which are monitored by the Council.

Healy and McMahon have been active publicists for the program since its inception. The first and second year, they convinced United Way to donate newspaper ads. Radio and television stations ran public service announcements, and Healy and McMahon wrote articles for the local paper. They sent letters to teachers asking them to recommend at-risk students. There are thirty schools serving 13,000 students in the Fairbanks North Star Borough, and approximately 15 percent of the students in the school district are from low-income families. The response from parents and others in search of tutoring services was so tremendous that Healy and McMahon had to turn people away.

At least half of the students in the program are referred by their teachers because they are having difficulty keeping up in school. Many of these students come from families in which little reading is done at home, and they lack literacy experiences such as bedtime stories, family visits to the library, or parent help with homework. They must rely almost exclusively on school for reading instruction and reinforcement. Healy and McMahon have found that these students frequently are the ones assigned to the remedial reading program at school because of poor reading scores. Once that decision is made, a vicious cycle often begins of low expectations reinforcing low achievement, and they become less and less motivated to improve their reading.

The tutoring program tries to counteract the effect of the labeling that these students have experienced in school. Many of the program's students are afraid they are having difficulty with reading because they are "stupid." Healy and McMahon work hard to build self-esteem in every student who enters the summer program.

Each student who is accepted into the program is tested on the Woodcock Reading Mastery Test and on the Wide Range Achievement Test (WRAT) Math Level I. (The majority at time of entry are reading one to two years below their peers, but some are 10th- and 12th-graders reading at 3rd-grade level.) Each is also asked to make a list of six things he or she would like to learn. This list is used as an informal writing sample, and it is also the source from which directors and tutors generate the weekly themes for the circle activities. The question on the post-test writing sample at the end of the summer—"The first day I came to this program I thought . . ."—also serves as an evaluation of the student and the program.

Tutors come into the program through a different route. The Private Industry Council screens and sends out candidates for all of the job training programs it sponsors. Eligibility for Council programs is linked to three criteria: participants must (1) be from a low-income family background, (2) have a juvenile court record, or (3) be under foster care. Healy and McMahon do further screening, giving each candidate tutor an oral and written interview. Written questions include: What do you think makes a good tutor? Have you ever helped someone with schoolwork? How did you help? Was your help effective? Oral questions probe further into the potential tutor's ways of working with others and resolving conflicts: Do you babysit? What do you do when the child screams? Have you ever had a really good (or bad) teacher? What were some of that teacher's qualities? Finally, candidates are asked to read a paragraph about the cross-age tutoring program and discuss it with the interviewer.

The directors have found that good tutors are patient and dependable but have high expectations for themselves and their students. Tutors also need to be perceptive enough to be able to recognize a student's needs, both personal and academic. When experienced tutors are asked what qualities they believe are most important to being a good tutor, they give very similar responses. Robert, 15, says, "Friendship, patience, willingness to learn as well as teach, and a willingness to face your mistakes." Mika sums it up as "being willing, having patience, and being crazy enough to teach." Mika also feels a teacher should not be stiff, but ought to relax and make things fun. The teacher should have a good time, too.

The new tutors' basic skills are also tested on the Woodcock Reading Mastery Test and the WRAT Level I Math test. Like the students, the majority of the new tutors are reading one to two years below grade level. The only requirement is that they be able to read at least two grade levels above their assigned students.

The program claims that through their participation in the program, 85 percent of both tutors and students will improve their skills in at least one of the parts of the Woodcock Reading Mastery Test: letter identification, word attack, word comprehension, and passage comprehension.

Tutors and students alike approach teaching and learning situations with a certain amount of trepidation, because of their previous—often unhappy—experiences with school and reading. The cross-age tutoring program has been successful in overcoming these fears and anxieties.

Ian, a student, didn't like school. He didn't want to do his work and frequently interrupted classroom instruction. Every year he fell further behind. His mother enrolled him in a summer school program in Virginia, where they were living at the time. The classrooms were designed with two-way mirrors, and students and teachers could not tell when they were being observed. Ian hated it. After his family moved to Alaska, his school performance did not improve. When his mother decided to send him to the cross-age tutoring program during the summer after 7th grade, he agreed to attend only if she could assure him there would be no two-way mirrors. To his surprise, as much as anyone's, he liked the program. He is reading more, and he likes it. Reading became a lot easier, he explains, when he discovered he liked his tutor and wanted to do well. He says he has read ten books since he started in the program.

Robert was a student in a different tutoring program during the school year, because of his poor academic marks. But he liked that tutoring experience so much that he decided to try becoming a tutor himself. This new role not only enables him to learn about teaching but also improves his reading and writing skills. Like Ian, he has been reading more and finding it easier. He thinks tutoring has given him a better understanding of why he makes certain mistakes.

Staff Training and Development

The program works because of the quality of the training and the supervision of the young tutors. Healy and McMahon rule with a firm but kind hand. "They are good about giving you help when you need it and not bothering you when you're getting along well. They supervise the tutors very closely at the beginning, but then back off once people get comfortable," says Roberta, another of the program's tutors. "They could easily sit at their desks and read all day, but they're always roaming around," says Robert. They offer "great" advice, and they "never make you feel stupid." "You can go to them when you have a problem, or run out of things to do," says Mika.

The tutors are oriented and trained in an exhaustive week-long workshop. The workshop focuses on two areas: the personal interactions between tutor and student, and how to teach reading instruction. There are also special sessions on writing, math, English as a second language, becoming familiar with computers, and learning disabilities. Because many who are enrolled in the program—both tutors and students—have either experienced child abuse or know others who have, the directors include a session on what child abuse is and the correct way to report it.

The training workshop helps the tutors to explore their own identities and to think about what they would like to do with their adult lives. They complete reading and writing interest inventories, make "passports," and discuss what they would like to do in the future. Considerable time is also spent role-playing situations that tutors might face with their students and how to resolve them appropriately.

In the part of their training that focuses on reading, the tutors learn several specific techniques for reading (and writing) instruction: sustained silent reading, reading aloud, student-dictated stories, and strategies for reading in subject areas. They are also taught to use a method called Directed Reading Thinking Activity (DRTA).[12] According to the program's adaptation, the tutor begins by dividing a short written passage into (numbered) paragraphs, with large spaces between. All but the first paragraph are then covered. The tutor and student read this first paragraph, discuss its meaning, and consider what might be in the next paragraph and why. Paragraph by paragraph, the two work through the passage, making guesses and then checking their guesses against the text. In the training workshop, time is allowed for tutors to practice doing the technique themselves.

The directors realize that their tutors and students, many of whom have been in remedial reading classes in school, have had far more practice in decoding and phonics than they have had with reading texts. Therefore, although the tutors are trained to teach decoding skills, the main emphasis is on teaching techniques that keep the focus on comprehension. In their training the tutors are encouraged to use learning games to build skills, as an alternative to traditional drills. Much time is spent becoming acquainted with existing games and inventing new ones.

As it prepares tutors to teach, the workshop also builds a cohesive work group. The workshop leaders model the way teachers work together, share ideas, and plan for their responsibilities. Sharing with colleagues is an important theme that carries through the six-week summer school session.

After the workshop, training continues in the form of supervision. Speakers are also brought in on special topics. Recently a staff member from Women in Crisis-Counseling Assistance spoke to tutors about abusive relationships and where to get help.

The final week of the program, after active tutoring is completed, incorporates several job-training activities for the tutors. One year tutors visited a college placement office, a day care center, a clerical skills school, and local art galleries. They spoke with a local artist and toured the local newspaper. They practiced job interviews, which were taped, and then reviewed their reactions to the tapes and discussed how they could improve their interviews. Other activities featured skills for "moving out on your own" and "keeping a budget."

Curriculum and Instruction

The effectiveness of the training and supervision can be observed in the tutoring sessions. The tutors readily use the techniques they have learned in the workshop; furthermore, they understand why they do what they do, and they can explain the rationale to visitors from outside the program. The workshop's emphasis on the "affective" element of tutoring is not misplaced. The tutors report that dealing with their students' fears and anxieties is one of the hardest parts of tutoring. "The most difficult thing is motivating the kids when they're in a bad mood," says Mika. Robert thinks the most difficult part is "remembering that I'm the role model. If I'm wild, they're wild. If I'm bored, they're bored." He agrees with Mika that it is not easy to be nice to a student who is irritating him.

The tutors and students all are anxious in the beginning. In the training workshop the tutors learn about getting off to a good start with their students. Mika reports that when she meets a student who seems scared, she says, "Hi, my name's Mika. Are you scared? I'm scared, too. Since we're both scared, let's be friends." Robert says he is as scared as the students when he starts. He breaks the ice by asking them questions about themselves and telling them about himself.

The first day together, tutors help their students make "passports," using those they made in the training workshop as an example. Every day the tutors and students all write in their journals on topics of their own choosing. Each student makes a book on a self-selected topic, to be displayed and shared at the potluck dinner at the end of the summer session.

The structured reading activities—sustained silent reading, reciprocal reading, and reading aloud—require the tutors and students to select and read books of their own choice. The large library the program has amassed ensures that there will be books to interest everyone. The students name *Garfield, Where the Red Fern Grows,* and *Little House on the Prairie* as some of their favorites. The tutors, too, are expanding their reading interests. Roberta recommends mysteries like *Blow Hot, Blow Cold.* Robert prefers nonfiction, biographies, and books about nature.

The tutors and students have grasped the principle the program advocates: reading is meaningful. Because he believes that comprehension is the most essential skill, Robert explains to his students that it is much more important to be able to understand the meaning of words and sentences than to be able to "call them out." George, a student, thinks the program puts a high value on students' understanding what they read. "Ways to understand better, like asking yourself questions, are very important," he says.

The tutors devise clever methods to involve their students in reading. Mika does dramatic readings with her students. During one session she takes the girls' parts, and her student, a boy, takes the male roles. She has also thought up a contest that incorporates individual reading with writing. She and a student choose a book together; both take home a copy, read it, and write a summary. Then another tutor judges which summary is the most interesting. Mika says the student usually wins.

Structuring and pacing lessons is one of the biggest problems that any new teacher faces; this problem is compounded when the teacher is a teenager. In the cross-age tutoring program, the carefully structured and timed activities ensure continuity between lessons. For two-thirds of each lesson, the tutors and students are reading and writing texts that are personally meaningful.

The last time slot of each tutoring session is devoted to skills work and special activities. From their pre-assessment information Healy and McMahon prepare a list of skills each student needs to work on. They put a copy of the list in the student's folder, along with the names of some games geared to teaching that skill. The tutor uses this list to plan lessons. Many of the game ideas come from teachers' magazines such as *Learning* and *Instructor.* The games are played individually, in pairs, or in a group. The students also have access to two computers and a variety of software that allow them to practice reading skills.

Young adolescents have a great need for physical activity, and active games are one way the program serves this need. "Cross the Creek" is a favorite group game that gets everyone involved and moving and helps students to practice reading skills. The tutors bring all their students together and divide them into two or more teams. The teams line up in queues, facing one edge of the "creek" (two long parallel strips of masking tape). One of the tutors then chooses a word, written on a piece of poster board, and puts it in the creek. In order to cross the creek, the student at the head of each queue has to say the word, use it in a sentence, think of a synonym or antonym, or think of a word that begins with the same letter. Whenever the word is "done" correctly, a new word is put into the creek. The first team whose members all get to the other side of the creek is the winner.

Collaboration is an important part of the training and the tutoring. The tutors learn that no teacher is an island. They have opportunities to share ideas before the students arrive in the morning, or in the afternoon after they leave. They also exchange information at a thirty-minute staff meeting every Friday.

Program Administration

The two program directors, Healy and McMahon, are both certified elementary teachers. Both have also had experience with a wide variety of the literacy needs of their community. Healy worked as an intern with the Literacy Council of Alaska. Besides supervising the summer tutoring program, she supervised the Council's Parents and Tots reading program. McMahon worked in an alternative elementary school sponsored by the Fairbanks Native Association and volunteered with the Literacy Council before working for the Council as a paid staff member. Though both directors have taken reading classes at the University of Alaska, they have learned much of what they know from professional journals like *The Reading Teacher* and *The Journal of Reading*. They designed the program, set it up under the aegis of the Literacy Council of Alaska, and administer its day-to-day operations.

Salaries are the major program expense. Costs of program space, utilities, and maintenance are absorbed by the state because the program is held at the community school. Tutor salaries are underwritten by funding from the Private Industry Council. The program is also assisted by donations from Standard Alaska Production Company, Exxon USA, MAPCO Petroleum, the United Way, and ARCO Alaska. Although the program is free, parents, like everyone else, are encouraged to make a contribution if they can. The Literacy Council has developed a creative donations campaign. By making a contribution of a certain amount, a donor may "adopt" a student. The student's identity is kept strictly secret, but the donor may receive regular progress reports on the student's work.

Involving the Parents

Parents' input is important in determining the instructional goals for each student. Every parent in the Fairbanks program is asked to fill out a questionnaire to provide important information that is conveyed to tutors before the tutoring sessions begin. Most of the students report talking to their parents about their work in the program. At the potluck dinner at the end of the six-week session parents can see their child's test scores and talk to the tutor.

Stronger parent involvement is on Healy and McMahon's "to do" list. They would like to make the program a year-round one, with an after-school schedule during the school year. If they can switch to that format, they plan to involve parents more. They have also considered making it mandatory for parents to visit the program, observe the tutoring process, and agree to work with their children at least ten minutes each night.

Healy and McMahon report that the parents of the children in their program want to be better advocates for their children, but often do not know how to do so. Uncertain of who to talk to or what to say to a teacher or school staff person, many of the parents feel they are unequal to the task of addressing their children's literacy problems.

Effectiveness

Students in the Fairbanks summer program receive tutoring help, at most, three times a week for an hour and a quarter each session, spread out over six weeks. This means that twenty-two hours and thirty minutes is the maximum amount of scheduled tutoring time one student can receive in one summer. It is obvious from observations and from interviews with participants that the program does help tutors and students to improve their reading skills as well as their self-esteem and perceptions of themselves as learners. However, it is doubtful whether that growth is accurately measured by the standardized tests the program uses to assess improvement. Students' and tutors' journals, lists of books read, writing samples, and students' and tutors' comments all provide much richer information on the progress of the program's participants than the movement they make on pre- and post-tests covering the six-week period.

The ultimate measure of the program's effectiveness, responsiveness, and success is its very high "happiness quotient." Jeremiah, a 7th-grader, says that what he likes best about the program is "the reading time you get in. You get away from the house, and the teachers are pretty nice." Carrie, a 5th-grader, says the program is "fun." She likes playing on the computer and making her book. She is looking forward to the potluck party, where she will display her book.

The tutors, too, are pleased with their learning and their work. Roberta believes that tutoring has made her more responsible. She has learned that consistent school attendance is necessary for academic achievement. Mika believes that tutoring will be a good reference and will enhance her employability in the future. It has also helped her to maintain some of the skills she would have otherwise lost during the summer, and she has made a lot of new friends, too.

Comprehensive Community Literacy Planning

The cross-age tutoring program in Fairbanks breaks new ground for community literacy planning. Communities across the country generally have approached literacy programming in piecemeal fashion, responding to a crisis, an age-group, or a special-interest group as particular needs become known. Often there is little communication between service providers in different community programs.

In contrast, the Literacy Council of Alaska has developed a comprehensive range of services for many different ages and different needs. Besides the usual adult literacy instruction provided by trained volunteers, the Council's programs also offer assistance for adult students in such skills as reading a bus schedule or making a shopping list. Council staff help adult students with referrals to community agencies, and they have developed materials for adult beginning readers about community characters in Fairbanks. Parents and Tots, a literacy program for parents who are new readers and their children, co-sponsored with the Fairbanks North Star Borough Library, and the cross-age tutoring program are the Council's two programs that involve younger students.

Literacy councils have traditionally focused on adults and not younger people because the question of who should provide services for illiterate school-age children is a sensitive policy area. In most cases communities leave the solutions to the schools. Protective of their "turf," schools can be hostile to other agencies moving into their arena. Yet the cross-age tutoring program in Fairbanks has worked compatibly with the local public schools, enhancing rather than threatening their work. Teachers have been eager to send students to the program.

The Literacy Council of Alaska has interpreted the term "literacy," and its own mission, in the broadest possible sense; it is committed to the belief that communities must plan for the reading and writing needs of all their members, not just adults. By meeting adolescents' literacy needs, good programs will alleviate the problem of providing services to them as adults.

Conclusions

Summer literacy programs have enormous potential. They can combine the best of in-school learning with the best of out-of-school programming. Not yet entrenched in a tradition, they can still develop and diversify in many directions.

The two programs reviewed here have many elements in common with the successful in-school and after-school programs mentioned earlier in this book. But they also have some special characteristics that highlight the value of summer programs in particular. First, they serve a critical need by keeping students' skills honed over the summer months, when much ground is otherwise lost. Second, unconstrained by a school-year schedule, they can arrange large blocks of time for a spectrum of activities (as New Orleans has) or work within intensive shorter sessions that can be geared towards a year-round after-school format (as Fairbanks hopes to do). Third, they can draw on a large pool of potential staff: professional teachers who are free for the summer, professors and graduate students who are free from university classes, and older adolescents and young adults who are eager to serve as teachers' aides and tutors.

Summer literacy programs can also serve as laboratories, pilot programs, or demonstration projects for programs and methods. The Kenosha Model and Learning to Read through the Arts, described elsewhere in this book, both began as summer programs before they were instituted as in-school reading programs.

The laboratory concept could be translated even further. Teacher-training programs could make excellent use of summer programs for in-service opportunities. Master teachers working with smaller-than-usual classes could use the extra time to supervise the development of teachers in training in the intensive way that Fairbanks and New Orleans have piloted. Summer literacy programs could also offer practicum and clinical training experience to graduate students in the fields of learning disabilities or reading specialization, by serving as field placements.

Summer literacy programs, like after-school literacy programs, could easily be sponsored by a range of agencies. Libraries, either alone or in conjunction with other community agencies, would make excellent sponsors of summer literacy programs. Other possibilities are religious organizations, recreation centers, and settlement houses.

As the nation's concern about illiteracy rises, and as minimum competency standards proliferate in school districts, summer literacy programs will become an increasingly important element in helping students to stay in school. These programs can be a powerful force in helping young adolescents develop, retain, and expand their literacy skills.

Notes

1. Barbara Heyns, *Summer Learning and the Effects of Schooling* (New York: Academic Press, 1978).

2. Launor F. Carter, "The Sustaining Effects Study of Compensatory and Elementary Education," *Educational Researcher* 13, no. 7 (1984): 11.

3. Barbara Heyns, "Summer Programs and Compensatory Education: The Future of an Idea," working paper prepared for the Office of Educational Research and Improvement, Chapter 1 Study Team, Conference on the Effects of Alternative Designs in Compensatory Education, Washington, D.C., 17–19 June 1986, 39.

4. Jay Neugeboren, "The Zodiacs," in his collection of stories *Corky's Brother* (New York: Farrar, Straus & Giroux, 1969); also in *Transatlantic Review* 20 (1966).

5. Albert Lamorisse, *The Red Balloon* (New York: Doubleday, 1978).

6. Southern Coalition for Educational Equity. *Annual Report 1983–84* (Jackson, Miss.: SCEE, 1985), 9.

7. See William Glasser, *Schools without Failure* (New York: Harper & Row, 1969), 21–24.

8. Southern Coalition for Educational Equity. *Annual Report,* 9.

9. See Annemarie Palinscar and Anne Brown, "Reciprocal Teaching: A Means to a Meaningful End," in *Reading Education: Foundations for a Literate America,* ed. Jean Osborn, Paul T. Wilson, and Richard Anderson (Lexington, Mass.: Lexington, 1985), pp. 299–310.

10. The Great Books Foundation was established in 1947 as an independent, nonprofit educational corporation. It promotes education through a program of reading and discussing great works of literature and trains some 18,000 discussion leaders per year toward this end. Junior Great Books began in 1962 as a program for parents who wanted to encourage their children's reading, but very soon began appearing in classrooms, grades 2–12, across the United States.

11. Foundations supporting this project include the Mary Reynolds Babcock Foundation, the Carnegie Corporation of New York, the D.H. Holmes Foundation of New Orleans, the RosaMary Foundation, and the Southern Education Foundation.

12. See Russell G. Stauffer, *Directed Reading Maturity as a Cognitive Process* (New York: Harper & Row, 1969).

SPECIAL FINDINGS

The preceding chapters have provided in-depth descriptions of three in-school programs, three after-school programs, and two summer programs that demonstrate innovative and successful ways of reaching out to young adolescents with literacy needs. These were only a few of the many programs that PAL staff visited during their field research. Many other programs that merit discussion cannot be fully described within the limits of this book. This chapter highlights some of our special findings from those programs.

Common themes introduced in earlier chapters resurface here. Nowhere is this more evident than with in-school programs. Young adolescents have special literacy needs that are a response to the varied and increased literacy demands of the middle grades. Here again, program directors report that many middle-grades students lack basic comprehension strategies, background knowledge, and subject-area requirements, as well as an elementary level of fluency in reading and writing.

Like those described in earlier chapters, the school and community programs touched on here seem unanimous in emphasizing literacy instruction that is integrated with the student's broader academic and personal experience, that is, put into a variety of meaningful contexts. They also reiterate that building the young person's self-assurance and self-esteem is a crucial part of the process.

A Comprehensive Classroom Program

BASIC, a program at Benjamin Franklin Middle School in San Francisco, is a comprehensive reading program geared to classroom teaching. Methods to help students bridge the gap between elementary and secondary school, reading instruction in the subject areas, and direct instruction in reading comprehension techniques are essential factors in BASIC's approach to helping middle-grades students improve their literacy skills.

The students at Benjamin Franklin are primarily foreign-born and from poor families. Seventy-five percent are eligible for Chapter 1 help, and 55 percent are enrolled in bilingual education classes. Once predominantly black in enrollment, the school now has large numbers of Chinese, Southeast Asian, and Hispanic students.

Every other year the 7th grade at Benjamin Franklin becomes the BASIC class, and the students continue with the BASIC program through their 8th-grade year. (Alternate, non-BASIC years provide a control group for comparison.) Like all students in the school, these students have one period of social studies and one period of English every day; but their social studies and English instruction is unified around the social studies curriculum and the teaching of reading and writing skills necessary to understanding subject-area material. For example, if the unit is on Africa, the social studies and English activities are organized around African topics.

BASIC teachers meet together during common planning periods to design the interrelated units. In class the teachers and their aides work with small groups, use materials and activities keyed to the students' differing levels of ability, and teach reading comprehension strategies in both the English and the social studies classes.

BASIC pays special attention to helping middle-grades students learn the skills they need to make the adjustment from the family-like elementary school setting to the more detached high-school setting. For example, most students who enter BASIC do not even know how to organize their notebooks for their different classes, much less how to organize materials to respond to different assignments. As part of instruction in BASIC, each student is required to purchase a loose-leaf notebook to be used for the social studies and English classes, and the teachers show their students exactly how to organize their notebooks.

Helping Students with Subject-Area Learning

The Middle School Reading Laboratory of the Jefferson County Schools in Louisville, Kentucky, serving about 2,250 adolescents in fifteen middle schools, has created a pullout program designed to give students extra literacy support and instruction in specific subject areas. Each Reading Laboratory teacher works with the subject area departments in his or her school to create a schoolwide plan for helping students improve their reading skills in these areas. For instance, Ellen Adams at Johnson Middle School reports that she may do a six- to eight-week unit in cooperation with the English department on library skills and the use of reference materials, then do a six-week unit with the science department, and then begin a test-taking unit to prepare students for the district's standardized testing.

Francis Bloom, a Chapter 1 teacher at Thomas Jefferson Middle School, finds that her students' lack of background knowledge is a problem, particularly in the specific subject areas. She clarifies her lessons by using examples and visual aids like films and computer programs. When her students read about London Bridge, she brings photographs, including those of the bridge after it was transported to Arizona. When they read about medieval England, she shows a number of filmstrips and pictures and helps the students make swords, a model of a castle, and other interesting items that reflect the period.

As a special response to middle-grades students' needs for help with homework, the school system has created a Homework Hotline. Staffed by student volunteers and supervised by paid teachers, the hotline helps students with questions about their homework. The center is stocked with the textbooks used in the school system.

Using Technology to Attract Interest

The Starpoint Secondary Reading Program, a Chapter 1 pullout program at Starpoint Central School in Lockport, New York, uses technology such as videodiscs and computers as a "hook" and a reinforcement to help middle-grades students learn and improve literacy skills.

Videodisc technology is new, exciting, and enticing. Students can freeze the action, play it in reverse, and replay any or all parts of the program. The benefits extend beyond the technical level, because hands-on use of the machinery also contributes to the students' self-assurance and hence their self-esteem. The popularity of the computers and videodiscs removes the stigma of attending the reading lab, where the equipment is located. In fact the participants, who soon learn to produce professional-looking papers by using the word-processing program, become the envy of their friends.

Technology has proven to be an effective means of securing the students' interest. Used in the context of class discussions and a variety of reading and writing activities, the video and computer machinery provides them with new experiences and new information and allows them to "see" things and places they could not otherwise, an especially important feature in building background knowledge. Lack of experience, the program's directors believe, is at the root of many students' reading problems. For instance, many of the Chapter 1 students have never seen Niagara Falls, although it is only a thirty-minute drive from Lockport.

Used to enhance and support literacy activities, technology can be a great asset. The Starpoint teachers are careful to select only the best materials for instruction—which can be surprisingly scarce. They avoid items that focus attention on factual recall of minor points, preferring those that promote more complex discussion and understanding of texts.

Improving the School Setting

Another theme that emerged in the course of PAL field research was the relationship of literacy instruction and achievement to other factors in school. A particularly good example is I.S. 158 (Theodore Gathings Middle School), in the Bronx, New York. Staff there found that by improving school organization and climate, they have also been able to improve schoolwide literacy achievement.

Making I.S. 158 a safe environment in which students feel free to learn has been a primary goal, and it is not an easy task. Although the South Bronx, where the school is located, is undergoing revitalization, dangers persist. In the lunchroom, teachers gossip about neighborhood gangs, who are now rumored to be armed with machine guns. At the high school that receives I.S. 158's graduates, armed guards patrol the halls, and only one-third of the freshman class continues through the senior year. The students at I.S. 158 come from low-income families (60 percent black, 40 percent Hispanic); nearly all qualify for government-sponsored free lunches. Only 19 percent of the entering 6th-graders read at grade level.

Administrators and teachers have worked together to implement a variety of changes to improve the climate and organization of the school as a whole. For instance, the students are divided into "families," each with their own corridor and group of teachers. One teacher in the corridor is designated the "father" or "mother" of the family. (This teacher is allowed an extra preparation period per day to make time for the additional responsibilities that come with the position.) A social worker is also assigned to each "family" and does counseling with small groups each week. All discipline starts within this "family." Any problem is referred first to the "mother" or "father," who, with the help of the other teachers in the family, makes a constructive plan for addressing the situation and dealing fairly with the student or students involved. The family head and teachers coordinate their work with the school's disciplinary dean.

A strategy that promotes unity within the school, bringing its different constituents together—from faculty and administrators to students and their parents—is the Comprehensive School Improvement Plan (CSIP). In New York state, schools that report poor reading or math scores, or poor attendance patterns, are required by the Regent's Action Plan to form a schoolwide committee to create a process to address school improvements. Every part of the school is represented on the committee, including paraprofessionals, parents, and a student council representative.

As improvements were made in the structure and organization of the school, reading levels also improved. In 1985, 44 percent of the 6th-graders were reading at grade level by the end of the school year. This demonstrates the importance of evaluating literacy needs within the context of the whole school, not just the reading program.

Responding to Special Needs: Vocational Training

Some literacy programs have developed specialized responses to special literacy needs of young adolescents. The Basic and Vocational Skills Program of Burlington, North Carolina, addresses a particularly acute need: the intertwined problems of low literacy skills, high dropout potential, and future employment prospects. Traditionally, vocational and job training programs have been offered only to older students, but this program focuses on 7th- and 8th-graders. The decision was made to target this age-group because of disturbing evidence uncovered in a study of students who had dropped out of schools in Burlington. Forty percent responded that their decision to drop out had been made while they were still in middle school (that is, well before they approached the legal age to do so), and one-third said that no one on the school staff had discussed the problem with them.[1]

The program serves about fifty students, who score between the 15th and 50th percentile in reading on the California Achievement Test (CAT). The students receive special help in reading along with vocational information and training in fields such as manufacturing, construction, communications, energy, and microcomputers. Burlington hopes that this literacy and job training will induce these at-risk middle-grades students to stay in school.

Responding to Special Needs: Creating Alternative Textbooks

The Na Pua a Pauahi program of the Kamehameha Schools in Hawaii is another example of a specialized response to a special need. A reading program situated in several middle-grades schools, it gives extra support to 7th-graders whose poor reading skills cause them to fall behind in their social studies classes. Na Pua a Pauahi serves about thirty students at each school, who attend the program four times a week for an hour each session in place of their regular social studies class.

The program's special response developed from these students' need for readable social studies materials. In Hawaii 7th-graders study the Hawaiian monarchy in their social studies classes.

Textbooks are available, but frequently even good students have difficulty making sense of the bland language in them. Seeking alternatives for their students with poor reading comprehension skills, the Na Pua a Pauahi teachers chose to write their own materials. For instance, in *Pikoi*, Hawaiian myths and legends are retold for middle-grades students. Several teacher-authored biographies of Hawaiian royal figures are also currently available, as well as volumes on ancient Hawaiian culture and the volcanic origins of the islands. Other titles include *The Water of Kane*, a collection of Hawaiian legends, and *Life in Old Hawaii*, a description of everyday life before the arrival of Captain Cook.[2]

Responding to Special Interests

Specialized programs need not arise only as a response to need but may also develop around special interests. Learning to Read through the Arts (LTRTTA), a Chapter 1 program that originated in New York City, provides students with enjoyable arts experiences that they can translate into reading skills. Students attend the program two days a week during school hours. All the art workshops—dance, film making, photography, drawing, sculpture, printmaking, painting, and mixed media—are reading-oriented. The students must listen carefully to instructions, talk about what they are going to do, and record information, directions, and descriptive paragraphs about each project in their individual journals, which are later reviewed by program staff. The art experience helps students to move from the concrete to the abstract, from looking and doing to thinking and conceptualizing.

The program's emphasis on creativity gives the students a positive feeling about learning and provides them with opportunities to experience success in the area of academic achievement as well as that of self-expression. Helping young people to feel successful is a key ingredient in programs that work with students who have suffered years of failure at school.

Community-Based Programs with Comprehensive Goals

In the realm of community-based literacy programs, comprehensive social-service agencies have great potential as providers of successful aid. Besides offering after-school or summer literacy instruction, they also sponsor a range of additional social services for participants and their families, such as counseling, referrals, recreation, and emergency clothing, food, and shelter.

Participants in community-based programs are, by and large, the poor. The need for these broader kinds of social services in addition to academic support and literacy instruction only serves to emphasize that point. After-school program directors believe that reading and school problems must be considered in the context of the individual and communal needs of the children and families in the neighborhoods they serve, and that programs to assist students in their academic work must be integrated with other services.

The Philadelphia Federation of Settlement Houses and the North Bronx Family Service Center are representative of the kinds of comprehensive social-service agencies that offer adolescent literacy instruction. These two agencies have more in common than their role in literacy assistance to young adolescents. When discussing their literacy programs, the two directors—Gerson Green in Philadelphia and Jim Marley in the Bronx—emphasize strikingly similar themes and concerns. As social workers, rather than educators, they bring a new perspective to the debate on what makes a good literacy program for young adolescents.

The lack of viable institutions in the poor communities they serve concerns both directors. The settlement houses in Philadelphia, Green explains, are neighborhood institutions operating exclusively in neighborhoods lacking in other strong institutions. They provide neighborhood residents, of all ages, with some of the few options for involvement that exist in many poorer communities. The North Bronx Family Service Center works similarly in a neighborhood otherwise "thin" in institutions. Its goal is to exert a positive "pull" on neighborhood residents. This pull is what Marley refers to as "social gravity—the climate in which kids have some foundation that keeps them going."

Both organizations exert this pull by providing programs for community residents of all ages, interests, and needs—from dropout prevention and job training to family counseling and recreation programs. One family member, or all, may be involved in one, or several, of the activities the agency offers. Integration of services is a hallmark of both agencies' approach.

Because of their concern for and their responsiveness to community needs, community-based agencies have addressed the literacy needs of many groups in their areas. They may teach English to new immigrants, provide preparation for the General Equivalency Diploma, and—as these two agencies have—develop programs that meet the literacy needs of young adolescents.

Though their concerns are similar, their responses to young adolescents' literacy needs differ. The Philadelphia Federation of Settlement Houses has developed an after-school, summer school, and summer camp program to enrich the literacy skills of young people in the communities it serves. The Mathematics, Arts, and Reading Camps (MARC) program is an integral part of the settlement-house philosophy of community empowerment.

The MARC summer day camp is a good example of innovative summer literacy programming: literacy enrichment activities are mixed with traditional summer camp activities such as swimming and arts and crafts. The program has also started to experiment with creating a week-long summer residential camp where literacy instruction is combined with counseling and outdoor activities.

Regardless of when the particular program is offered, in the summer or after school, all MARC teachers are committed to making learning stimulating and fun. For instance, they teach skills through games or introduce literature through drama.

Because the program directors discovered that many of the participants had seldom ventured outside their own neighborhoods, expanding young people's experiences has become an important element in all MARC programs. "They live with a small world concept. Many kids feel trapped and don't know why," explains Green. Hence field trips are part of MARC instruction both after school and during the summer. They give young adolescents a chance to learn about the world outside their neighborhoods and also help break down the spatial and conceptual barriers that poverty too often builds.

The North Bronx Family Service Center began its after-school tutoring program as part of its effort to support students in the local schools, where reading levels are among the lowest in the city. Center staff also provide support services to the children and family at the school. "Failure is almost ordinary; it's not exotic," says Marley of the situation in the local schools. "Economically and culturally these students lead chaotic, marginal personal lives. They are not socialized to institutions and the institutions themselves are profoundly weak." The tutoring program serves about 65 students aged 7 to 14 who are reading at least two grades below their expected level. About half are young adolescents, many of whom are reading at the very beginning levels.

The purpose of the program is both social and academic: to help students improve their academic skills, and to improve the self-esteem of those who are suffering failure at school. As with all the Center's services, the academic and social goals of the program are interlocking. Students may come into the tutoring program through other services the Center offers, or they may begin with tutoring and then join other programs, such as counseling or recreation.

The tutoring program is a cross-age program. The tutors are drawn from the local community college. Primarily women who are neighborhood residents, many of the tutors are themselves attending remedial classes in reading, math, or composition that prepare them for their junior college courses. They come to the Center either as work-study students or as interns placed by the Human Services Department at the community college.

Conclusions

Perhaps more than any other in this book, this chapter shows that good adolescent literacy programs come in many sizes and shapes. The two criteria for such programs—an organization that is responsive to the developmental needs of young adolescents; and good, solid literacy instruction—can be met in more than one fashion. The needs and resources of an agency or a community must be the starting point for drawing up a plan for addressing the literacy needs of young adolescents.

Postscript

Despite the overwhelmingly positive tone of this chapter, a report of the PAL research team's special findings would not be complete without serious mention of one particularly disturbing problem: the uneasy climate that surrounds programs for young people whose native language is not English. A hot issue in many communities, "bilingual education" touches on many volatile political questions of our time, from foreign policy to domestic tax cuts. In trying to provide the best possible educational plan for each child who enters their doors, schools frequently find themselves caught between the demands of federal immigration officials, angry parents, wavering school boards, and court rulings.

Tucson, Arizona, is a microcosm of the problems that school systems across the country face as they try to provide services for students with limited English proficiency. The Tucson Unified School District serves 53,000 students, 5,500 of whom have limited English proficiency. Although the overall student population in Tucson is not increasing, the proportion of students who must learn to speak English as well as learn to read and write it is rising rapidly. In 1985 the non-English-speaking population in the schools rose by 17 percent. Students from Mexico and Central America predominate, but enrollment also includes a growing number of students from the Middle East, Indochina, and other areas of Asia. Some of the students, especially those from Mexico, have never before attended school. Twenty unaccompanied Southeast Asian orphans who have been adopted by American families recently entered the school system.

"Politics really do impact the curriculum," says Kathy Escamilla, director of the Department of Bilingual Education in the Tucson Unified School District. "Principals have accused immigration officials of staking out schools to catch entire families." She explains that after a Friday raid by immigration officials, a school may open on Monday with one-third fewer students.

While the government is looking for illegal aliens, schools are trying to give students the instruction the courts have mandated they are all to receive regardless of their families' residence status. "The field of bilingual education, in general, is lacking in support," says Escamilla. "It's thought of as a compensatory poverty program. The politics are fear of the 'brown wave' of illegal immigration."

The Tucson program and many others that serve students for whom English is a second language are charged with a difficult task. But under circumstances such as these even the best-planned and most lavishly funded literacy program for young people would have difficulty functioning happily. And all too often, in too many places, "lack of support" refers not only to public moral support but to community allocations. As with many other political issues that affect them, ultimately the young people—who have the least voice and the most to lose—are the ones who suffer from this atmosphere of anger and uncertainty.

Models for effective programs that help students to learn English as a second language and become integrated into school life are readily available. The HILT program in El Paso, described earlier in this book, is one such model. But all of the programs mentioned throughout this book adhere to a philosophy and use instructional approaches that can be used effectively with students who are learning to speak English as well as read and write it.

Notes

1. See Ellen S. Pittillo, principal researcher, *Dropout Research* (Burlington, N.C.: Burlington Public Schools, 1982), 22.

2. The materials cited here are all published by Kamehameha School Press, Kamehameha Schools Store, Honolulu, HI 96817.

WHAT WORKS AND WHY

Successful compensatory literacy programs for young adolescents are complex organisms. They are bigger than one good teacher or one good director, one pleased student, or one active parent. They have many supporters in all walks of life in their communities, who have been affected or involved in the programs in some way. Their success is dependent on their ability to engage, instruct, and develop the strengths and interests of many individuals at many levels.

These programs coalesce around an ideal: the belief that each of their students *can* and, with their help, *will* learn to read. That ideal works like a magnetic force to bind the parts of the program into a whole. Successful programs share not only this common philosophy but also a common core of beliefs about what is effective curriculum and instruction for young adolescents with literacy needs.

Successful compensatory literacy programs for young adolescents are both good literacy programs and good adolescent programs. They have successfully integrated effective instruction within a format tailored to fit the characteristics and needs of young adolescents. The evidence of their success takes many forms. Most important, the students in these programs are reading and writing. They can talk about what they read, and they can show observers what they have written. In successful programs the participants—students, teachers, parents, and administrators—are pleased with the program. The students who participate in them experience personal as well as academic growth.

The purpose of the Project on Adolescent Literacy study was to explore the ways in which successful compensatory literacy programs for young adolescents create and sustain young people's interest and academic growth. Project researchers studied in-school and out-of-school programs, using two questions to guide them in their pursuit of successful programs: (1) Is the program developmentally responsive and (2) Is it academically effective? The previous case studies provide numerous examples of the ways that successful programs meet these two goals. In this chapter, the project's underlying guidelines are revisited in light of what was learned through the site visits and numerous discussions with experts around the country, and the findings from three years of work are refined and clarified.

As staff reviewed the findings, it quickly became apparent that the two original criteria for success—academic effectiveness and developmental responsiveness—were too broad to serve alone as a framework for understanding what made good programs successful. Three more items were added to the list of essentials. Thus, the five components of successful compensatory literacy programs for young adolescents are:

1. Vision and definition
2. Developmental responsiveness
3. Academic effectiveness
4. Access to the world of the written word
5. Organization to ensure success for all

Vision and Definition

Staff in successful literacy programs believe that their students are capable, with help, of learning to read and write. They may offer different explanations why the students who come to them have not already learned to do so, but it is a basic and unshakable tenet of their faith that these students *will* learn. This means that staff in effective programs also believe that they can teach these students. They believe they are in control of the outcome and will be successful in their job. They do not start off with an attitude of defeat, as many teachers of students with these problems do, who shrug their shoulders and offer excuses such as, "There's nothing you can do now—they're too angry to learn," "What do they expect me to do? I'm just babysitting," or "I'm not worried about skills. I just want them to feel good about themselves." Staff in effective programs believe their students can learn to read and will learn to read, and that their own contribution as educators will be a significant one. This is a positive and affirming belief, and it shapes the definition of roles, the methods of instruction, the organization, and the outcomes of each program in a positive and affirming manner.

In these programs staff acknowledge that illiteracy's complex origins may lie in a variety of areas, such as poverty or a lack of access to experienced readers and writers who could serve as role models. They understand that complex problems demand complex solutions that address more than the immediate problem that brings the student to a literacy program. Even the most committed students will have difficulty learning if they have not eaten all day or are not sure there will be a roof over their heads the next day. Poverty and other personal worries are learning problems when they interfere with a student's education. However, staff in successful programs do not use these social problems as an excuse to abdicate their responsibility of ensuring that all students, regardless of their socioeconomic or ethnic backgrounds, progress at an equal rate in their program.

Besides a shared belief in students' ability to learn to read and write, practitioners in successful programs share a common definition of reading and writing as meaningful activities. Making sense of text, they believe, is the primary task of a reader or writer.

Developmental Responsiveness

"What shows you that you are having success? What is your first piece of evidence?" PAL staff asked this question in some form of every teacher, tutor, and administrator interviewed in the course of their research.

"I see it in their faces," some answered.

"In their attitude," was another common answer.

Agreement was unanimous that the first sign of success showed up in a student's behavior. Some described how students begin to sit differently as they become involved. Before, they slumped in their chairs; now they lean forward attentively. Before, they were silent; now they offer suggestions in group discussions or offer to help a fellow student with a project. These students have begun to engage as readers and writers. They are beginning to see reading and writing as meaningful activities, and to believe that they are capable of creating and deciphering text. This has to happen for the instruction to be effective.

This change does not occur by accident. Successful literacy programs for young adolescents consciously create consistent, caring environments that acknowledge and respond to the developmental characteristics of their young participants as well as provide instruction in literacy. Staff in these programs recognize that poor self-esteem, anger, depression, or self-destructive behavior often accompanies reading failure in young adolescents, but they rechannel the energy that went into these negative outlets, into new and positive directions.

It is assumed by many that young adolescents, known for their hypersensitivity to the opinions of their peers, are reluctant to attend remedial programs because of the stigma they feel is attached to being singled out as a person who has reading problems. PAL staff found this was not so with the successful programs described in this book. Students assigned to these programs are eager to come. In school settings, students who are not assigned to these programs often beg their teachers to allow them to attend the "remedial" classroom. In after-school and summer programs, where attendance is voluntary, high attendance is a sure sign that the program is meeting intended goals in the participants' eyes.

This evidence of students' eagerness to attend successful literacy programs belies the commonly held assumption that these students cannot be reached. When asked why they come, they not only respond, "It's fun," "I get to talk to my friends," or "I like the teacher," but also, "This is going to help me in the future," or "You can't get a job if you can't read. This program is helping me to be a better reader." It is clear that these students understand and appreciate the long-range consequences of effective literacy programs.

In these programs there is a great respect for the individual student. The students' capabilities and competencies are recognized by giving them the chance to participate in many aspects of class decision making; their opinions are solicited, listened to, and responded to; and they are allowed to make their own choices whenever possible. Class activities are planned to give everyone a chance to incorporate personal knowledge and experience with the new learning.

Good programs see literacy as a forum where students can interact with peers and adults around matters of concern and interest to young adolescents. Literacy activities that give young adolescents chances for this kind of meaningful interaction include joint projects, reciprocal reading, peer editing, and experience-based learning, of which many examples are given in this book.

Staff in these programs recognize that just as there are differences in physical, social, and emotional growth among young adolescents, there is also great variety in cognitive and linguistic growth. They recognize the difference between an individual's cognitive development, reflecting the human potential, and that same individual's level of conceptual development: the unique intersection of thought, language, and experience in each person's life. They understand that anything that enhances the individual's language development or expands his or her experience will consequently enhance conceptual development.

Students with literacy needs often lack exposure to the forms of language and literacy that schools conventionally expect students to have encountered. They also lack exposure to knowledge of many of the specific subject areas—science, math, social studies— taught in schools. Faced with a student who lacks many basic concepts that schools take for granted, a teacher too often assumes that the lack of conceptual development is the same as lack of cognitive ability. These students are labeled "slow" and shunted to remedial classes, where skills rather than concepts are too often the main fare.

In contrast, educators in effective literacy programs for young adolescents focus on concepts. They work to overcome their students' lack of conventional background knowledge by teaching new literacy skills in the context of a stimulating and meaningful curriculum.

Staff in these programs recognize the importance and value of "talk" in young adolescents' lives. These are not silent classrooms. They hum with purposeful activity and conversation. In these programs talk is incorporated into literacy activities, rather than banned from the classroom. These educators see spoken language as an important tool for young adolescents to use in integrating new knowledge and skills into their understanding. The programs do this in many ways. They encourage students to ask each other when they don't know an answer before asking the teacher. Reciprocal reading encourages students to discuss books together. Writing workshops encourage students to serve as editors and critics for their fellow students.

The variety of groupings also responds well to young adolescents' need for physical activity. The majority of programs PAL staff visited have a "workshop" atmosphere, relaxed but purposeful. When group discussions are not in session, students are allowed to move about the room. Places for different materials are clearly defined, and the students know where these are and how to use them. Allowing students to move around and collect their own materials not only fulfills their need for physical movement but fosters their independence and frees teachers to deal with more important matters. Some programs, like the cross-age tutoring service in Fairbanks, Alaska, have even incorporated vigorous physical games into reading instruction.

Unfortunately, the number and kinds of literacy programs available for young adolescents do not meet the need. Of those that PAL staff reviewed, in-school programs offer the most in the way of literacy programs for young adolescents. The PAL survey located no after-school programs and only one summer school program that was designed for the age-group.

Academic Effectiveness

Instruction is essential if young adolescents with literacy needs are to achieve the levels of literacy that society demands. But surprisingly enough, instruction in reading and writing is an element missing in most classrooms today.

A recent review of research on the characteristics of literacy instruction in our schools concludes:

> Collectively, these studies of literacy instruction suggest that teachers perceive themselves as evaluators of student learning, using brief answers to brief questions as indicators of learning. . . . Furthermore, the focus is on "coverage" of content as opposed to student learning, and evaluation is

dominated by an implicit belief that coverage itself in some way constitutes (rather than correlates with) learning.[1]

Instruction is not lacking in effective literacy programs. The school-based programs PAL staff visited naturally did a better job of providing extended blocks of structured instructional time with experienced teachers than did the nonschool programs. Nonschool programs provide less structured instruction for several reasons: a different definition of their role and purposes, shorter terms of service with fewer class sessions per term, and lack of highly trained staff. However, nonschool programs can provide students with personal support and incentives for learning that they often lack in school.

Just as instruction is not lacking in effective programs, neither is curriculum. Good administrators lead the way in curriculum planning, but the key rests with the teacher. Successful teachers involve themselves in the content and concepts of the curriculum they teach. Their preparation is thorough, including background reading from a variety of sources. These teachers possess a deep curiosity toward the world and a special thoughtfulness toward the presentation of that world to young people. Teachers with these qualities tend to enroll in a variety of continuing education experiences and pursue a wide range of personal interests and hobbies that they are able to relate to the curriculum in some way (for instance, photography, space travel, art, or classical ballet). Students catch the enthusiasm their instructors feel for such self-chosen subjects and respond eagerly. In these classes students explore new topics and concerns with courage and vigor, building conceptual information while improving basic skills.

In successful school-based programs, curriculum (what one teaches) and instruction (how one teaches) are the primary domain of teachers, and they jealously guard these rights. These literacy programs do not try to "teacher-proof" instruction by using packaged lessons that guarantee that "anyone" can deliver the lesson. Because teachers in such programs are concerned with the overall design of the curriculum, rather than merely delivering specific bits and pieces of content information, there is an integrity to their lessons that is often lacking in the average classroom. "Curriculum" and "instruction" are words that live and breathe life in these teachers' minds.

The middle grades present special literacy hurdles to many young adolescents, and effective programs recognize and respond to these needs. This is the time when many students, particularly those from minority or low socioeconomic backgrounds, show a decline in reading scores. Good programs are especially sensitive to addressing young adolescents' need for support in learning advanced literacy skills beyond the level of basic fluency.

Diverse as these programs may be, the educators who work in them seem to share a core of beliefs about what constitutes good instruction. Although some of the programs reviewed in this book may stress one element more than another, most of the following suggestions for effective instruction can be observed in the majority of successful programs.

1. *Spend a high proportion of time on reading and writing.* In successful programs the proportion of time spent on reading, writing, and discussing what one reads and writes far outweighs time spent on drills designed to enhance specific skills. This is in direct opposition to procedures in most middle-grades classrooms and remedial programs. Many activities in these successful literacy programs foster reading real books: by sustained silent reading, through 100-minute clubs that encourage reading at home, by creating one's own book for others to read, and by reading books to answer questions and do projects. Students are eager to talk about the books they have read. There is also much evidence of the writing that goes on in these programs. Student-authored journals, autobiographies, poetry, novels, and nonfiction items such as travel brochures, menus, and informational pieces are displayed on bookshelves, stored in writing folders, and proffered to visitors by students eager to share their work. This is not the usual fare one expects from "remedial" students.

2. *Teach skills in context.* In successful programs literacy skills such as phonics, spelling, and punctuation are taught in context. Skills work is integrated into the curriculum through games, reading opportunities, and writing projects, thereby providing students with a meaningful context for practicing their new learning. Students in these programs show significant increases in their skills levels, good retention of their skills learning, and the ability to apply these skills to a wide range of tasks.

3. *Stress silent reading.* In most good literacy programs the majority of reading is done silently, not in round-robin reading groups. This increases the amount of time students actually spend reading.

When students do read aloud, the ground rules are clear. A student seldom reads aloud to a group unless he or she has requested to do so; more often the student reads to a partner (who may be the teacher or may be another student). The student chooses the book that is to be read from. Usually this book is one written at a level the student can handle comfortably. Before reading aloud the student usually reads the material silently.

There is one important exception: students often read aloud pieces that they have written themselves. Because they have written them, they can handle the material even when it does not fall into the convenient graded levels that traditional reading textbooks require.

4. *Teach strategies for reading comprehension.* Successful programs emphasize strategies for reading comprehension. This is an especially important objective for middle-grades students, who face continually escalating demands on their reading skills in specific subject areas. Good literacy teachers make explicit to older beginning readers and writers the strategies that experienced readers and writers use to decipher text and read for a purpose. They teach strategies on all levels, from such simple lessons as how to figure out a word one does not know by reading to the end of the sentence, or how to find the fiction books in the library, to the more complex strategies involved in writing a research paper using several sources. These teachers want their students to know *how* to solve problems, not just what the right answer is.

5. *Build on background information and experience.* Researchers have become increasingly aware of the crucial role that background knowledge plays in literacy: "A clear finding from research of the past decade is that young readers and poor readers of every age do not consistently see relationships between what they are reading and what they already know."[2] Good literacy programs recognize these difficulties and develop methods to help students cope. In some cases literacy students lack the vocabulary and concepts necessary to understanding. In other cases they simply have not been shown how to take what they already know and bring it to bear efficiently on what they read.

In effective literacy programs assessment of each student's knowledge and experience of the topic at hand is an essential beginning to any reading or writing activity. Pre-reading and pre-writing discussions give students a forum in which they can consider what they already know about the subject and use that information to make predictions about the new material they will encounter. Post-reading and post-writing discussions help students to see the relationships between their knowledge and the new learning. The old and new are connected in meaningful and accessible patterns.

6. *Integrate speaking and listening with reading and writing.* Speaking and listening are powerful tools for literacy learning, and successful programs integrate them equally with reading and writing. Reading aloud by teachers or tutors is a popular activity in effective adolescent literacy programs, and an excellent example of how these programs integrate the different language areas. Hearing books read aloud provides all students in the class, regardless of their individual levels of literacy, with a common text to discuss, as well as introduces vocabulary, literary forms, topics, and authors they might not have approached on their own. Hearing a book read aloud also makes them aware of language in new and special ways, piquing their interest in and excitement with books. Students often go on to read a book on their own after they have heard it read aloud. They may buy or borrow the book, or incorporate the plot, characters, or settings in stories of their own. They learn to enjoy reading to each other from books they have chosen themselves, or from their own writing.

    Other activities that integrate speaking and listening with reading and writing include discussion, group projects, and experience-based literacy activities. Some programs, especially those that serve young people for whom English is a second language (such as the HILT program profiled in this book), emphasize that a student's ability to speak and to comprehend spoken language is a special kind of literacy, and encourage their students to work from listening to speaking to reading and writing.

7. *Focus on writing.* Since the mid-1970s the teaching of writing has become a major focus of concern in education. Recent research in writing has given educators new information on the developmental sequence of writing acquisition, instructional techniques, and curriculum guidelines. New research findings also point to the effectiveness of integrating writing with reading instruction, using each to strengthen learning in the other.[3] Staff in literacy programs that have effective writing components have used this new research to inform their practice. School-based

literacy programs have been strongest in developing good writing components; nonschool programs have barely touched the subject.

One point that correlates consistently with the quality of writing instruction is the quality of staff training in teaching writing. Programs that have tried teaching writing but have failed to teach it successfully are usually working without support or inspiration. The staff are uninformed about the theoretical information on teaching writing and do not have access to professionals who could guide them in improving writing instruction. The Kenosha Model, profiled here, offers an excellent example of the kind of teacher training and support needed to create a good writing program.

8. *Use modeling as a teaching technique.* In successful programs teachers "show" rather than "tell" whenever possible. They model for students how experienced readers and writers plan and execute their goals. Step by step, they lead their students through the process involved in each task. Teachers often "talk through" their strategies so that students can hear the rationale behind a process while they observe it in action.

9. *Use involvement- or experience-based curriculum approaches that foster conceptual development.* "Doing" rather than "drilling" is important in successful literacy teaching. Through field trips, interviews, observations, experiments, or discussion, students experience what they will read or write about, and then incorporate the experience into a literacy activity. For instance, in a study of dogs, Kenosha students observed a dog groomer, and in a study of rockets, they built rockets. In New York City's Learning to Read through the Arts program, students keep notebooks on their artwork just as a real artist would.

10. *Facilitate discussions rather than lead them.* In successful literacy programs teachers facilitate discussion rather than lead discussion—an important distinction. Whether it takes place orally in a group, or in a shared written journal, discussion occurs in an atmosphere of mutual trust and regard. Discussion provides a place for students to explore their ideas, not to be assessed. The teacher's questions are often open-ended. The right answer (if there is one) is not always the goal; understanding is. All have a chance to express themselves, and each is encouraged to participate; but no one is required to speak.

As with most aspects of effective programs, this kind of discussion does not happen by accident. Teachers must be trained to use discussion in this way.

11. *Use varied groupings, and value collaborative learning.* In the successful programs PAL staff visited, groupings were heterogeneous (that is, without regard to the individual's grade level or age). Groupings also varied in size depending on the activity in progress, and participants were grouped and regrouped as the activity changed.

Remedial educators have long extolled the virtues of homogeneous grouping, but in the successful programs visited for this study, teachers and administrators emphasized the importance of heterogeneous arrangements. "Students have a lot to learn from each other," and "They need to learn how to rely on each other, not just on the teacher," were reasons educators gave for the value of mixed-level groupings. These instructors remark that "homogeneous" groupings are, after all, really a mirage. Even in a group of students who have all received the same score on a standardized reading test, there is a wide range of diversity in background, learning strengths and weaknesses, and interests—factors critical to determining an individual's true reading abilities.

Heterogeneous groupings work in these classrooms because the activities allow students who read and write at many different levels to participate in a common curriculum of study. For instance, in an experience-based curriculum a class may share in rocket building, or dog grooming, and then follow up that experience with projects that allow each student to work at his or her own level. Teachers teach strategies that each student can use regardless of individual level.

Small class size and more personal attention are important factors in successful literacy programs. Fifteen to twenty students per classroom was the maximum observed in any program, and most groups were smaller; this is far fewer than a regular classroom, for which thirty-five students is the norm. Nonschool tutoring programs usually provided one-to-one instruction.

As PAL staff interviewed teachers and administrators in these programs, it became clear that they kept in mind a sharp distinction between "individualized" instruction and "one-to-one" instruction. Several of those who were interviewed had formerly worked in "individualized" remedial programs, where they supervised a group of students who worked alone in sequenced, commercially prepared texts or workbooks. They voiced strong criticism of those methods, insisting that such tactics isolate students and ignore the value of discussion and collaboration between students. As teachers, they had to learn the hard way that there is great value to what students learn from each other.

Access to the World of the Written Word

In real life, as opposed to school life, readers have to deal with many different forms of print: newspapers, magazines, and books; fiction or nonfiction. In real life literacy serves many purposes—to find bargains at the supermarket, to find out what is going to be on television, or to find out what movie one wants to see. Writing keeps one in touch with friends and family; it also sets up savings accounts and responds to credit inquiries. Reading and writing are used as entertainment and creative outlets. Yet in school, as opposed to real life, literacy is often used within a tightly restricted range of purposes and cultivated within a tightly restricted range of materials.

In successful literacy programs, as in real life, students have access to many materials and are exposed to a wide range of purposes for using literacy. Few of the successful programs PAL staff observed used traditional reading textbooks or workbooks, and those that did had clearly defined for their staff how such materials were to be used in conjunction with real books and real writing activities.

When visiting schools, one often hears teachers complain that they would like to have their students read books, but they don't have the budget to provide these materials, or they lack a school library or a nearby public library. Teachers in successful literacy programs don't wait for someone to supply the books; they get the books. Books, not standard textbooks, are a budget item they request. They are ruthless in their search for books and magazines: they raid locked closets where retired teachers have left books long forgotten, beg from businesses, haunt garage sales, and demand donations from friends whose children have gone off to college leaving behind their outgrown personal libraries.

Good school libraries would insure every student's access to a variety of reading materials, but many schools do not have libraries or only have inadequate ones. A report published in 1981 revealed that "fully 15% of the nation's schools do not have libraries. In most of the remaining schools the collections are small, averaging just over 13 volumes per student."[4] Where school libraries do not exist, good programs make use of public libraries whenever possible.

Computers and other modern technologies are often cited by educators and policymakers as magic-workers in literacy programs, providing great access to all students. They are touted as "nonthreatening," "individualized," "self-paced," "high-interest," and most important to many administrators, "cost-effective." But this study did not find any effective literacy program that relied exclusively on technology. Computers, where they were available, were used as a tool for writing, or for skills practice, but they in no way substituted for a teacher and classroom instruction. Compensatory literacy programs have not yet begun to creatively explore the potential of the computer.

Organization to Ensure Success for All

Staff Development

Just as successful programs have a high degree of respect for their students, they also have a high degree of respect for the teachers. In good programs teachers are more than mere proctors of workbooks. They create curriculum, work with school teams to assess students' literacy abilities, have an active voice in developing school and district reading policy, and are involved in their professional communities. High-quality professionals are attracted to good programs by the chance to work under such conditions, and they stay with these programs because of the continuing support they receive. Administrators in many different programs report that the one essential quality they look for in teachers is this sense of commitment: to the program, to the young people, and to the profession. "You can't teach commitment," says one principal.

Staff diversity is an important quality in these programs. One of the exciting elements PAL staff discovered in observing the programs is the range of individual strengths and interests one finds in each. Good programs encourage their teachers to share and use those diverse abilities in their classrooms.

There is a strong positive correlation between the quality of a program and the quality and quantity of the training and development activities offered to the staff. In good programs staff are not working in isolation. They have regular opportunities, built into their schedules, for sharing with their co-workers.

The same qualities and values that make good programs so effective for students are the same qualities and values that make them effective for teachers. Respect for the individual's knowledge and professionalism, discussion, modeling, a chance for meaningful participation, and a high degree of "ownership" in the proceedings are key features of staff development in these programs. This book has described a range of staff development models for school-based programs: teacher swap days, breakfast meetings, buddy systems, monthly in-service meetings, in-house teacher newsletters, learning fairs, and intensive pre–school-term workshops.

Successful community-based, after-school, and summer literacy programs likewise offer creative models for staff development, carefully tailored to meet the needs of staff in each specific program. The cross-age tutoring programs described in this book have devised a variety of formats for intensive staff development and supervision to train young people as effective tutors. Giving experienced and inexperienced tutors a chance to talk together is a method that the Montgomery Ward-Cabrini Green program has found to be successful; to encourage interest in such meetings and give them less of a pedagogical atmosphere, participants are regaled with pizzas and hamburgers donated by local businesses.

In good programs teachers are not only supported in their own personal growth and development as professionals but are also expected to help other teachers to learn and develop. The highly trained teachers in these effective programs are often tapped as resource specialists in their schools and districts, and even serve as outside trainers. Their skills and expertise bring them special recognition in their field. In many schools in New York City's District 4, the Chapter 1 teacher assists classroom teachers in improving their teaching of reading and their assessment of students' literacy skills. They may observe lessons, help in writing lesson plans, teach in-service workshops, and recommend materials for the classroom teacher. In community-based after-school and summer programs, directors with backgrounds as professional educators create special training programs for nonprofessionals. And school-based summer literacy programs are good potential laboratories for training new teachers and providing experienced teachers with information on new techniques in effective literacy approaches.

Access to professional materials is an important aspect of staff development. Many American communities do not have bookstores; some only have bookstores that are oriented to general interests and stock no specialized materials. Public libraries similarly tend to buy for the general reading public, although they can order specific materials when needed. Many professionals who would like to be better informed find themselves hampered by the difficulty of obtaining the materials they need.

In good literacy programs professionals have many strategies for staying on top of the news in their field. They belong to professional organizations and attend local meetings, as well as regional and national conferences. They personally subscribe to a variety of publications that alert them to new materials, and they share this information with their colleagues. Some school districts have developed strong collections of professional publications, from which staff may borrow freely. Generally speaking, however, professionals greatly need to have broader exposure to research and writing on educational issues than is currently available to most of them.

Successful teachers or tutors in successful programs model a successful attitude toward life and learning. They believe that they can control the options and the outcomes in their work, and they convey this positive attitude to their students.

Organization and Administration

Administrators in good programs can teach what they preach. In good school-based programs administrators are, in general, successful classroom teachers who have moved up to new tasks because of their abilities, rather than failing teachers who are pulled out of classroom service. Because they are comfortable with the classroom setting and with young people, successful administrators seem to spend a proportionately large amount of time in the classroom. They have a finger on the pulse of the students and teachers they supervise.

In nonschool programs staff rate good administrators high for their availability, the appropriateness of their suggestions, and their ability to provide clear structure to the program and build a cohesive work team.

Good administrators have a strong command of the issues that surround literacy instruction. They can translate their broad theoretical understanding into classroom practice and are thus able to offer real direction to the teachers, as well as to overall program development and policies. These directors believe that educators, as professionals, have an obligation to know why they do what they do. In their programs teachers are not frustrated by theory but enriched.

The challenge of translating research into practice seems greatest in community-based programs. To make new concepts understandable, successful administrators have used role playing, guided practice, and tying research ideas into tutors' own experiences with education. Administrators in community-based reading programs come from a variety of backgrounds, and they may or may not have formal credentials in reading instruction. However, all have had to avail themselves of opportunities to learn more about effective reading instruction and program administration. Like their teachers, they subscribe to professional journals, attend special conferences, and meet with a network of local educators involved in similar programs.

These administrators feel they have control over the goals and outcomes of their programs, and they act clearly and decisively to meet the goals they have established. This means that although they give excellent support to their staff, they are not afraid to fire those who cannot, or will not, meet their standards. As advocates for their students and their students' families, administrators must insure that their students' needs are being met first.

Good management is an attribute of both teachers and administrators in these programs. They manage their time very well. Moreover, they constantly work to create better and more efficient systems, whether for managing a classroom, a set of tutors, or a full program. They design record-keeping systems that facilitate rather than hinder their jobs, and they allocate their resources rather than allow the resources to allocate them.

Good management is directly related to the issue of clear program structure and good communication. Lack of these assets has led to many of the complaints one hears about school-based compensatory "pullout" programs. Teachers say that such programs disrupt the flow of classroom life, stigmatize the students assigned to them, and breed jealousy among the staff toward the special reading teacher, who usually teaches smaller classes and may have more money allotted for materials. These criticisms are often a result of poor communication.

In effective literacy programs clear structure and good lines of communication alleviate this distress. Good administrators develop systems that include both the classroom teachers and the program teachers in decisions about their students, and they institute communication channels that will keep all teachers conveniently informed about special program activities and each student's progress. They help their teachers find ways to become part of the entire school team, often by using their staff in the schools as resource people who are there to offer support to the classroom teacher. Regular school staff who work with the special program—classroom teachers, janitors, librarians, and other school helpers—express satisfaction with the communication process. They believe that the program is of benefit to their students. If trouble does arise, good lines of communication encourage cooperation in resolving problems quickly.

Good administrators make sure that the communication channels are open and working, not only within school but also toward the community. They know that the survival of a program is dependent on its becoming accepted and recognized throughout the school system and the community.

Like good teachers and tutors, good administrators not only teach what they preach, they model it. By example, they show the staff and students in their program the values, beliefs, and standards they wish to see implemented.

Assessing Success

In successful literacy programs for young adolescents both teachers and administrators are guided by what Tierney and Cunningham have called a "vision"—a vision of the goal they are striving to accomplish and of the ecology of the program, which must be working harmoniously to make that goal a reality. This vision has four tiers: a vision of learners, of learning groups, of teachers, and of teacher support and change.[5] One could add a fifth tier to their description: a vision of parents and community. It is this complex vision that guides the assessment design in successful programs. Just as the vision is comprehensive and multilayered, so, too, is the assessment process.

Furthermore, the assessment focus of the successful programs reviewed in this book reflects practices at the cutting edge of evaluation research.

> The most important developments in evaluation have been (1) the focus on decision making as the purpose of conducting an evaluation, (2) the acknowledgment that both process and product information are important for educational decision making, (3) the use of a variety of information collected continuously, and (4) an approach to evaluation that has allowed both the goals of evaluation and the issues studied to emerge from the context.[6]

The programs studied here have used a variety of instruments to elicit the information they need, such as standardized tests, teacher-made tests, informal assessment, oral and written language samples, interest inventories, teacher ratings, questionnaires, interviews, and reports from outside evaluators. They solicit information from the full range of program participants. Decisions that affect their students, both individually and collectively, and decisions that affect the program as a whole are never made solely on the basis of one measure or one individual's opinion.

Although the staff of the school-based and community-based programs that PAL staff visited shared similar philosophies about assessment, the two types of programs have developed markedly different systems of assessment. The school-based programs use more "hard" measures, such as standardized tests, but supplement these with a variety of other measures, many designed to meet the needs of the individual program. The Kenosha program is a particularly good example of an in-school comprehensive assessment plan that validates success, serves as an information document for community members, and provides a basis for innovation and future growth. Because they are still a fairly new phenomenon, after-school and summer literacy programs for young adolescents must tailor their assessment tools even more closely to their particular needs and goals, for reliable external standards are as yet scarce. Many ingenious techniques that they have developed have been mentioned in this book. For instance, the Friendly Place, a literacy center in a library-bookstore, relies heavily on book circulation figures as a measure of students' participation. The Montgomery Ward-Cabrini Green Tutoring Program, an academic encouragement program, considers tutor and student attendance a critical measure of success, and attendance statistics are carefully monitored by computer.

Surprisingly, PAL staff discovered that although instruments and tools abound to assess the many discrete parts of a literacy program, there appears to be no tool to help educators or youth workers assess the whole. Clearly, there is a need for an assessment tool that will help programs understand how well the various interconnecting parts of their literacy environments fit together and function together.

Involving Parents

Good programs not only acknowledge parents' interests and inform them of their children's progress, but also involve parents in all aspects of program development and assessment. However, in the historical development of most programs, parents are the last group to receive attention. And when resources are cut back, attention to parents' involvement is one of the first aspects of the program to suffer.

Successful programs are attentive to parents' need to help their children become readers and writers and to learn to be their advocates at the school and community level. They are aware that the parents of their students often lack basic skills and self-esteem, just as their children do. They understand that these parents may enter academic situations with their own cache of unpleasant memories about teachers and schools.

Among the programs PAL staff visited, several have reached a good understanding of what kinds of literacy experiences parents can best help students with, such as encouraging and praising students' successes, reading aloud or being read to, or making sure all family members get library cards. In these programs, staff have personally explained to parents how they can help their children despite a lack of skills, so that even parents who cannot read themselves can participate. The programs communicate with parents orally as well as in writing. They communicate frequently, not waiting until the child's negative behavior or academic failure precipitates a meeting.

The Montgomery Ward-Cabrini Green Tutoring Program has created an impressive example of a powerful parent group. This program's experience indicates that parents can and should play a much more active role in literacy programs for young people. Parents can and will respond to programs that approach them as competent adults capable of generating solutions to the problems they face.

Curiously enough, many programs that are otherwise doing a good job seem never to have bridged the gap between understanding their students and understanding their students' parents. Fliers, letters, and other information distributed to parents are often densely written in educational jargon. Some programs present to parents workshops that expect the parent to instruct the child as a classroom teacher would. Other programs approach parents' lack of participation in a punitive fashion, threatening to exclude the child if the parent does not come and observe the program, come to school to pick up the report card, or read so many minutes every evening with the child. Such actions only serve to widen the gap between parents and the program.

A few programs have addressed the literacy needs of parents as well as students. These programs gather referral information, make contact with local adult literacy groups and other adult continuing education providers in the area, and most important, make it known to parents that their children's program can help them find assistance in that direction. Involving parents in their

own literacy learning is one of the most powerful means of helping
their children.

Conclusions

Successful adolescent literacy programs respond with grace
and vigor to the characteristics and needs of the young adolescent
age-group. These programs engage students who have been
alienated from reading and build self-esteem by showing them that
they can become successful learners. They expose their students to
a wide range of literacy experiences; at the same time, they build a
repertoire of strategies that facilitate reading and writing. Most
important, however, in successful adolescent literacy programs
students who were not reading or writing before are now doing so,
and enjoy doing so. These programs also strengthen their students'
conceptual development.

These students now have hope that they will be able to make
choices and have more options in the future. They know that they
can read the want ads, fill out a job application, and read the
instructions needed for the job. They know they will be able to read
to their children, apply for a library card, and use the library. They
have discovered that there is joy, excitement, and new knowledge
hidden inside the cover of a good book. They have also learned to
share their own feelings and interests with others through writing.
All these and many other possibilities are open to them because
they can read and write and because they have the self-confidence
to use their skills.

Not surprisingly, students in good literacy programs for
young adolescents seem animated and purposeful. To parents and
teachers who remember the angry or frightened student before this
change occurred, the transformation in behavior is dramatic.

The small selection of successful programs, both school-based
and community-based, that have been surveyed in this book
demonstrates the potential that good programs could have in
attacking the problem of adolescent's unmet literacy needs. They
provide important information on what is effective in teaching these
young people to read and write, and why.

Notes

1. Judith Langer, "Literacy Instruction in American Schools: Problems and Perspectives," in *Literacy in American Schools: Learning to Read and Write*, ed. Nancy L. Stein (Chicago: University of Chicago Press, 1984), 118.

2. Richard Anderson et al., *Becoming a Nation of Readers: The Report of the Commission on Reading* (Washington, D.C.: National Institute of Education, 1984), 55.

3. See Jane Hansen, *When Writers Read* (Portsmouth, N.H.: Heinemann Educational Books, 1987).

4. Anderson et al., *Becoming a Nation of Readers*, 78, citing R.A. Heintze and L. Hodes, *Statistics of Public School Libraries/Media Centers 1978 Fall* (Washington, D.C.: National Center for Education Statistics, 1981).

5. Robert J. Tierney and James W. Cunningham, "Research on Teaching Reading Comprehension," in *Handbook of Reading Research*, ed. P. David Pearson (New York: Longman, 1984), 639–41.

6. Roger Farr and Robert Carey, *Reading: What Can Be Measured?* 2d ed. (Newark, Del.: International Reading Association, 1986), 2.

TRANSLATING WHAT WORKS
INTO PROGRAMS AND POLICIES

In initiating the investigation into compensatory literacy programming for young adolescents in 1985, the Center for Early Adolescence began with a set of assumptions and concerns about literacy and young adolescents. The accuracy of these assumptions has been borne out by the findings of the study, the Center's subsequent work on those conclusions, and the growth of a number of independent initiatives that have sprung up over the last few years to address these very same issues.

The first assumption staff made was that early adolescence is a critical stage in the development of a literate individual and, as it is with many aspects of adolescent life, a time of both opportunity and vulnerability. During the ages 10 to 15, young people are expected to attain adept or proficient levels of literacy achievement, characterized by speed and fluency, flexibility, and the ability to use reading and writing as tools for inquiry and enjoyment. These literacy skills underlie future school and employment opportunities, and they are critical for participating in daily life and enjoying many of the pleasures available to people in a literate society.

Evidence from many sources indicated that, unfortunately, many young people were not making this transition from beginning-level to proficient-level readers and writers. The majority of this group comprised young people whose disadvantaged status could be seen both as a consequence and as a cause of their reading failure. These same young adolescents with low literacy achievement were also found in high numbers among youth with a range of other problems, from being teen parents to dropouts. The second assumption was that among the many young adolescents who should be, but are not, achieving proficient levels of literacy achievement expected at the middle grades, it is this failure to achieve that puts these young people in jeopardy of many other serious problems.

The third assumption, based on extensive information from research and hands-on experience in schools and community agencies, was that the knowledge and expertise of successful practitioners and programs needed to be shared with others wrestling with the same concerns. Individual teachers or youth workers do not have the time nor money to seek out, identify, visit, and study the best programs; however, the Center for Early Adolescence staff could create a resource that would share information on "what works" with educators and others around the country. In beginning the search for programs, staff assumed that school programs would be in the majority. The kind and quality of community programs that would emerge was unknown, but a part of the third assumption was that community agencies could play an important role in the development of young people's literacy development.

Adolescent Literacy: What Works and Why was released in 1988, and soon thereafter information on its impact began to filter back in many different forms—in letters, conversations, and reviews. The feedback validated the initial assumptions outlining the project and the importance of the findings and the case study approach for educators, youth workers, parents, policymakers, and others concerned with these issues. Even more heartwarming, readers began to contact the Center to share the ways in which they were using the information presented in *Adolescent Literacy: What Works and Why* as the basis for changing and improving their classrooms or after-school programs or, in many cases, as a resource for establishing new programs.

In like fashion, Center staff built on the findings of this study, using the conclusions as the assumptions for the next stages of their own work. For instance, recognizing from the study that a major barrier to student success in reading and writing at the middle grades is a lack of schoolwide vision and planning around adolescent literacy needs, Center staff developed a schoolwide assessment and planning tool. *Literacy Assessment for the Middle Grades* is designed to assist middle-grades schools in surveying their responsiveness to adolescents' reading and writing needs and in developing a blueprint for improving the kinds of literacy learning supports the school provides.[1] Responding to the study's findings that community agencies could make a larger contribution to young people's reading and writing development, Center staff developed, tested, and produced a new resource, *Building Youth Literacy: A Training Curriculum for Community Leaders.*[2] The research and testing for these new products gave Center staff many opportunities to put the findings of *Adolescent Literacy: What Works and Why* to work in dynamic and practical ways, reaffirming their belief in the validity of the study's conclusions.

This final chapter, reviewing the implications of "what works" with an eye toward "what needs to be done now," builds not only from the knowledge presented in the case studies but also on the knowledge gained as a result of the release of the first edition of *Adolescent Literacy: What Works and Why* and further work exploring its conclusions. While in many ways the plight of young adolescents with compensatory literacy needs has increased since 1988, interest in early adolescence and issues related to the education, health, and well-being of 10- to 15-year-olds has also risen dramatically. As a consequence, there are a number of new and important initiatives designed to address this age-group that deserve special consideration here as part of a discussion of "what needs to be done now."

Section I. Translating What Works

There are several conclusions from this study that bear careful examination in order to frame prescriptions for how "what works" can be translated into programs and policies. These conclusions include the following:

- There are far too few compensatory literacy programs available for the numbers of youth in need.
- Young adolescents often have less access to compensatory literacy services than younger or older youth.
- The majority of young people needing compensatory literacy programs are economically disadvantaged.
- Within this group of disadvantaged youngsters, there are a number of groups with legitimate claims to special attention. These include blacks, Hispanics, immigrant youth, and homeless youth.
- Good compensatory literacy programs connect the developmental needs of young adolescents with literacy learning.

- In schools, there is an over-reliance on traditional remedial structures and a lack of comprehensive schoolwide approaches to addressing adolescents' literacy learning needs.
- Community agencies can make important contributions to supporting adolescents' literacy learning, but the potential of these agencies is not being fulfilled.
- Many young adolescents lack access to the world of the written word.

Although on the one hand it is frustrating to consider what is not present, on the other hand this list of what is missing can serve as the foundation for recommendations of what needs to be done to translate the findings of *Adolescent Literacy: What Works and Why* into the kinds of programs and policies that will improve the lives of young people.

Section II. Recommendations

If young people's literacy needs are to be met, there are three major recommendations that deserve special consideration:

1. Increase the quantity and quality of school-based support for young adolescents with compensatory literacy needs.
2. Help community agencies to support young adolescents' literacy development.
3. Increase all young people's access to the world of the written word.

These three broad and general recommendations will be meaningless, however, if they are implemented without acknowledgment of and attention to the special needs of particular groups of youth. These include the needs of youth who have grown up in the shadow of institutional racism, the needs of immigrant youth to gain English-language as well as literacy skills, and the needs of homeless youth who struggle to gain literacy skills without the safety and comfort of a roof over their heads.

Increase the Quantity and Quality of School-Based Support for Young Adolescents with Compensatory Literacy Needs

Two issues are at stake here. One is the level of support for school-based compensatory literacy programming as it is traditionally constituted, and another is the need for broader, more flexible, and more comprehensive approaches to literacy education in middle-grades schools.

The federal government's Chapter 1 program is the country's largest school-based compensatory literacy program. Five million school-age children living in 14,000 school districts receive Chapter 1 assistance. Congress reauthorized the program in 1988, reaffirming its importance and contribution over the last quarter century. In reauthorizing Chapter 1, Congress also acted upon recommendations for its improvement. These recommendations include a new focus on accountability and an emphasis on flexibility in pursuing outcomes, greater coordination between Chapter 1 and other school components, and heightened parent involvement. Chapter 1 in its new form will also stress critical thinking and schoolwide appreciation of the learning potential of disadvantaged youth.[3]

These are steps in the right direction. Unfortunately, Chapter 1 funding levels are not sufficient for the numbers of children in need of these services. A Chapter 1 official who asked to remain unnamed explained that the varying eligibility criteria used by districts make it difficult to provide a "clear" answer to the question of how many are not being served. According to this official, the Department of Education guesses that 40 to 70 percent of those students who are eligible actually receive Chapter 1 services. This means that 30 to 60 percent of those eligible do not receive services.[4]

The problem, however, is not just the level of funding; it is also the distribution of funds. Traditionally, 70 percent of Chapter 1 funding has gone to grades 1–6 and only 18 percent to grades 7–9.[5] This inequity has long been recognized but allowed to persist. As early as 1975 the authors of the landmark study *Compensatory Education and Early Adolescence* reported that "disadvantaged students in the intermediate and secondary grades have been neglected by our national policy of compensatory education. Only a small (and declining) fraction of federal money for compensatory education is spent on providing children beyond the age of ten with compensatory help in basic academic and cognitive skills."[6]

Compensatory literacy programs that take young people out of the classroom to provide special services can be very effective but, for a number of reasons, may not be as viable as more comprehensive approaches. The term "comprehensive" when applied to compensatory literacy programs can mean several things. For instance, it may refer to full-day literacy learning programs, as opposed to thirty-minute sessions. It may also refer to a schoolwide focus on reading. Examples would be projects that address reading and writing across the curriculum, involving all faculty members, not just the language arts staff. Schoolwide restructuring projects to increase faculty leadership and improve school performance can also fall within this category. Regardless of the form, comprehensive approaches share a focus on intensive schoolwide remedies to address the literacy needs of young adolescents.

In this study there are several examples of successful comprehensive approaches. The schools in New York City's District 4 that have adapted the STAR approach as a schoolwide reading program demonstrate remarkable success with a comprehensive outlook. The HILT program in Texas is another example of success when intensive, high-quality supports are offered to young people over an entire school day, rather than in thirty-minute blocks once a day.

Over the last several years, concerns about disadvantaged youth and their educational needs have joined forces with concerns about the schooling of young adolescents, and this marriage of interests has led to several new initiatives that meet the criteria for comprehensive approaches. These initiatives are distinguished and united by their focus on developing "whole schools" that provide young people with challenging curriculum and a vision for the future, regardless of their economic circumstances. Individual school districts have been the catalysts for developing many of these projects. However, it should be noted that private philanthropy has taken the lead in raising these critical concerns about young adolescents and keeping them before the public, as well as in supporting creative and innovative attempts to change and reorganize schools. It is a sad comment on our times that the federal government has been conspicuously absent as a leader in addressing these problems.

Lilly Endowment Inc., through the Middle Grades Improvement Program, spurred middle-grades school improvement at select sites throughout Indiana and is now working to network project schools together. The Edna McConnell Clark Foundation's Program for Disadvantaged Youth targeted twelve middle-grades schools in five major urban school districts for school-restructuring assistance. Additional grants to local and national agencies provided technical assistance, developed new resources to aid disadvantaged youth, and stimulated discussion of the best ways to assist disadvantaged youth. *Turning Points*, a recent report released by the Carnegie Council on Adolescent Development, drew national attention to the broad range of adolescent needs that middle-grades schools failed to address.[7] A subsequent grant program from Carnegie Corporation of New York directed attention to improvement of middle-grades education. The members of the numerous statewide task forces created as a result of this initiative quickly found themselves confronting not only middle-grades education issues in their respective states, but also the desperate educational needs of disadvantaged young adolescents. The Annie B. Casey Foundation, the DeWitt Wallace-Reader's Digest Fund, and others have also undertaken major middle-grades reform projects, all of which are directly or indirectly concerned with the literacy needs of disadvantaged young adolescents. These projects are also similar in that they stress the importance of broad, comprehensive approaches, as opposed to narrow or categorical ones.

Schools: Recommendations

Young adolescents need more and better school-based literacy learning supports. To achieve this goal we must:

- Increase federal, state, and local financial support for compensatory literacy programs like Chapter 1;
- Adhere to the recommendations for improvements that have been made for Chapter 1 and other similar compensatory programs; and
- Support comprehensive or schoolwide approaches to school improvement through district encouragement, financial assistance,

flexible policies, and acknowledgement of the contribution teachers, principals, and others are making in undertaking the challenge.

Help Community Agencies to Support Young Adolescents' Literacy Development

Community agencies can be partners with schools and families in the work to support young adolescents' literacy development. The work they perform in enriching, remediating, or advocating for young adolescents' literacy needs often goes unacknowledged. Lacking knowledge of what literacy is and how literacy is supported, youth workers are themselves often unaware of the important ways they are contributing and supporting young people to become readers and writers. Many community agencies would like to play an even larger and more intentional part in this effort, but they are unsure of the role they should assume, wary of conflicts with educators and concerned that they lack sufficient expertise. "We're not reading specialists," they say. "How can we be sure that we're helping and not damaging young readers?"

A shortage of resources also hinders community agencies in their attempts to gain a toehold as youth literacy supporters. They lack dollars for staff, materials, and training. The programs they are able to establish often exist on precarious bases, and every year there is a new scramble for support.

The results of this study demonstrate, however, that community agencies can be very important literacy learning resources for young people. This is particularly true for disadvantaged youth living in neighborhoods and attending schools that are lacking in such supports. It is time that community agencies emerge from the shadows to become full partners with schools and parents in the work of guiding young people through this critical period in literacy learning.

To effectively become full partners, however, community agencies need not only financial support for program staffing and materials, but also opportunities at many levels to explore and define their understanding of their potential. The role each agency assumes will be closely intertwined with the agency's mission and the definition of literacy it accepts as its own. These discussions about community agencies' role and purpose in young people's literacy development need to occur among staffs, within the field of community agencies, within communities (with schools and parents), and with professionals in the literacy field.

In developing the *Building Youth Literacy* training curriculum, Center for Early Adolescence staff have participated in many such discussions and have worked with youth workers from a broad range of agencies. The Center's staff have helped community leaders explore definitions of literacy and apply information about young people's reading and writing development to their program planning. Data gained from these efforts demonstrate that information on youth literacy needs and opportunities to integrate and explore the most appropriate ways for each program result in enthusiasm and creativity to develop excellent responses that fit the community's needs and the agency's mission.

The *Building Youth Literacy* project is only one of a handful of encouraging initiatives and experiments seeking to increase the role community agencies can play in this field. The Bowne Foundation in New York City provides grants to develop compensatory literacy programs for young adolescents in that city's community agencies. The foundation also provides potential and current grantees with a number of rich staff development opportunities and technical assistance support from literacy experts. The San Francisco Foundation recently supported the development of the Bay Area Youth Literacy Network. Through a comprehensive yearlong leadership experience that combined training in adolescent literacy needs and program planning techniques for community agencies, participants have gone on to develop an advocacy group that is beginning to raise awareness about youth's literacy needs and the role community agencies can play in meeting these needs.

Becoming literate is a complex task, and the middle grades represent difficult and unique challenges in this process. Schools play an absolutely critical role, particularly for disadvantaged youth, in helping to develop the broader and more varied skills that distinguish proficient readers and writers. However, schools cannot do it alone, and community agencies are partners in the effort. The strengths of community agencies—their flexibility and knowledge of neighborhoods and families and of what works with young people— can be valuable assets to the literacy movement and to educators.

Community Agencies: Recommendations

If we are to support community agencies to engage productively in youth literacy work, we must:

- Acknowledge the important role they can play in supporting young people's literacy development;
- Increase federal, state, local, and private financial support for community agency youth literacy work;
- Support technical assistance to agency staff; and
- Provide opportunities for discussions at many levels regarding the roles and contributions of youth agencies in this field.

Increase Young People's Access to the World of the Written Word

A typical portrait of a young adolescent with compensatory literacy needs reveals a young person with few points of access to the world of the written word. Young people with literacy needs more often than not attend schools with economic and other needs. In such schools it is unusual to find classrooms stocked with paperbacks and periodicals that will entice young teenagers. The school library will often be inadequate to the size of the school and the needs of the students.

Books and reading materials are not foreign to community agencies. Early in this century, settlement houses developed their own reading collections and assisted in the development of neighborhood "block" collections, and they founded neighborhood reading clubs around these local libraries.[8] Many of today's youth service agencies also have book collections, and even a room designated as a library. The fact that books or magazines are present in today's youth programs does not, however, guarantee access. Center for Early Adolescence staff visited the library of the local affiliate of a national youth organization. The room was filled with young people waiting to attend their next set of activities. They chatted in small groups and some played board games, but no one was reading. The books that lined the walls of the room were ancient, dusty, and unused.

Although young people may lack access to books through their schools or local community agencies, they may be lucky enough to have a local public library with a good young adult collection. If they are very, very lucky, the young people will have access to a collection with its own space and a young adult librarian who likes young adolescents and provides active programming for teens. Unfortunately, this scenario only occurs in select libraries. In recent years, many libraries have had to cut back, folding adolescent services under the wing of children or adult services. As a result, collections and programming for young adolescents are curtailed.

Access to a wide range of well-written, appealing, and diverse kinds of reading materials is essential to the development of strong readers and writers. There is absolutely no dissension on this point among researchers and educators. They are also in agreement that it is not just the collections that are needed, but also the trained staff and the vision that will help link young people with the books. Classroom teachers and youth workers need assistance in learning how to incorporate fiction and nonfiction trade books and other materials into their programs and how to develop on-site collections for young people.

Throughout this study there are numerous examples of individuals who believe in books and share their love of books with young people. The student-authored books that form the backbone of the Kenosha approach allow young people to explore the authorial process in depth. In Texas, students in the HILT program read daily in English and Spanish as suits their needs. The Adventures in Excellence program buys substantial amounts of paperbacks each year for the summer reading program and shares the collection with teachers and students to use during the school year. The Highline Indian Tutoring Program recognizes the needs that Indian youth have for information about their heritage and has developed a large resource collection on Indian culture and history. Agnis Ennis of the STAR program teaches in a classroom that is virtually a small lending library. The Friendly Place in East Harlem bills itself as an "informal, for pleasure library-bookstore."

Providing young adolescents with access to books and other important reading materials is an issue that cuts across institutional boundaries. Young people need to be surrounded by diverse and well-written reading materials. Federal, state, and local districts have an obligation to make sure this occurs. Professional organizations can lobby to widen awareness of the need and urge reforms and improvements. Communities can form creative partnerships to make sure that books are not only available but also used.

Access to Books: Recommendations

If young adolescents are to have access to the world of the written word, we must:

- Dramatically increase funding to school and public libraries for collection development, personnel, staff development, and active programming for young adolescents;

- Increase support for the purchase of excellent fiction and nonfiction reading materials (such as trade books and periodicals) for classroom use; and

- Support community agencies to provide young adolescents with access to the world of the written word (e.g., finance community agency book collections, promote creative links to school and public libraries, and support youth work staff development opportunities).

Conclusions

The foregoing recommendations focus on ways to improve the literacy support and instruction that young people with compensatory literacy needs receive in schools and community agencies and ways to increase their access to excellent reading resources. The emphasis throughout has been on *more* and *better*. Given the link between poverty and low literacy achievement, the evidence of greater numbers of youth falling into poverty, and our knowledge of the levels of literacy achievement that will be needed in the future, it is clear that the nation is on the brink of a serious youth literacy crisis. Providing *more* and *better* services and resources to disadvantaged young people is the only way to successfully meet the crisis.

Schools, community agencies, and public libraries must be the focal point of any effort to improve youth literacy. If these institutions are to succeed, they must have assistance from the federal government, as well as state and local governments. This help must include more dollars for programs, materials, and staff development—not just praise and a plaque for meritorious service.

The young adolescents, teachers, and youth workers described in these case studies struggle daily against tough odds. For the young people attending the programs catalogued here, gaining the adequate literacy skills may be only one of many hurdles to overcome. However, literacy is the critical tool for accomplishing many objectives; reading and writing underlie almost all activities.

This study demonstrates that young people can succeed in improving their reading and writing skills. Furthermore, we know what works to help them achieve their goals. It remains to be seen if we will be able to translate that knowledge of what works to programs and policies that meet the needs of *all* young adolescents.

Notes

1. Judith Davidson and Robin Pulver, *Literacy Assessment for the Middle Grades: User's Manual* (Carrboro, N.C.: Center for Early Adolescence, University of North Carolina at Chapel Hill, 1991).

2. Judith Davidson and Robin Pulver, *Building Youth Literacy: A Training Curriculum for Community Leaders* (Carrboro, N.C.: Center for Early Adolescence, University of North Carolina at Chapel Hill, 1991).

3. Mary Jean LeTendre, "Improving Chapter 1 Programs: We Can Do Better," *Phi Delta Kappan* 72 (1991): 576–80.

4. U.S. Department of Education, "Chapter 1 of the Education Consolidation and Improvement Act of 1981," December 1986 (report on file at the Center for Early Adolescence).

Meredith A. Larson and Freya Dittmann, *Compensatory Education and Early Adolescence: Reviewing Our National Strategy* (Menlo Park, Calif.: Stanford Research Institute, 1975), xi.

Children's Defense Fund, *A Children's Defense Budget* (Washington, D.C.: Children's Defense Fund, 1986), 49.

Children's Defense Fund, *A Children's Defense Budget*, 149.

5. U.S. Department of Education, "Chapter 1 of the Education Consolidation and Improvement Act of 1981."

6. Larson and Dittmann, *Compensatory Education and Early Adolescence*, xi.

7. *Turning Points: Preparing American Youth for the 21st Century* (Washington, D.C.: Carnegie Council on Adolescent Development, 1989).

8. Robert A. Woods and Albert J. Kennedy, *The Settlement Horizon: A National Estimate* (New York: Russell Sage Foundation, 1922), 67.

APPENDIX:
TEST INSTRUMENTS CITED IN THIS BOOK

California Achievement Test
1985 edition
No authors listed
Available from: CTB/McGraw Hill
                  2500 Garden Road
                  Del Monte Research Park
                  Monterey, CA 93940

Comprehensive English Language Test
1986 edition (currently out of stock)
Principal author: David P. Harris
Available from: Attention: International Division
                  McGraw-Hill Book Company, Inc.
                  Princeton Road
                  Heightstown, NJ 08520

Iowa Test of Basic Skills
1985 edition
Principal authors: A.N. Hieronymus and H.D. Hoover
Available from: Riverside Publishing Company
                  8420 Bryn Mawr Avenue
                  Chicago, IL 60631

Reading Miscue Inventory: Alternative Procedures
1987 edition
Principal authors: Yetta M. Goodman, Dorothy J. Watson,
                  Carolyn L. Burke
Available from: Richard C. Owen Publishers, Inc.
                  Rockefeller Center, Box 819
                  New York, NY 10185

Stanford Test of Academic Skills
1982 edition
Principal authors: Eric F. Gardner, Robert Callas, Jack C.
                                      Merwin, Herbert C. Rudman
Available from: The Psychological Corporation
                                      P.O. Box 9954
                                      San Antonio, TX 78204

Wide Range Achievement Test
Revised 1984 edition
Principal authors: Sarah Jastak and Gary Wilkinson
Available from: Jastak Associates
                                      P.O. Box 4460
                                      Wilmington, DE 19807

Woodcock Reading Mastery Test
1987 edition
Principal author: Richard Woodcock
Available from: American Guidance Service, Inc.
                                      Publisher's Building
                                      P.O. Box 99
                                      Circle Pines, MN 55014

AN ANNOTATED RESOURCE LIST

This annotated resource list is adapted from: Davidson, Judith, and Robin Pulver. *Literacy Assessment for the Middle Grades: User's Manual.* Carrboro, N.C.: Center for Early Adolescence, University of North Carolina at Chapel Hill, 1991. Used with permission.

Adolescent Development and Language Development

Benson, Peter, Dorothy Williams, and Arthur Johnson. *The Quicksilver Years: The Hopes and Fears of Early Adolescence.* San Francisco: Harper and Row, 1987.

This book reports the responses of youth from a national survey of thirteen youth-serving organizations about the thoughts, beliefs, values, and behaviors of young adolescents from 5th through 9th grade and their parents. The major findings reveal important connections between parental modeling and family atmosphere that have measurable impact on what adolescents value, believe, and do.

Cole, Michael, and Sheila R. Cole. *The Development of Children.* New York: Scientific American Books, 1989.

This developmental psychology textbook reviews research on human development, placing special emphasis on the role of social and cultural contexts. Two chapters discuss adolescent development, one highlighting biological and social foundations and the other reviewing psychological achievements.

Csikszentmihalyi, Mihaly, and Reed Larson. *Being Adolescent: Conflict and Growth in the Teenage Years.* New York: Basic Books, 1984.

The authors present the findings of a survey of seventy-five teenagers who carried beepers for one week and filled out questionnaires about their activities each time they were paged. Charts and graphs, amplified with narrative material obtained from the questionnaires, provide a vivid portrait of the behavior, inner feelings, and daily activity of these adolescents.

Hill, John P. *Understanding Early Adolescence: A Framework.* Carrboro, N.C.: Center for Early Adolescence, University of North Carolina at Chapel Hill, 1980.

The purpose of Hill's book is to define the classic issues of adolescent development and to put the issues in a framework that makes sense out of adolescence as a whole. Hill tells the concerned professional, parent, or policymaker what is known about the primary and secondary changes of early adolescence that lead to healthy growth and maturation. The framework serves as a guide to understanding the adolescent in the context of daily life—family, peer group, school, and community.

Jones, Reginald L., ed. *Black Adolescents.* Berkeley, Calif.: Cobb & Henry, 1989.

This resource provides up-to-date research on black adolescents. It includes an overview section reviewing the field, as well as sections on youth in diverse settings, physical and mental health, psychosocial development and socialization, educational issues and programs, career development and employment, counseling and psychotherapy, and special issues (teen pregnancy, substance use, and youth in the criminal justice system).

Menyuk, Paula. *Language and Maturation.* Cambridge, Mass.: The MIT Press, 1977.

This book is a detailed, specific study of language acquisition and development from infancy to adulthood. It summarizes findings on the language behavior of children and adults during different stages of development.

Steinberg, Laurence. *Adolescence.* New York: Alfred A. Knopf, 1985.

Steinberg provides us with a realistic understanding of adolescents by focusing his college text on developmental changes within the meaningful context of the lives of adolescents. He concentrates on such psychosocial issues as identity, autonomy, intimacy, sexuality, and achievement.

Reading, Writing, and the Young Adolescent

Andrasick, Kathleen Dudden. *Opening Texts: Using Writing to Teach Literature*. Portsmouth, N.H.: Heinemann, 1990.

In keeping with the subtitle of the book—Using Writing to Teach Literature—the author provides detailed discussions of the most up-to-date techniques for teaching literature. She examines the theoretical base for using writing as a tool for teaching literature and provides concrete descriptions of many ways to do so: dialogue journals, process logs, and reading responses. The book also provides information on ways to deepen initial writing forays into literature and combine writing techniques in meaningful sequences.

Atwell, Nancie. *In the Middle: Writing, Reading, and Learning with Adolescents*. Portsmouth, N.H.: Boynton Cook, 1987.

Atwell, an experienced middle-school reading and writing teacher at Boothbay Harbor Grammar School in Maine, developed a successful workshop to teach reading and writing to her 8th graders. The book records and recounts her decision to abandon the standard curriculum and begin learning with her students through reading and writing workshops. As she tells how to establish a workshop routine, she gives examples of conversations with students, samples of their writing, and samples of forms needed to manage the workshop.

Atwell, Nancie, ed. *Coming to Know: Writing to Learn in the Intermediate Grades*. Portsmouth, N.H.: Heinemann, 1990.

This is a practical book for teachers and planners who wish to develop ways for children to use writing to learn throughout the school day. It explores alternatives to "report" writing, the uses of learning logs, and making connections among reading, writing, and learning.

Calkins, Lucy McCormick. *The Art of Teaching Writing.* Portsmouth, N.H.: Heinemann, 1986.

This book focuses on Calkin's techniques for getting students involved in writing. The essentials of teaching writing are brought to life with illustrations from real classrooms on the reading-writing connection, report writing, writing development, and teacher-student conferences. It is filled with suggestions to improve literacy learning for young adolescents.

Duffy, Gerald G., ed. *Reading in the Middle School.* 2d ed. Newark, Del.: International Reading Association, 1990.

This is a collection of essays on a broad range of topics related to reading in the middle grades. It covers many aspects, from classroom instruction and assessment to program planning and staff development. The authors focus heavily on the special content area reading tasks required of middle-grades students.

Flood, James, Julie M. Jensen, Diane Lapp, and James R. Squire, eds. *Handbook of Research on Teaching the English Language Arts.* New York: Macmillan, 1991.

This is an omnibus of articles on research in English language arts. It includes sections on the theoretical bases for English language arts teaching, research methods, and research on language learners, teaching environments, and specific aspects of instruction and curriculum.

Hansen, Jane. *When Writers Read.* Portsmouth, N.H.: Heinemann, 1987.

Hansen demonstrates the importance of providing frequent opportunities for students to practice writing. She advocates a student-centered, response-oriented reading program that connects reading to writing. This instruction focuses on letting readers read and on content, rather than the mechanical conventions of reading and writing.

Moore, David W., Sharon A. Moore, Patricia M. Cunningham, and James W. Cunningham. *Developing Readers and Writers in the Content Areas: K–12.* White Plains, N.Y.: Longman, 1986.

This textbook uses an integrated approach in teaching reading and writing. Even though separate chapters are devoted to comprehension and composition, reading and writing are combined in each chapter. Through expository and narrative accounts, the authors show how the principles and strategies of instruction operate in the classroom. Learning activities and suggested readings are included.

Newkirk, Thomas, and Nancie Atwell, eds. *Understanding Writing: Ways of Observing, Learning, and Teaching K–8.* 2d ed. Portsmouth, N.H.: Heinemann, 1988.

The articles collected in this book offer insights into how students develop writing skills. This book also includes chapters on students with special needs and shows how they can achieve success in the reading and writing class.

Perl, Sondra, and Nancy Wilson. *Through Teachers' Eyes: Portraits of Writing Teachers at Work.* Portsmouth, N.H.: Heinemann, 1986.

Through in-depth case studies, Perl and Wilson provide the reader with portraits of six writing teachers at work. The authors lived in the homes and classrooms of these teachers for two years, interviewing, observing, and gathering data. Intensely revealing and thought-provoking, the case studies provide many insights into the factors that make a writing class successful.

Probst, Robert E. *Response and Analysis: Teaching Literature in Junior and Senior High School.* Portsmouth, N.H.: Boynton Cook, 1988.

This book argues that literature is experience, not information, that students gain as they interact with the text in the process of reading. It demonstrates how teachers can encourage students to respond to literature so they can learn to analyze and understand what they read. The book also includes several lists of recommended adolescent literature.

Smith, Frank. *Joining the Literacy Club: Further Essays into Education.* Portsmouth, N.H.: Heinemann, 1988.

The focus of this collection of essays is making literacy learning a meaningful, purposeful activity. Smith proposes that learning is a social accomplishment. Students first see others engage in literate behavior before they learn to become readers and writers themselves. Teachers play a critical role in providing young people with opportunities to join a "literacy club" whose membership requires them to learn how to read and write and be critical thinkers.

Smith, Frank. *Reading without Nonsense.* 2d ed. New York: Teachers College Press, 1985.

Smith's theme is that children learn only when helped to use spoken and written language in meaningful ways. Smith clearly contrasts factors that facilitate language learning with those that create difficulties for all children.

Tchudi, Stephen N., and Margie C. Huerta. *Teaching Writing in the Content Areas: Middle School/Junior High.* Washington, D.C.: National Education Association, 1983.

To become effective writers, students need help using language in more than just isolated language arts exercises. This book offers teachers basic principles, procedures, ideas, and examples on how to incorporate content writing into their classes.

Tsujimoto, Joseph I. *Teaching Poetry Writing to Adolescents.* Urbana, Ill.: ERIC Clearinghouse on Reading and Communication Skills and the National Council of Teachers of English, 1988.

Tsujimoto approaches his task from the dual perspective of a poet and a junior high school teacher. He provides the reader with a rich, step-by-step account of his poetry curriculum, illustrated with numerous examples of student poetry.

Compensatory Literacy Programs and Strategies

Beck, Judith S. "A Problem Solving Framework for Managing Poor Readers in Classrooms." *The Reading Teacher* 41, no. 8 (April 1988): 774–79.

Beck offers ideas and suggests steps for intervening to change specific behaviors in poor readers. Many poor readers hold negative attitudes about themselves and school that prevent them from benefiting from literacy instruction.

Brozo, William G. "Learning How At-Risk Readers Learn Best: A Case for Interactive Assessment." *Journal of Reading* 33, no. 7 (April 1990): 522–27.

In this article, Brozo supports assessments of high-risk students that are more interactive. He presents an example of administering an informal reading inventory interactively and explains how it leads students to improve performance and attitudes about themselves as readers.

Coley, Joan Develin, and Dianne M. Hoffman. "Overcoming Learned Helplessness in At-Risk Readers." *Journal of Reading* 33, no. 7 (April 1990): 497–502.

This article discusses a model program developed for 6th-grade students classified as "at risk" in reading. The program aims to enhance the self-concept of young people so they will view themselves as competent, capable learners and offers methods to do so.

Heller, Mary F. "Comprehending and Composing through Language Experience." *The Reading Teacher* 42, no. 2 (November 1988): 130–35.

This article describes the Language Experience Approach (LEA) to remedial reading instruction, its problems, and some responses to those problems. It includes a description and analysis of a language dictation with practical suggestions for modifying the LEA approach.

Helmstetter, Ann. "Year-long Motivation in the 8th Grade Reluctant Class." *Journal of Reading* 31, no. 3 (December 1987): 244–47.

Helmstetter discusses how she used positive reinforcement to change her at-risk 8th-graders into active literacy learners.

Kohl, Herbert. *Reading, How To.* Milton Keynes, England: Open University Press, 1988.

Kohl advocates an alternative method of reading instruction based on a caring, nonthreatening learning environment and on respect for the culture, mind, and abilities of older beginning readers and writers.

McKenna, Michael C. "Reading Interests of Remedial Secondary School Students." *Journal of Reading* 29, no. 4 (January 1986): 346–51.

McKenna reports on an investigation to identify universal reading interests of low-achieving adolescents. Determining areas of interest was found to be a useful first step in motivating these reluctant readers. This study looked for universal preferences but also revealed measured differences related to sex and age. Tables with the interest topics are included.

Reed, Sally, and R. Craig Sautter. "Children of Poverty: The Status of 12 Million Young Americans." *Phi Delta Kappan* 71, no. 10 (June 1990): K1–K12. (Available from: Special Report Reprints, *Phi Delta Kappan*, P.O. Box 789, Bloomington, IN 47402.)

This special report on children of poverty provides overwhelming evidence of the crisis we face. It is filled with up-to-date facts and figures. To improve student achievement, the report asserts that schools, communities, and families must cooperate and work together.

Rhodes, Lynn K., and Curt Dudley-Marling. *Readers and Writers with a Difference: A Holistic Approach to Teaching Learning Disabled and Remedial Students.* Portsmouth, N.H.: Heinemann, 1988.

The authors contend that holistic teaching makes learning meaningful to students with special learning needs. They present strategies to encourage the reading and writing development of learning disabled and remedial readers.

Rose, Mike. *Lives on the Boundary: The Struggles and Achievements of America's Underprepared.* New York: The Free Press, 1989.

Mike Rose has worked for twenty years with children and adults deemed remedial or underprepared. Using himself as an example, he writes of his struggle to become literate and overcome class and culture barriers.

Vacca, Richard T., and Nancy D. Padak. "Who's At Risk in Reading?" *Journal of Reading* 33, no. 7 (April 1990): 486–88.

The authors discuss what it means to be at risk in school, and they connect school failure to reading failure. They offer suggestions for teachers to help at-risk readers rethink the reading process and their roles as readers and learners.

Wheelock, Anne, and Gayle Dorman. *Before It's Too Late: Dropout Prevention in the Middle Grades.* Carrboro, N.C.: Center for Early Adolescence, University of North Carolina at Chapel Hill; Boston: Massachusetts Advocacy Center, 1988.

This is a landmark report that describes why the middle grades deserve special focus if we are to address the problem of school dropouts. It provides practical information for teachers and administrators on restructuring schools to meet young adolescents' needs.

Schoolwide Literacy Planning

Binkley, Marilyn R. *Becoming a Nation of Readers: What Principals Can Do.* Washington, D.C.: U.S. Department of Education, 1989.

This book is a distillation of the findings from the influential 1984 report *Becoming a Nation of Readers: The Report of the Commission on Reading.* It contains ideas every principal can use to enhance reading instruction in school. Essential information about reading research and practice is included.

Blau, Sheridan. "Teacher Development and the Revolution in Teaching." *English Journal* 77, no. 4 (April 1988): 30–35.

This article focuses on the evolution and impact of the professional development model James Gray laid out in the Bay Area Writing Project in 1974. He recognized the expertise and professionalism of classroom teachers and helped make them accepted as expert practitioners, writers, and agents of change.

Daniels, Harvey, and Steven Zemelman. *A Writing Project: Training Teachers of Composition from Kindergarten to College.* Portsmouth, N.H.: Heinemann, 1985.

This book presents various workshops the Illinois Writing Project prepared to change classroom teaching methods and improve writing by students. Writing and practice, as well as theory and research examples, are used to prove the effectiveness of in-service programs to teach writing.

Gee, Thomas C., and Nora Forester. "Moving Reading Instruction beyond the Reading Classroom." *Journal of Reading* 36, no. 6 (March 1988): 505–11.

The results of a questionnaire regarding the extent to which schools emphasized reading/learning skills are discussed in this article. The authors suggest how school districts can develop ways for reading-and-content teachers to work together to implement content reading programs.

Irvin, Judith L., and Neila A. Connors. "Reading Instruction in Middle Level Schools: Results of a U.S. Survey." *Journal of Reading* 32, no. 4 (January 1989): 306–11.

Current practices in reading organization and instruction were surveyed in schools recognized for having quality reading instruction programs and in randomly selected schools. The authors conclude that in the majority of U.S. middle-level schools reading practice seems to lag far behind reading theory.

Samuels, S. Jay, and P. David Pearson, eds. *Changing School Reading Programs: Principles and Case Studies.* Newark, Del.: International Reading Association, 1988.

This book contains theories on introducing change in school reading programs and examples of how changes have been achieved. Case studies provide ideas about how to change reading programs so that all students become literate.

Tchudi, Stephen. "How Do Good English Curricula Develop?" *English Journal* 79, no. 6 (October 1990): 16–24.

This article examines a survey of 132 National Council of Teachers of English (NCTE) Centers of Excellence to learn how to plan and develop good English-language arts curricula projects. Centers with successful programs had grassroots planning by a highly professional, collegial staff with fiscal support from administrators.

Assessment Issues

"Assessing Bilingual Students for Placement and Instruction." *ERIC Clearinghouse on Urban Education Digest* 65 (May 1990): 1–3. (Available from: ERIC Clearinghouse on Urban Education, Institute for Urban and Minority Education, Box 40, Teachers College, Columbia University, New York, NY 10027.)

The difficulties of administering and interpreting tests for bilingual students are discussed in this digest. The authors conclude that we do not yet know how to measure the extent to which one of the languages of a bilingual student influences the other or how to describe bilingual competence.

Flood, James, and Diane Lapp. "Reporting Reading Progress: A Comparison Portfolio for Parents." *The Reading Teacher* 42, no. 7 (March 1989): 508–14.

A helpful way for teachers to chart students' progress for parents is to place tangible examples of standardized tests, informal assessments, and writing samples in portfolios. When teachers confer with parents, comparisons can readily be made using the examples.

Goswami, Dixie. "Assessing Assessment." *Bread Loaf News* (Fall/Winter 1989, Spring 1990): 20–21, 22. (Available from: Bread Loaf Office, Tilden House, Middlebury College, Middlebury, VT 05753.)

These articles provide detailed information on the ways that teachers in the Boothbay Writing Across the Curriculum program found to demonstrate or assess student success through project work.

Krest, Margie. "Adapting the Portfolio to Meet Student Needs." *English Journal* 79, no. 2 (February 1990): 29–34.

The author discusses how portfolios can be used to promote the holistic paradigm in teaching and assessing writing. Portfolios have flexibility and can be adapted to students' different grade, motivational, and ability levels.

Pikulski, John J. "The Assessment of Reading: A Time for Change?" *The Reading Teacher* 43, no. 1 (October 1989): 80–81.

In this article, the author discusses changes needed in the way reading assessment is conceptualized and the way tests are constructed, administered, and interpreted.

Schell, Leo M. "Dilemmas in Assessing Reading Comprehension." *The Reading Teacher* 42, no. 1 (October 1988): 12–16.

Schell challenges traditional reading comprehension diagnostics by the interactive model of reading. He includes examples and recommendations to revise diagnostic procedures.

Spandel, Vicki, and Richard J. Stiggins. *Creating Writers: Linking Assessment and Writing Instruction*. White Plains, N.Y.: Longman, 1990.

This book focuses on how teachers and students use good writing assessment to improve the writing process. The authors describe, and provide practice for, linking assessment and instruction to teach writing more effectively.

Taylor, Denny. "Teaching without Testing: Assessing the Complexity of Children's Literacy Learning." *English Education* 22, no. 1 (February 1990): 4–74.

This article deals with the issue of assessment in whole language teaching. The results are useful to modify and encourage teacher's professional growth and collaboration to reform instruction in language arts at the grassroots level.

Valencia, Sheila. "A Portfolio Approach to Classroom Reading Assessment: The Whys, Whats, and Hows." *The Reading Teacher* 43, no. 4 (January 1990): 338–40.

This article offers theoretical and pragmatic reasons for using a portfolio approach to reading assessment. Portfolios appeal to students and teachers because they provide opportunities for them to discuss literacy activities. They also help students accept assessment to guide learning.

Wade, Suzanne E. "Using Think Alouds to Assess Comprehension." *The Reading Teacher* 43, no. 7 (March 1990): 442–51.

This article describes an informal assessment procedure that uses think alouds: readers' verbal self-reports about their thinking process.

Wolf, Dennie Palmer. "Opening Up Assessment." *Educational Leadership* 45, no. 4 (December 1987/January 1988): 24–34.

This article focuses on an innovative portfolio assessment model developed by Harvard University researchers. Pittsburgh art teachers are using ARTS PROPEL methods to assess their students' learning and growth.

Wolf, Dennie Palmer. "Portfolio Assessment: Sampling Student Work." *Educational Leadership* 46, no. 7 (April 1989): 35–39.

Wolf states that when students maintain portfolios of their work, they learn to assess their own progress as learners. Teachers also gain new perspectives on their accomplishments in teaching.

Organizations and Journals

American Library Association, Young Adult Library Services Association (YALSA)
50 East Huron Street
Chicago, IL 60611
(800) 545-2433

The goal of this division of the American Library Association (ALA) is to advocate, promote, and strengthen services to young adults through special programs and publications. YALSA advocates for the young adult's right to free and equal access to materials and services and assists librarians in handling access problems. ALA publishes several resources of particular interest to those working with young adolescents. Included are lists of books of interest to young adolescents and the publication *Book Links.*

ERIC Clearinghouse on Reading and Communication Skills
Indiana University
Smith Research Center, Suite 150
2805 East 10th Street
Bloomington, IN 47408–2698
(812) 855–5847

This ERIC Clearinghouse provides a database of relevant information on research and practice in the language arts. Abstracts of journal articles, papers, conference proceedings, literature reviews, and curriculum materials are available that deal with topics such as reading and communication skills; instruction development in reading, writing, speaking, and listening; and remediation. The Clearinghouse also publishes a variety of products, including summaries and bibliographies, and offers reference and referral services.

International Reading Association
800 Barksdale Road
P.O. Box 8139
Newark, DE 19714–8139
(302) 731–1600

The International Reading Association (IRA) has three goals: (1) to improve knowledge of the reading process, (2) to promote reading as a lifetime habit, and (3) to develop the full potential of every reader. The organization holds an annual conference at which researchers, teachers, and national leaders meet to discuss new trends and concerns. IRA publishes numerous books, monographs, and other materials related to reading. The organization publishes several journals of interest to those working at the middle-grades level, including *Journal of Reading* and *The Reading Teacher.* In addition, the Special Interest Group on Literature for the Adolescent Reader produces the newsletter *SIGNAL.*

National Council of Teachers of English
1111 Kenyon Road
Urbana, IL 61801
(217) 328–3870

The National Council of Teachers of English (NCTE) addresses the broad issues of English education. The organization provides two conferences each year, at which members meet to discuss issues of concern and learn about new developments in theory and practice. NCTE also prepares a number of publications that are useful to middle-grades educators. *English Journal, The ALAN Review, Language Arts,* and *The Idea Factory* provide information on research, curriculum issues, instructional design, and instructional methods and strategies pertinent to language arts in the middle grades.

National Middle School Association
4807 Evanswood Drive
Columbus, OH 43229–6292
(614) 848–8211

The National Middle School Association (NMSA) addresses the concerns of educators, parents, and others who are interested in middle-grades education. NMSA promotes the growth of the middle-school concept and provides information on innovative programs and projects in middle schools. NMSA publishes the *Middle School Journal.*

Voice of Youth Advocates (VOYA)
Scarecrow Press, Inc.
52 Liberty Street
P.O. Box 4167
Metuchen, NJ 08840
(800) 537–7107

This publication is written primarily for young adult librarians, but it offers information and items of interest for professionals in other disciplines. Middle-grades educators will find reviews of literature written for young adults and of professional literature written for those who work with them. *VOYA* is an excellent resource for people interested in improving media centers and library programs for young adolescents.

GENERAL BIBLIOGRAPHY

"Adult Functional Illiteracy: On the Verge of Crisis." *Business Council for Effective Literacy: A Newsletter for the Business Community* 1 (September 1984): 2–3.

Allen, R.R., and Robert W. Kellner. "Integrating the Language Arts." In *Speaking and Writing, K–12: Classroom Strategies and the New Research*, edited by Christopher J. Thaiss and Charles Suhor. Urbana, Ill.: National Council of Teachers of English, 1984.

Allen, Roach Van, and C. Allen. *Language Experiences in Reading: Teacher's Resource Book.* Chicago: Encyclopedia Britannica Press, 1966.

Allington, Richard L. "Amount and Mode of Contextual Reading as a Function of Reading Group Membership." Paper presented at the National Council of Teachers of English, Washington, D.C., 1982; cited in Richard C. Anderson et al., *Becoming a Nation of Readers: The Report of the Commission on Reading.* Washington, D.C.: National Institute of Education, 1984, 52.

————. "How Well Are the Remedial and Special Education Programs Working in Your School?" *School Administrator* 1 (1988): 33–34.

————. "If They Don't Read Much, How They Ever Gonna Get Good?" *Journal of Reading* 21 (1977): 57–61.

————. *Poor Readers Don't Get to Read Much.* Occasional Paper, no. 31. East Lansing, Mich.: Institute for Research on Teaching, Michigan State University, 1980.

————. "Teacher Interruption Behaviors during Primary-Grade Oral Reading." *Journal of Educational Psychology* 72 (1980): 371–77.

————. "What Have We Done in the Middle?" In *Reading in the Middle School*, edited by Gerald G. Duffy. 2d ed. Newark, Del.: International Reading Association, 1990.

Allington, Richard L., and Peter Johnston. "Coordination, Collaboration and Consistency: The Redesign of Compensatory and Special Education Interventions." In *Preventing School Failure: Effective Programs for Students at Risk*, edited by R. Slavin, N. Madden, and N. Karweit. Boston: Allyn & Bacon, 1989.

Allington, Richard L., Helen Stuetzel, Mary Shake, and Sharon Lamarche. "What Is Remedial Reading? A Descriptive Study." *Reading Research and Instruction* 26, no. 1 (1986): 15–30.

Alvine, Lynne B. "Buena Vista Writing to Learn: Teachers as Agents for Educational Change." In *Reclaiming the Classroom: Teacher Research as an Agency for Change*, edited by Dixie Goswami and Peter R. Stillman. Portsmouth, N.H.: Boynton Cook, 1987.

American Library Association. Young Adult Library Services Association. *Quick Picks for Great Reading*. Chicago: American Library Association, 1991.

Anderson, Beverly. "Test Use Today in Elementary and Secondary Schools." In *Ability Testing: Uses, Consequences, and Controversies*, edited by Alexandra K. Wigdor and Wendell R. Garner, vol. 2. Washington, D.C.: National Academy Press, 1982.

Anderson, Judith I., and Robert M. Stonehill. "Twenty Years of Federal Compensatory Education: What Do We Know about the Program?" Paper presented at the annual meeting of the American Educational Research Association, San Francisco, April 1986.

Anderson, Richard C. "The Necessity of Promoting Voluntary Reading." Paper presented at a meeting of the International Reading Association, Philadelphia, April 1986.

Anderson, Richard C., Elfrieda H. Hiebert, Judith A. Scott, and Ian A.G. Wilkinson. *Becoming a Nation of Readers: The Report of the Commission on Reading*. Washington, D.C.: National Institute of Education, 1984.

Anderson, Richard C., Jean Osborn, and Robert J. Tierney, eds. *Learning to Read in American Schools: Basal Readers and Content Texts.* Hillsdale, N.J.: Lawrence Erlbaum, 1984.

Apodaca, Rosita. "How We Educate Non-English Speaking Students Successfully." Paper presented at the annual convention of the National School Boards Association, Anaheim, Calif., March 1985.

Applebee, Arthur N. *The Child's Concept of Story: Ages Two to Seventeen.* Chicago: University of Chicago Press, 1978.

Applebee, Arthur N., and Judith A. Langer. "Instructional Scaffolding: Reading and Writing as Natural Language Activities." *Language Arts* 60, no. 2 (1983): 168–75.

Applebee, Arthur N., Judith A. Langer, and Ina V.S. Mullis. *Who Reads Best?: Factors Related to Reading Achievement in Grades 3, 7, and 11.* Princeton, N.J.: National Assessment of Educational Progress, 1988.

———. *Writing: Trends across the Decade, 1974–84.* Princeton, N.J.: National Assessment of Educational Progress, 1986.

Applebee, Arthur N., Judith A. Langer, Ina V.S. Mullis, and Lynn B. Jenkins. *The Writing Report Card, 1984–88: Findings from the Nation's Report Card.* Princeton, N.J.: National Assessment of Educational Progress, 1990.

Applebee, Arthur N., Judith A. Langer, Lynn B. Jenkins, Ina V.S. Mullis, and Mary A. Foertsch. *Learning to Write in Our Nation's Schools: Instruction and Achievement in 1988 at Grades 4, 8, and 12.* Princeton, N.J.: National Assessment of Educational Progress, 1990.

Armbruster, Bonnie B., Catharine H. Echols, and Ann L. Brown. *The Role of Metacognition in Reading to Learn: A Developmental Perspective.* Reading Education Report, no. 40. Champaign, Ill.: Center for the Study of Reading, University of Illinois at Urbana-Champaign, 1983.

Armbruster, Bonnie B., Jean H. Osborn, and Alice L. Davison. "Readability Formulas May Be Dangerous to Your Textbooks." *Educational Leadership* 42, no. 7 (1985): 18–20.

Armor, David, Patricia Conry-Oseguera, Millicent Cox, Nicelma King, Lorraine McDonnell, Anthony Pascal, Edward Pauly, and Gail Zellman. *Analysis of the School Preferred Reading Program in Selected Los Angeles Minority Schools.* Santa Monica, Calif.: Rand Corporation, 1976.

Armstrong, Liz Schevtchuk. "Census Confirms Remarkable Shifts in Ethnic Makeup." *Education Week,* 20 March 1991, 1, 16.

Ashton-Warner, Sylvia. *Teacher.* New York: Simon & Schuster, 1963.

Atwell, Nancie, ed. *In the Middle: Writing, Reading, and Learning with Adolescents.* Portsmouth, N.H.: Boynton Cook, 1987.

Aulls, Mark W. *Developmental and Remedial Reading in the Middle Grades.* Abridged ed. Boston: Allyn & Bacon, 1978.

Baez, Tony. "Desegregation and Bilingual Education: Legal and Pedagogical Imperatives." *Interracial Books for Children Bulletin* 17, no. 3/4 (1986): 22–23.

Barr, Rebecca. "Beginning Reading Instruction: From Debate to Reformation." In *Handbook of Reading Research,* edited by P. David Pearson. New York: Longman, 1984.

Bartlett, Elsa Jaffe, and Sylvia Scribner. "Text and Content: An Investigation of Referential Organization in Children's Written Narratives." In *Writing: Process, Development and Communication,* edited by Carl H. Frederiksen and Joseph F. Dominic. Hillsdale, N.J.: Lawrence Erlbaum, 1981.

Bates, Gary W., and Sally L. Navin. "Effects of Parent Counseling on Remedial Readers' Attitudes and Achievement." *Journal of Reading* 30 (1986): 254–57.

Bates-Watkins, Sue Ann, and Thomas F. Diener. "Kenosha ECIA Program Review, March 25–28, 1985." Kenosha, Wis., 1985.

Bauman, Richard, and Joel Sherzer, eds. *Explorations in the Ethnography of Speaking.* New York: Cambridge University Press, 1974.

Becker, Wesley C. "Teaching Reading and Language to the Disadvantaged—What We Have Learned from Field Research." *Harvard Educational Review* 47 (1977): 518–43.

Beckerman, Ellen L. "Who Put the Bureaucracy in the Bureau: Federal Involvement in Indian Education." *Future Choices* 1, no. 2 (Fall 1989): 8.

Berger, Allen, and Alan H. Robinson, eds. *Secondary School Reading: What Research Reveals for Classroom Practice*. Urbana, Ill.: National Council of Teachers of English, 1982.

Berger, Dan. *Guggenheim Museum Children's Program: Learning to Read through the Arts, School Year 1974–1975*. Brooklyn: New York City Board of Education, Office of Educational Evaluation, 1975.

Berlin, Gordon, and Andrew Sum. "American Standards of Living, Family Welfare and the Basic Skills Crisis." Paper based on a speech delivered by Berlin at a Conference of School and Employment and Training Officials, December 1986.

Bessai, Frederick, and Con Cozac. "Gains of Fifth and Sixth Grade Readers from In-School Tutoring." *The Reading Teacher* 33 (1980): 567–70.

Bilingual Education: A New Look at the Research Evidence, Briefing Report to the Chairman, Committee on Education and Labor, House of Representatives. GAO/PEMD-87-12/BR. Gaithersburg, Md.: General Accounting Office, 1987.

Bilingual Education Pilot Programs: Interim Study Report. Report to the Texas State Board of Education, Austin, Tex., 1985.

Bond, Guy L., Miles A. Tinker, Barbara B. Wasson, and John B. Wasson. *Reading Difficulties: Their Diagnosis and Correction*. 5th ed. Englewood Cliffs, N.J.: Prentice-Hall, 1984.

Bormuth, John R. "Reading Literacy: Its Definition and Assessment." *Reading Research Quarterly* 9 (1973–74): 7–66.

The Bottom Line: Chicago's Failing Schools and How to Save Them. Chicago School Watch Research Report, no. 1. Chicago: Designs for Change, 1985.

Bowen, Ezra. "For Learning or Ethnic Pride?" *Time* 126, no. 1 (8 July 1985): 80–81.

Brown, Rexford G. *Schools of Thought: How the Politics of Literacy Shape Thinking in the Classroom*. San Francisco: Jossey-Bass, 1991.

Calfee, Robert, and Priscilla Drum. "Research on Teaching Reading." In *Handbook of Research on Teaching*, edited by Merlin C. Wittrock. 3d ed. New York: Macmillan, 1986.

———, eds. *Teaching Reading in Compensatory Classes.* Newark, Del.: International Reading Association, 1979.

Calkins, Lucy McCormick. *The Art of Teaching Writing.* Portsmouth, N.H.: Heinemann, 1986.

Carroll, John B., and Jeanne S. Chall, eds. *Toward a Literate Society.* New York: McGraw-Hill, 1975.

Carter, Launor F. "The Sustaining Effects Study of Compensatory and Elementary Education." *Educational Researcher* 13, no. 7 (1984): 4–13.

Cazden, Courtney B., Vera P. John, and Dell Hymes, eds. *Functions of Language in the Classroom.* Prospect Heights, Ill.: Waveland Press, 1972.

"CBO's: Reaching the Hardest to Reach." *Business Council for Effective Literacy: A Newsletter for the Business Community* 1 (April 1986): 1, 4–5.

"Center for Early Adolescence Studies Adolescent Literacy." *Common Focus* 7, no. 1 (1986): 1, 8.

Chall, Jeanne S. "Literacy: Trends and Explanations." *American Education* 20, no. 9 (1984): 16–22.

———. *Stages of Reading Development.* New York: McGraw-Hill, 1983.

Chesson, Gail Smith, and Ed Maxa. *River's Edge: A 4-H Environmental Science Adventure.* Raleigh, N.C.: N.C. Agricultural Extension Service, 1991.

"Chicago Researchers Cite Reading Skills in Dropout Study." *Report on Education Research* 17, no. 13 (19 June 1985): 4.

"Children in Poverty." *Education Week,* 1 November 1989, 3.

Children's Defense Fund. *A Children's Defense Budget.* Washington, D.C.: Children's Defense Fund, 1986.

————. *A Vision for America's Future: An Agenda for the 1990s: A Children's Defense Budget.* Washington, D.C.: Children's Defense Fund, 1989.

Chomsky, Carol. "After Decoding: What?" *Language Arts* 53 (1976): 288–96.

Church, Joseph. *Language and the Discovery of Reality: A Developmental Psychology of Cognition.* New York: Random House, 1961.

Clark, Christopher M., and Susan Florio-Ruane. *The Written Literacy Forum: Combining Research and Practice.* Research Series, no. 138. East Lansing, Mich.: Institute for Research on Teaching, Michigan State University, 1984.

Clark, Margaret M., ed. *New Directions in the Study of Reading.* Philadelphia: Falmer Press, 1985.

"Cloze Procedure as Applied to Reading." In *Mental Measurements Yearbook,* edited by Oscar K. Buros, vol. 2. 8th ed. Highland Park, N.J.: Gryphon Press, 1978.

Cohen, Peter A., James A. Kulik, and Chen-Lin C. Kulik. "Educational Outcomes of Tutoring: A Meta-analysis of Findings." *American Educational Research Journal* 19 (1982): 237–48.

Coleman, James. "Summer Learning and School Achievement." *The Public Interest* 66 (1982): 140–44.

"A Commitment to Literacy." Cleveland, Ohio: Greater Cleveland Communications Skills Study Group, n.d.

Committee of Inquiry. *A Language for Life.* London: Her Majesty's Stationery Office, 1975.

Communication Arts Department, Community School District 4, City of New York. *STAR: Structured Teaching in the Areas of Reading and Writing: Teacher Manual for Communication Arts.* 2 vols. New York: Office of Communication Arts, Community School District 4, 1981.

Compaine, Benjamin M. "The New Literacy." *Daedalus* 112 (1983): 129–42.

Condon, Mark W.F., and Ric A. Hovda. "Reading and Writing and Learning: Skill Flexibility for Middle School." *Approaches to Teaching Reading/Writing* 16, no. 1 (1984): 14–21.

Corbett, Edward P.J. "The Status of Writing in Our Society." In *Variation in Writing: Functional and Linguistic-Cultural Differences*, edited by Marcia Farr Whiteman. Hillsdale, N.J.: Lawrence Erlbaum, 1981.

Cornwell, Linda. Director of Reading Excitement and Paperback Project and consultant, Indiana State Department of Education. Telephone conversation with author, June 1991.

Cowles, Nancy. *A Teacher's Guide for Environment Skill Book.* Irving, Tex.: Boy Scouts of America, 1980.

Cracking the Code: Language, Schooling, Literacy. Special issue, *Education Week*, 5 September 1984, L1–L72.

Crawford, James. "Bilingual Education: Language, Learning, and Politics." *Education Week*, 1 April 1987.

Cummins, Jim. "Bilingual Education and Anti-Racist Education." *Interracial Books for Children Bulletin* 17, no. 3/4 (1986): 9–12.

———. *Interdependence and Bicultural Ambivalence: Regarding the Pedagogical Rationale for Bilingual Education.* Rosslyn, Va.: National Clearinghouse for Bilingual Education, 1982.

Cummins, Jim, and Merrill Swain. *Bilingualism in Education: Aspects of Theory, Research and Practice.* New York: Longman, 1986.

Cunningham, James W., Patricia Cunningham, and Sharon V. Arthur. *Middle and Secondary School Reading.* New York: Longman, 1981.

Daniel, Milly Hawk, and Martha Jo Dennison. *Right to Read: Contemporary Issues: Literacy.* New York: Girl Scouts of the U.S.A., 1990.

Davidson, Judith, and Robin Pulver. *Building Youth Literacy: A Training Curriculum for Community Leaders.* Carrboro, N.C.: Center for Early Adolescence, University of North Carolina at Chapel Hill, 1991.

————. *Literacy Assessment for the Middle Grades: User's Manual.* Carrboro, N.C.: Center for Early Adolescence, University of North Carolina at Chapel Hill, 1991.

Deay, Ardeth M. *Considerations on Selection of Reading and Math Remediation Programs for Kentucky Schools.* Charleston, W.Va.: Appalachian Educational Laboratory, 1979.

De La Rosa, Denise, and Carlyle E. Maw. *Hispanic Education: A Statistical Portrait 1990.* Washington, D.C.: National Council of La Raza, 1990.

Diehl, William A., and Larry Mikulecky. "The Nature of Reading at Work." *Journal of Reading* 24 (1980): 221–27.

Dillner, Martha H., and Joanne P. Olson. *Personalizing Reading Instruction in Middle, Junior and Senior High Schools: Utilizing a Competency-Based Instructional System.* New York: Macmillan, 1982.

DiPerna, Paula. *Functional Literacy: Knowledge for Living.* New York: Public Affairs Pamphlets, 1984.

Doheny-Farina, Stephen, and Lee Odell. "Ethnographic Research on Writing: Assumptions and Methodology." In *Writing in Nonacademic Settings,* edited by Lee Odell and Dixie Goswami. New York: Guilford Press, 1985.

Dorman, Gayle. *Improving Middle-Grade Schools: A Framework for Action.* Carrboro, N.C.: Center for Early Adolescence, University of North Carolina at Chapel Hill, 1987.

————. "Issues in Middle-Grades Education." Carrboro, N.C.: Center for Early Adolescence, University of North Carolina at Chapel Hill, 1986.

————. *Middle Grades Assessment Program: User's Manual.* 2d ed. Carrboro, N.C.: Center for Early Adolescence, University of North Carolina at Chapel Hill, 1981.

Dorman, Gayle, and Anne Wheelock. "Middle Schools: An Intervention Point for Dropout Prevention." New York: Manpower Demonstration Research Corporation, 1987.

Dorman, Gayle, Dick Geldof, and Bill Scarborough. *Living with 10- to 15-Year-Olds: A Parent Education Curriculum.* 2d ed. Carrboro,

N.C.: Center for Early Adolescence, University of North Carolina at Chapel Hill, 1984.

Dougherty, John C., IV. *A Matter of Interpretation: Changes under Chapter 1 of the Education Consolidation and Improvement Act.* Report prepared for the Subcommittee on Elementary, Secondary, and Vocational Education of the House Committee on Education and Labor. 99th Cong., 1st sess., 1985.

Dougherty, John W. *Summer School: A New Look.* Fastback, no. 158. Bloomington, Ind.: Phi Delta Kappa Educational Foundation, 1981.

Downing, John, and Che Kan Leong. *Psychology of Reading.* New York: Macmillan, 1982.

Dryfoos, Joy G. *Adolescents At Risk: Prevalence and Prevention.* New York: Oxford University Press, 1990.

Duffy, Gerald G. *Reading in the Middle School.* Perspectives in Reading, no. 18. Newark, Del.: International Reading Association, 1974.

———, ed. *Reading in the Middle School.* 2d ed. Newark, Del.: International Reading Association, 1990.

———. *Teacher Effectiveness Research: Implications for the Reading Profession.* Occasional Paper, no. 45. East Lansing, Mich.: Institute for Research on Teaching, Michigan State University, 1981.

Duffy, Gerald C., and Laura R. Roehler. *Improving Classroom Reading Instruction: A Decision-making Approach.* New York: Random House, 1986.

Dupuis, Mary M., ed. *Reading in the Content Areas: Research for Teachers.* Newark, Del.: International Reading Association, 1984.

Durkin, Dolores. *A Study of Poor Black Children Who Are Successful Readers.* Reading Education Report, no. 33. Cambridge, Mass.: Bolt, Beranck & Newman, 1982.

————. "What Classroom Observations Reveal about Reading Comprehension Instruction." *Reading Research Quarterly* 14 (1978–79): 481–538.

Earle, Richard A. *Teaching Reading and Mathematics.* Newark, Del.: International Reading Association, 1976.

Early, Margaret. *Reading to Learn in Grades 5 to 12.* San Diego: Harcourt Brace Jovanovich, 1984.

"Economic Disparity Gap between Blacks and Whites Widens: Blacks Share Less of Economic Growth." *American Family* 12, no. 1 (January 1989): 20.

Edelsky, Carol, Kelly Draper, and Karen Smith. "Hookin' 'Em In at the Start of School in a 'Whole Language' Classroom." *Anthropology and Education Quarterly* 14 (1983): 257–81.

Ekwall, Eldon E., and James L. Milson. "When Students Can't Read Textbooks and Lab Manuals." *School Science and Mathematics* 80, no. 2 (1980): 93–96.

Elley, Warwick B., and Francis Mangubhai. "The Impact of Reading on Second Language Learning." *Reading Research Quarterly* 19 (1983): 53–67.

Entwisle, Doris R. "Implications of Language Socialization for Reading Models and for Learning to Read." *Reading Research Quarterly* 7 (1971): 111–67.

————. "Semantic Systems of Children: Some Assessments of Social Class and Ethnic Differences." In *Language and Poverty: Perspectives on a Theme,* edited by Frederick Williams. Chicago: Markham, 1970.

"EPIC Events Newsletter." Washington, D.C.: English Plus Information Clearinghouse.

Erickson, Judith B. Indiana Youth Institute, expert on the history of American youth organizations. Conversation with author, 6 June 1991.

————. "Non-Formal Education in Organizations for American Youth." *Children Today* 15, no. 1 (January–February 1986): 17–25.

————. "Of Dicky Birds, Go-Hawks, and Junior Birdmen of America: Periodical-Sponsored Clubs for Children. Part I: Newspapers." St. Paul: Center for Youth Development and Research, University of Minnesota, 1983. Draft copy.

Esworthy, Helen Feaga. "Parents Attend Reading Clinic, Too." *Reading Teacher* 32 (1979): 831–34.

Fader, Daniel. *The New Hooked on Books.* New York: Berkley, 1976.

Fagan, Thomas W., and Camilla A. Heid. "Chapter 1 Program Improvement: Opportunity and Practice." *Phi Delta Kappan* 72 (1991): 583.

Fallon, Berlie J., and Dorothy J. Filgo, eds. *Forty States Innovate to Improve School Reading Programs.* Bloomington, Ind.: Phi Delta Kappa, 1970.

Farr, Roger, and Robert F. Carey. *Reading: What Can Be Measured?* 2d ed. Newark, Del.: International Reading Association, 1986.

First, Joan McCarty, and John Willshire Carrera. *New Voices: Immigrant Students in U.S. Public Schools.* Boston: National Coalition of Advocates for Students, 1988.

Five, Cora Lee. "Fifth Graders Respond to a Changed Reading Program." *Harvard Educational Review* 56 (1986): 395–405.

Five Million Children: A Statistical Profile of Our Poorest Young Citizens. New York: National Center for Children in Poverty, Columbia University, 1990.

Fleming, David. "Challenge from the Inner City." *Youth Policy* 8, no. 6 (June 1986): 1, 3.

Flood, James, ed. *Promoting Reading Comprehension.* Newark, Del.: International Reading Association, 1984.

Flood, James, Julie M. Jensen, Diane Lapp, and James R. Squire, eds. *Handbook of Research on Teaching the English Language Arts.* New York: Macmillan, 1991.

Foley, Eileen. *Peer Tutoring: A Step-by-Step Guide.* New York: Public Education Association, 1983.

Foley, Jonathan. "When Street Signs Are Mysteries." *Youth Policy* 7, no. 6 (1985): 23–27.

Fraatz, Jo Michelle Beld. *The Politics of Reading: Power, Opportunity and Prospects for Change in America's Public Schools.* New York: Teachers College Press, 1987.

Freed, Barbara F. "Secondary Reading—State of the Art." *Journal of Reading* 17 (1973): 195–201.

Freire, Paulo. *Pedagogy of the Oppressed.* Translated by Myra Bergman Ramos. New York: Herder & Herder, 1970.

Fuentes, Luis. "The Parent-School Partnership and Bilingual Education." *Interracial Books for Children Bulletin* 17, no. 3/4 (1986): 20–21.

Gans, Roma. *Guiding Children's Reading through Experiences.* New York: Teachers College Press, 1979.

Gardner, Howard. *Developmental Psychology: An Introduction.* 2d ed. Boston: Little, Brown, 1982.

Gay, Carol. "Reading, Writing, and the Community." *Children's Literature in Education* 16 (1985): 110–20.

Gentile, Lance M., Michael L. Kamil, and Jay S. Blanchard, eds. *Reading Research Revisited.* Columbus, Ohio: Charles E. Merrill, 1983.

Gersten, Russell. "Structured Immersion for Language Minority Students: Results of a Longitudinal Evaluation." *Educational Evaluation and Policy Analysis* 7, no. 3 (1985): 187–96.

Giving Youth a Better Chance: Options for Education, Work, and Service. San Francisco: Jossey-Bass, 1979.

Glasser, William. *Schools without Failure.* New York: Harper & Row, 1969.

Goelman, Hillel, Antoinette A. Oberg, and Frank Smith, eds. *Awakening to Literacy.* The University of Victoria Symposium on Children's Response to a Literate Environment: Literacy before Schooling. London: Heinemann, 1984.

Goldman, Susan R. *Acquisition of Literacy Skills in First and Second Languages: Knowledge Utilization in Understanding.* N.p.: National Clearinghouse for Bilingual Education, 1983.

Gonzalez, Josue M. "Why We Should Not Adopt an Official Language." *IDRA Newsletter* (Intercultural Development Research Association) (January 1987): 1–2.

Goodman, Kenneth S. "A Linguistic Study of Cues and Miscues in Reading." In *Reading Research Revisited*, edited by Lance M. Gentile, Michael L. Kamil, and Jay S. Blanchard. Columbus, Ohio: Charles E. Merrill, 1983.

————. "On Being Literate in an Age of Information." *Journal of Reading* 29 (1985): 388–92.

————. *What's Whole in Whole Language?* Portsmouth, N.H.: Heinemann, 1986.

Goodman, Kenneth S., and Yetta M. Goodman. *A Whole-Language, Comprehension-Centered Reading Program.* Occasional Paper, no. 1. Tucson, Ariz.: Program in Language and Literacy, Arizona Center for Research and Development, University of Arizona, 1981.

Goodman, Kenneth S., Yetta M. Goodman, and Barbara Flores. *Reading in the Bilingual Classroom: Literacy and Biliteracy.* Rosslyn, Va.: National Clearinghouse for Bilingual Education, InterAmerica Research Associates, 1978.

Goodman, Yetta M., and Carolyn Burke. *Reading Strategies: Focus on Comprehension.* New York: Holt, Rinehart & Winston, 1980.

Graves, Donald H. *Writing: Teachers and Children at Work.* Portsmouth, N.H.: Heinemann, 1986.

Graves, Michael F. *The Classroom Teacher's Role in Reading Instruction in the Intermediate and Secondary Grades.* Minneapolis: University of Minnesota, 1982.

————. "The Roles of Instruction in Fostering Vocabulary Development." University of Minnesota, Minneapolis, 1984. Photocopy.

Greer, R. Douglas, and Susan Rovet Polirstok. "Collateral Gains and Short-Term Maintenance in Reading and On-Task Responses by Inner-City Adolescents as a Function of Their Use of Social Reinforcement While Tutoring." *Journal of Applied Behavior Analysis* 15 (1982): 123–39.

Griswold, Philip A., Kathleen J. Cotton, and Joe B. Hansen. *Effective Compensatory Education Sourcebook.* 2 vols. Washington, D.C.: U.S. Government Printing Office, 1986.

Gruber, Howard E., and J. Jacques Voneche, eds. *The Essential Piaget.* New York: Basic Books, 1977.

Guthrie, John T., Mary Seifert, and Lloyd W. Kline. "Clues from Research on Programs for Poor Readers." In *What Research Has to Say about Reading Instruction,* edited by S. Jay Samuels. Newark, Del.: International Reading Association, 1978.

Hakuta, Kenji. *Mirror of Language: The Debate on Bilingualism.* New York: Basic Books, 1986.

Hakuta, Kenji, and Laurie J. Gould. "Synthesis of Research on Bilingual Education." *Educational Leadership* 44, no. 6 (March 1987): 38–45.

Hall, Mary Anne. *Teaching Reading as a Language Experience.* Columbus, Ohio: Charles E. Merrill, 1970.

Hall, William S., and Roy O. Freedle. *Culture and Language: The Black American Experience.* Washington, D.C.: Hemisphere Publishing, 1975.

Hallinger, Philip, and Joseph Murphy. "Characteristics of Highly Effective Elementary School Reading Programs." *Educational Leadership* 42, no. 5 (1985): 39–55.

Hansen, Jane. *When Writers Read.* Portsmouth, N.H.: Heinemann, 1987.

Harris, Albert J. "Progressive Education and Reading Instruction." *The Reading Teacher* 18 (1964): 128–38.

Harste, Jerome C., and Carolyn L. Burke. "Examining Instructional Assumptions: The Child as Informant." *Theory into Practice* 19 (1980): 170–78.

———. "A New Hypothesis for Reading Teacher Research: Both Teaching and Learning of Reading Are Theoretically Based." In *Reading: Theory, Research, Practice,* edited by P. David Pearson and Jane Hansen. Clemson, S.C.: National Reading Conference, 1977.

Heath, Shirley Brice. "Critical Factors in Literacy Development." In *Literacy, Society, and Schooling: A Reader*, edited by Suzanne De Castell, Allan Luke, and Kieran Egan. New York: Cambridge University Press, 1986.

————. "The Functions and Uses of Literacy." *Journal of Communication* 30 (1980): 123–33.

————. "Literacy or Literate Skills? Considerations for ESL/EFL Learners." In *On TESOL '84: A Brave New World for TESOL*, edited by Penny Larson, Elliot L. Judd, and Dorothy S. Messerschmitt. Washington, D.C.: TESOL (Teachers of English to Speakers of Other Languages), 1985.

————. *Teacher Talk: Language in the Classroom.* Language in Education: Theory and Practice, no. 9. Arlington, Va.: Center for Applied Linguistics, 1978.

————. "Toward an Ethnohistory of Writing in American Education." In *Variation in Writing: Functional and Linguistic-Cultural Differences*, edited by Marcia Farr Whiteman. Hillsdale, N.J.: Lawrence Erlbaum, 1981.

————. *Ways with Words: Language, Life, and Work in Communities and Classrooms.* New York: Cambridge University Press, 1983.

Heilman, Arthur W., Timothy R. Blair, and William H. Rupley. *Principles and Practices of Teaching Reading.* Columbus, Ohio: Charles E. Merrill, 1986.

Henry, Marcia. "One Parent's Experience with Bilingual Education." *Youth Law News* 7, no. 2 (1986): 17–19.

Herber, Harold L. *Teaching Reading in Content Areas.* Englewood Cliffs, N.J.: Prentice-Hall, 1970.

Herber, Harold I.., and Joan Nelson. *Network of Secondary School Demonstration Centers for Teaching Reading in Content Areas.* Syracuse University; State University of New York, Binghamton, 1984. Photocopy.

Herber, Harold L., and Joan Nelson-Herber. "Planning the Reading Program." In *Becoming Readers in a Complex Society*, edited by Alan C. Purves and Olive Niles. Chicago: University of Chicago Press, 1984.

Heyns, Barbara. "Schooling and Cognitive Development: Is There a Season for Learning?" *Child Development* 58 (1987): 1151–60.

———. *Summer Learning and the Effects of Schooling.* New York: Academic Press, 1978.

———. "Summer Programs and Compensatory Education: The Future of an Idea." Working paper prepared for the Office of Educational Research and Improvement, Chapter 1 Study Team, Conference on the Effects of Alternative Designs in Compensatory Education, Washington, D.C., 17–19 June 1986.

High Intensity Language Training: Program Information 1983–84. El Paso, Tex.: El Paso Independent School District, 1983.

Hillocks, George, Jr. *Research on Written Composition: New Directions for Teaching.* Urbana, Ill.: National Council of Teachers of English, 1986.

———. "Synthesis on Teaching Writing." *Educational Leadership* 44, no. 8 (1987): 71–82.

Holdaway, Don. *The Foundations of Literacy.* New York: Ashton Scholastic, 1979.

———. *Stability and Change in Literacy Learning.* Portsmouth, N.H.: Heinemann, 1984.

Holdzkom, David, Linda J. Reed, E. Jane Porter, and Donald L. Rubin. *Research within Reach: Oral and Written Communication, A Research-Guided Response to the Concerns of Educators.* St. Louis: CEMREL (1982).

"Homeless Children in School." *Aware* (Virginia Department for Children) 13, no. 9 (December 1989): 4.

Hoover, Mary Rhodes. "Characteristics of Black Schools at Grade Level: A Description." *The Reading Teacher* 31 (1978): 757–62.

Horowitz, Rosalind. "Toward a Theory of Literacy." *Harvard Educational Review* 54 (1984): 88–97.

How to Start and Run a School Paperback Bookstore. New York: American Reading Council, 1977.

Hughes, Mark Alan. *Poverty in Cities.* Washington, D.C.: National League of Cities, 1989.

Humphrey, Jack W. "Do We Provide Children Enough Books to Read?" *The Reading Teacher* 44, no. 2 (October 1990): 94.

Hunter, Madeline. "What's Wrong with Madeline Hunter?" *Educational Leadership* 42, no. 5 (1985): 57–60.

Hyde, Arthur A., and Donald R. Moore, "Reading Services and the Classification of Students in Two School Districts." *Journal of Reading Behavior* 20, no. 4 (1988).

Jacobs, W.W. *The Monkey's Paw.* Mankato, Minn.: Creative Education, 1986.

Jenkins, Joseph R., and Darlene Pany. *Teaching Reading Comprehension in the Middle Grades.* Reading Education Report, no. 4. Cambridge, Mass.: Bolt, Beranek & Newman, 1978.

Jenkins, Joseph R., and Linda M. Jenkins. "Making Peer Tutoring Work." *Educational Leadership* 44, no. 6 (1987): 64–68.

John, Vera P. "Styles of Learning—Styles of Teaching: Reflections on the Education of Navajo Children." In *Functions of Language in the Classroom,* edited by Courtney B. Cazden, Vera P. John, and Dell Hymes. Prospect Heights, Ill.: Waveland Press, 1972.

Johnson, Dale D., and P. David Pearson. *Teaching Reading Vocabulary.* New York: Holt, Rinehart & Winston, 1978.

Johnson, David W. "Student-Student Interaction: The Neglected Variable in Education." *Educational Researcher* 10, no. 1 (1981): 5–10.

Johnston, Peter H. "Assessment in Reading." In *Handbook of Reading Research,* edited by P. David Pearson. New York: Longman, 1984.

———. *Reading Comprehension Assessment: A Cognitive Basis.* Newark, Del.: International Reading Association, 1983.

Johnston, William B., and Arnold H. Packer. *Workforce 2000: Work and Workers for the Twenty-first Century.* Indianapolis: Hudson Institute, 1987.

Joseph, Carole Berotte. "Bilingual Education and Creole Languages." *Interracial Books for Children Bulletin* 17, no. 3/4 (1986): 13–14.

Judy, Stephen N. *The ABCs of Literacy: A Guide for Parents and Educators.* New York: Oxford University Press, 1980.

Kadavy, Rhonda, ed. *Reducing Functional Illiteracy: A National Guide to Facilities and Services.* Lincoln, Neb.: Contact Center, Inc., 1985.

Kaston, Carren O. *The Community of the Book: A Directory of Selected Organizations and Programs.* Washington, D.C.: Library of Congress, 1986.

Kean, Michael H., Anita A. Summers, Mark J. Raivetz, and Irvin J. Farber. *What Works in Reading?* Philadelphia: Office of Research and Evaluation, The School District of Philadelphia, 1979.

Kenosha Unified School District. "Children at Risk Program Plan." Prepared for the Wisconsin Department of Public Instruction, July 1986.

Kett, Joseph F. *Rites of Passage: Adolescence in America—1790 to the Present.* New York: Basic Books, 1977.

Kirsch, Irwin, and Ann Jungeblut. *Literacy: Profiles of America's Young Adults.* Princeton, N.J.: National Assessment of Educational Progress, 1986.

Kopfstein, Robert W. "Review of *Stages of Reading Development* by Jeanne S. Chall." *Harvard Educational Review* 54, no. 4 (1984): 468–73.

Kozol, Jonathan. *Illiterate America.* New York: Doubleday, 1985.

———. "Teaching Johnny to Read." *The New Republic* 27 (May 1983): 36–38.

Krashen, Stephen D. *The Input Hypothesis: Issues and Implications.* New York: Longman, 1985.

———. *Principles and Practice in Second Language Acquisition.* New York: Pergamon, 1982.

Labov, William. "The Logic of Nonstandard English." In *Language and Poverty: Perspectives on a Theme*, edited by Frederick Williams. Chicago: Markham, 1970.

Lamorisse, Albert. *The Red Balloon*. New York: Doubleday, 1978.

Langer, Judith A. "Literacy Instruction in American Schools: Problems and Perspectives." In *Literacy in American Schools: Learning to Read and Write*, edited by Nancy L. Stein. Chicago: University of Chicago Press, 1984.

Langer, Judith A., Arthur N. Applebee, Ina V.S. Mullis, and Mary A. Foertsch. *Learning to Read in Our Nation's Schools: Instruction and Achievement in 1988 at Grades, 4, 8, and 12.* Princeton, N.J.: National Assessment of Educational Progress, 1990.

Langer, Judith A., and M. Trika Smith-Burke, eds. *Reader Meets Author/Bridging the Gap: A Psycholinguistic and Sociolinguistic Perspective*. Newark, Del.: International Reading Association, 1982.

Lapp, Diane, and James Flood. *Teaching Reading to Every Child.* 2d ed. New York: Macmillan, 1983.

Larson, Meredith A., and Freya Dittmann. *Compensatory Education and Early Adolescence: Reviewing Our National Strategy*. Menlo Park, Calif.: Stanford Research Institute, 1975.

Lee, Valerie. "Catholic School Minority Students Have 'Reading Proficiency Advantage.'" *Momentum* 17, No. 3 (1986): 20–24.

Lefstein, Leah M. "Effective After-School Programs for Young Adolescents." In *3:00 to 6:00 P.M.: Young Adolescents at Home and in the Community*, edited by Leah M. Lefstein, William Kerewsky, Elliott A. Medrich, and Carol Frank. Carrboro, N.C.: Center for Early Adolescence, University of North Carolina at Chapel Hill, 1982.

————. "School Improvement and After-School Programs: Making the Connection." Carrboro, N.C.: Center for Early Adolescence, University of North Carolina at Chapel Hill, 1986. Photocopy.

Lefstein, Leah M., and Joan Lipsitz. *3:00 to 6:00 PM: Programs for Young Adolescents*. 2d ed. Carrboro, N.C.: Center for Early

Adolescence, University of North Carolina at Chapel Hill, 1983.

Lenneberg, Eric H., and Elizabeth Lenneberg, eds. *Foundations of Language Development: A Multidisciplinary Approach.* 2 vols. New York: Academic Press, 1975.

Lerner, Janet W. "Remedial Reading and Learning Disabilities: Are They the Same or Different?" *Journal of Special Education* 9 (1975): 119–31.

LeTendre, Mary Jean. "Improving Chapter 1 Programs: We Can Do Better." *Phi Delta Kappan* 72 (1991): 576–80.

Levine, Daniel U. *Improving Student Achievement through Mastery Learning Programs.* San Francisco: Jossey-Bass, 1985.

Levine, Daniel U., and Joyce Stark. *Instructional and Organizational Arrangements and Processes for Improving Academic Achievement at Inner City Elementary Schools.* Kansas City: University of Missouri-Kansas City, School of Education, Center for the Study of Metropolitan Problems in Education, 1981.

Levine, Daniel U., Rayna F. Levine, and Eugene E. Eubanks. "Characteristics of Effective Inner-city Intermediate Schools." *Phi Delta Kappan* 65 (1984): 707–11.

———. *Instructional and Organizational Characteristics of Unusually Effective Inner City Intermediate Schools.* Kansas City: University of Missouri, 1983.

Levine, Kenneth. "Functional Literacy: Fond Illusions and False Economics." *Harvard Educational Review* 52 (1982): 249–66.

Lippitt, Peggy, Ronald Lippitt, and Jeffrey Eiseman. *Cross-Age Helping Program: Orientation, Training, and Related Materials.* Ann Arbor, Mich.: University of Michigan, 1971.

Lipsitz, Joan. *After School: Young Adolescents on Their Own.* Carrboro, N.C.: Center for Early Adolescence, University of North Carolina at Chapel Hill, 1986.

———. *Successful Schools for Young Adolescents.* New Brunswick, N.J.: Transaction Books, 1984.

Loban, Walter. *Language Development: Kindergarten through Grade Twelve.* Research Report, no. 18. Urbana, Ill.: National Council of Teachers of English, 1976.

MacIver, Douglas J. "Helping Students Who Fall Behind: Remedial Activities in the Middle Grades." CDS Report, no. 22. Baltimore: Center for Research on Effective Schooling for Disadvantaged Students, The Johns Hopkins University, 1991.

"The Main Basic Skills Programs: An Introduction." *Business Council for Effective Literacy: A Newsletter for the Business Community* 1 (September 1984): 4–9.

Mallett, Graham. "Using Language Experience with Junior High Native Indian Students." *Journal of Reading* 21 (1977): 25–28.

Mann, Dale. "Can We Help Dropouts? Thinking about the Undoable." *Teachers College Record* 87 (Spring 1986): 307–23.

Martin, James G., and Richard H. Meltzer. "Visual Rhythms: Report on a Method for Facilitating the Teaching of Reading." *Journal of Reading* 8 (1976): 153–60.

Martin, Nancy, Pat D'Arcy, Bryan Newton, and Robert Parker. *Writing and Learning across the Curriculum 11–16.* Glasgow, Scotland: Ward Lock Educational, 1976.

Mason, Jana, and Jean Osborn. *When Do Children Begin "Reading to Learn"? A Survey of Classroom Reading Instruction Practices in Grades Two through Five.* Technical Report, no. 261. Champaign, Ill.: Center for the Study of Reading, University of Illinois at Urbana-Champaign, 1982.

McCullough, Constance M., ed. *Inchworm, Inchworm: Persistent Problems in Reading Education.* Newark, Del.: International Reading Association, 1980.

McEwin, C. Kenneth, and Michael G. Allen. "Moving toward Middle Level Teacher Certification." *Middle School Journal* 16, no. 4 (August 1985): 18–20.

McEwin, C. Kenneth, and Robin M. Clay. *A National Comparative Study of Practices and Programs of Middle and Junior High Schools.* Boone, N.C.: Appalachian State University, 1983.

McGowan, William. "Corporations Aim to Wipe Out Illiteracy." *Business and Society Review* no. 44 (1983): 37–40.

McGuire, C. Kent. *State and Federal Programs for Special Student Populations.* Denver: Education Commission of the States, 1982.

McNaughton, S., T. Glynn, and V.M. Robinson. *Parents as Remedial Reading Tutors: Issues for Home and School.* Studies in Education no. 28. Wellington, New Zealand: New Zealand Council for Educational Research, 1981.

Meek, Margaret. *Achieving Literacy: Longitudinal Studies of Adolescents Learning to Read.* London: Routledge & Kegan Paul, 1983.

Menyuk, Paula. *The Acquisition and Development of Language.* Englewood Cliffs, N.J.: Prentice-Hall, 1971.

———. *Language and Maturation.* Cambridge, Mass.: MIT Press, 1977.

Meyer, Linda A., Russell M. Gersten, and Joan Gutkin. *Direct Instruction: A Project Follow-Through Success Story.* Technical Report, no. 302. Champaign, Ill.: Center for the Study of Reading, University of Illinois at Urbana-Champaign, 1983.

Micklos, John J., Jr. "The Facts, Please, about Reading Achievement in American Schools." *Journal of Reading* 24 (1980): 41–45.

Mihaly, Lisa Klee. *Homeless Families: Failed Policies and Young Victims.* Washington, D.C.: Children's Defense Fund, 1991.

Mikulecky, Larry. "Job Literacy: The Relationship between School Preparation and Workplace Actuality." *Reading Research Quarterly* 17 (1982): 400–419.

Mobile Reading Centers, Dade County, Florida: Program Conspectus. New York: Center for Urban Education, [1969].

Model Programs: Reading, School-within-a-School, Keokuk, Iowa. Washington, D.C.: U.S. Government Printing Office, 1971.

Morrison, Beverly. *Content-Area Reading Staff Development for Secondary Teachers: Comments and Guidelines for the Reading Specialist.* Practical Paper, no. 23. Madison, Wis.: Research and

Development Center for Individualized Schooling, University of Wisconsin, 1980.

Mosenthal, Peter. "Defining Reading Program Effectiveness: An Ideological Approach." *Poetics* 13 (1984): 195–216.

Mullis, Ina V.S., and Lynn B. Jenkins. *The Reading Report Card, 1971–88: Trends from the Nation's Report Card.* Princeton, N.J.: National Assessment of Educational Progress, 1990.

Nasworthy, Carol, and Magdalena Rood. *Bridging the Gap between Business and Education: Reconciling Expectations for Student Achievement.* Critical Issues in Student Achievement, no. 4. Austin, Tex.: Southwest Educational Development Laboratory, 1990.

National Assessment of Educational Progress. *Profiles of Literacy: An Assessment of Young Adults.* Princeton, N.J.: National Assessment of Educational Progress, 1985.

————. *The Reading Report Card: Progress toward Excellence in Our Schools; Trends in Reading over Four National Assessments, 1971–1984.* Princeton, N.J.: National Assessment of Educational Progress, 1985.

National Commission on Resources for Youth. *An Evaluation of the Youth Tutoring Youth Model for In-School Neighborhood Youth Corps.* New York: National Commission on Resources for Youth, 1972.

National Diffusion Network. *Educational Programs That Work: A Collection of Proven Exemplary Educational Programs and Practices.* 12th ed. Longmont, Colo.: Sopris West, 1986.

Negin, Gary A., and Dee Krugler. "Essential Literacy Skills for Functioning in an Urban Community." *Journal of Reading* 24 (1980): 109–15.

Nelson, Jeffrey B. "Big Hit in the Inner City." *American Education* 14, no. 10 (1978): 23–27.

Neugeboren, Jay. "The Zodiacs." In *Corky's Brother* by Jay Neugeboren. New York: Farrar, Straus & Giroux, 1969.

Neuman, Susan B. "Reading Performance." *Society* 21, no. 6 (1984): 14–15.

Newkirk, Thomas, and Nancie Atwell, eds. *Understanding Writing: Ways of Observing, Learning, and Teaching K–8.* 2d ed. Portsmouth, N.H.: Heinemann, 1988.

Nicholson, Tom. "Experts and Novices: A Study of Reading in the High School Classroom." *Reading Research Quarterly* 19 (1984): 436–51.

Nieto, Sonia. "Annotated Bibliography." *Interracial Books for Children Bulletin* 17, no. 3/4 (1986): 29–30.

———. "Equity in Education: The Case for Bilingual Education." *Interracial Books for Children Bulletin* 17, no. 3/4 (1986): 4–8.

———. "Guidelines for Evaluating Bilingual Classrooms." *Interracial Books for Children Bulletin* 17, no. 3/4 (1986): 26–28.

———. "Organizational Resources." *Interracial Books for Children Bulletin* 17, no. 3/4 (1986): 31–32.

Oakes, Jeannie. *Keeping Track: How Schools Structure Inequality.* New Haven, Conn.: Yale University Press, 1985.

Odell, Lee. "Planning Classroom Research." In *Reclaiming the Classroom: Teacher Research as an Agency for Change,* edited by Dixie Goswami and Peter R. Stillman. Upper Montclair, N.J.: Boynton Cook, 1987.

Odell, Lee, and Dixie Goswami. *Writing in Nonacademic Settings.* New York: Guilford Press, 1985.

Okedara, J.T. *Concepts and Measurements of Literacy, Semi-literacy and Illiteracy.* Ibadan Literacy Series, no. 1. Ibadan, Nigeria: Ibadan University Press, 1981.

Olson, Lynn. "A Prominent 'Boat Rocker' Rejoins the Fray." *Education Week,* 14 January 1987, 14–16.

The 100 Minute Club Handbook. Kenosha, Wis.: Kenosha Unified School District, n.d.

Orasanu, Judith, ed. *Reading Comprehension: From Research to Practice.* Hillsdale, N.J.: Lawrence Erlbaum, 1986.

Orum, Lori S. *The Education of Hispanics: Selected Statistics.* Washington, D.C.: National Council of La Raza, 1985.

Osborn, Jean, Paul T. Wilson, and Richard C. Anderson, eds. *Reading Education: Foundations for a Literate America.* Lexington, Mass.: Lexington Books, 1985.

Palinscar, Annemarie Sullivan, and Ann L. Brown. "Reciprocal Teaching of Comprehension-Fostering and Comprehension-Monitoring Activities." *Cognition and Instruction* 1 (1984): 117–75.

Palmer, Julia Reed. *Read for Your Life: Two Successful Efforts to Help People Read and an Annotated List of the Books That Made Them Want To.* Metuchen, N.J.: Scarecrow Press, 1974.

Palmer, Julia Reed, and Sara Schwabacher. *How to Start and Run a Book and Game Club.* New York: American Reading Council, 1985.

Paolitto, Diana Pritchard. "The Effect of Cross-Age Tutoring on Adolescence: An Inquiry into Theoretical Assumptions." *Review of Educational Research* 46, no. 2 (Spring 1976): 215–37.

Park, Jeanne S., ed. *Winners, All! 41 Outstanding Education Projects That Help Disadvantaged Children.* Washington D.C.: U.S. Government Printing Office, 1978.

Pearson, P. David. "Assessment, Accountability, and Professional Prerogative." Speech delivered at the National Reading Conference, Austin, Tex., December 1986.

————. "Broad Trends in Reading Research during the 1980s." In *Encyclopedia of Educational Research,* 1992.

————. *A Context for Instructional Research on Reading Comprehension.* Technical Report, no. 230. Champaign, Ill.: Center for the Study of Reading, University of Illinois at Urbana-Champaign, 1982.

————, ed. *Handbook of Reading Research.* New York: Longman, 1984.

Pearson, P. David, and Dale D. Johnson. *Teaching Reading Comprehension.* New York: Holt, Rinehart & Winston, 1978.

Perfetti, Charles A. *Reading Ability.* New York: Oxford University Press, 1985.

Perfetti, Charles A., and Thomas Hogaboam. "Relationship between Single Word Decoding and Reading Comprehension Skill." *Journal of Educational Psychology* 67 (1975): 461–69.

Perl, Sondra, and Nancy Wilson. *Through Teachers' Eyes: Portraits of Writing Teachers at Work.* Portsmouth, N.H.: Heinemann, 1986.

Pialorsi, Frank. *Teaching the Bilingual: New Methods and Old Traditions.* Tucson, Ariz.: University of Arizona Press, 1974.

Pink, William T., and Robert E. Leibert. "Reading Instruction in the Elementary School: A Proposal for Reform." *The Elementary School Journal* 87 (1986): 50–67.

Pittillo, Ellen S. *Dropout Research.* Burlington, N.C.: Burlington Public Schools, 1982.

Porter, Kathryn H. *Poverty in Rural America: A National Overview.* Washington, D.C.: Center on Budget and Policy Priorities, 1989.

"The Potential of Middle Schools to Engage Youth-at-Risk." Report of a meeting of the Carnegie Council on Adolescent Development, Washington, D.C., 22 May 1987. Draft.

Project READ. *Designing a Paperback Book Program.* Silver Spring, Md.: READ, 1979.

———. *Motivational Activities for Reluctant Readers.* Silver Spring, Md.: READ, 1979.

———. *To Make a Difference.* Silver Spring, Md.: READ, 1978.

Pulte, William. "What is Bilingual Immersion?" *IDRA Newsletter* (Intercultural Development Research Association) (October 1986): 3–5.

Purves, Alan C., and Olive Niles, eds. *Becoming Readers in a Complex Society.* Eighty-third Yearbook of the National Society for the Study of Education, pt. 1. Chicago: University of Chicago Press, 1984.

Read, Charles. *Children's Creative Spelling.* Boston: Routledge & Kegan Paul, 1986.

Reed, Sally, and R. Craig Sautter. "Children of Poverty: The Status of 12 Million Young Americans." *Phi Delta Kappan* 90, no. 10 (June 1990): K3.

Remer, Victor. "'Take a Giant Step': A Remedial Reading Program in a Camp Setting." *Child Welfare* 49 (1970): 270–74.

Resnick, Daniel P., and Lauren B. Resnick. "The Nature of Literacy: An Historical Exploration." *Harvard Educational Review* 47 (1977): 370–85.

Rom, Alan Jay. "Bilingual Education and the Law." *Interracial Books for Children Bulletin* 17, no. 3/4 (1986): 24–25.

Romaine, Suzanne. *The Language of Children and Adolescents: The Acquisition of Communicative Competence.* New York: Basil Blackwell, 1984.

Rose, Mike. *Lives on the Boundary: The Struggles and Achievements of America's Underprepared.* New York: The Free Press, 1989.

Rosenbaum, Peter S. *Peer-mediated Instruction.* New York: Teachers College Press, 1973.

Rowan, Brian, and Larry F. Guthrie. *The Quality of Chapter 1 Instruction: Results from a Study of 24 Schools.* San Francisco: Far West Laboratory for Educational Research and Development, 1988.

Russell, David H. "Reading and Child Development." In *Reading in the Elementary School.* Forty-eighth Yearbook of the National Society for the Study of Education, pt. 2. Chicago: University of Chicago Press, 1949.

Salisbury, Lois. "Bilingual Education Gets Underway in Oakland." *Youth Law News* 7, no. 2 (1986): 14–17.

Samuels, S. Jay. "Automatic Decoding and Reading Comprehension." *Language Arts* 53 (1976): 323–25.

————. "Characteristics of Exemplary Reading Programs." In *Comprehension and Teaching,* edited by John Guthrie. Newark, Del.: International Reading Association, 1981.

————, ed. *What Research Has to Say about Reading Instruction.* Newark, Del.: International Reading Association, 1978.

Santa, Carol M. "Changing Teacher Behavior in Content Reading through Collaborative Research." In *Changing School Reading Programs: Principles and Case Studies,* edited by S. Jay Samuels and P. David Pearson. Newark, Del.: International Reading Association, 1988.

SARI: Systematic Approach to Reading Improvement: Student Placement Test, Levels 1.0 through 7.0. Bloomington, Ind.: Phi Delta Kappa, 1973.

Schardt, Arlie. "The Kids Need Help, Too—And They Get Plenty from 'RIF.'" *Foundation News* 24, no. 1 (1983): 16–17.

Schieffelin, Bambi B., and Perry Gilmore, eds. *The Acquisition of Literacy: Ethnographic Perspectives.* Norwood, N.J.: Ablex, 1986.

Schneider, S. *HILT Follow-Up Study.* El Paso, Tex.: El Paso Independent School District, n.d.

Schooling and Language Minority Students: A Theoretical Framework. Los Angeles: Evaluation, Dissemination and Assessment Center, California State University, 1981.

Schools That Succeed beyond Expectations in Teaching. Studies in Education Technical Report, no. 1. Washington, D.C.: National Institute of Education, 1979.

Schwartz, Alvin, ed. *Scary Stories to Tell in the Dark.* New York: Harper & Row Junior Books, 1981.

Scollon, Ron, and Suzanne B.K. Scollon. *Narrative, Literacy and Face in Interethnic Communication.* Norwood, N.J.: Ablex, 1981.

Scribner, Sylvia, and Michael Cole. *The Psychology of Literacy.* Cambridge, Mass.: Harvard University Press, 1981.

Seager, Andrew. *A Practitioner's Sourcebook: Effective Educational Practices in Chapter 1 Programs in Maine, New Hampshire, and Vermont.* Concord, N.H.: New Hampshire Department of Education, 1984.

Shake, Mary C., and Richard L. Allington. "Where Do Teachers' Questions Come From?" *The Reading Teacher* 38 (1985): 432–38.

Shaver, James P. *Tutorial Students Two Years Later: A Report on the Logan-Cache Tutorial Center for Underachieving Readers and Writers.* Salt Lake City: Utah State Department of Public Instruction, 1969.

Sheppard, Ronnie. *Enhancing Learning through Oral and Written Expression: Strategies for Subject Area Teachers.* Columbus, Ohio: National Middle School Association, 1985.

Shuman, Amy. *Storytelling Rights: The Uses of Oral and Written Texts by Urban Adolescents.* New York: Cambridge University Press, 1986.

Silverstein, Barry, and Ronald Krate. *Children of the Dark Ghetto: A Developmental Psychology.* New York: Praeger, 1975.

Slavin, Robert E. "Chapter 1: A Vision for the Next Quarter Century." *Phi Delta Kappan* 72 (1991): 587.

Sloan, Charles A., and James E. Walker. "Perceptions of and Practices in Middle/Junior High School Reading Instruction." *Journal of the Association for the Study of Perception* 14, no. 2 (1979): 16–21.

Smith, Carl B., and Leo C. Fay. *Getting People to Read: Volunteer Programs That Work.* New York: Delacorte, 1973.

Smith, David M. "The Anthropology of Literacy Acquisition." In *The Acquisition of Literacy: Ethnographic Perspectives,* edited by Bambi B. Schieffelin and Perry Gilmore. Norwood, N.J.: Ablex, 1986.

Smith, Frank. *Essays into Literacy: Selected Papers and Some Afterthoughts.* Portsmouth, N.H.: Heinemann, 1983.

————. *Insult to Intelligence: The Bureaucratic Invasion of Our Classrooms.* New York: Arbor House, 1986.

————. *Psycholinguistics and Reading.* New York: Holt, Rinehart & Winston, 1973.

————. *Understanding Reading: A Psycholinguistic Analysis of Reading and Learning to Read.* 3d ed. New York: Holt, Rinehart & Winston, 1971.

Solorzano, Lucia. "Bilingual Services: Educating the Melting Pot." *U.S. News & World Report,* 31 March 1986, 20–21.

Sorenson, Aage B., and Maureen T. Hallinan. "Effects of Ability Grouping on Growth in Academic Achievement." *American Educational Research Journal* 23 (1986): 519–42.

Southern Coalition for Educational Equity. *Annual Report 1983–84.* Jackson, Miss.: Southern Coalition for Educational Equity, 1985.

Starr, Jerold M. "American Youth in the 1980's." *Youth and Society* 17 (June 1986): 323–45.

Staton, Jana. *Dialogue Journals: A New Tool for Teaching Communication.* 1983. ERIC ED 227 701.

————. "Thinking Together: Interaction in Children's Reasoning." In *Speaking and Writing, K–12: Classroom Strategies and the New Research*, edited by Christopher J. Thaiss and Charles Suhor. Urbana, Ill.: National Council of Teachers of English, 1984.

Stauffer, Russell G. *Directed Reading Maturity as a Cognitive Process.* New York: Harper & Row, 1969.

————. *The Language-Experience Approach to the Teaching of Reading.* New York: Harper & Row, 1980.

Steffensen, Margaret S., and Larry Colker. *The Effect of Cultural Knowledge on Memory and Language.* Technical Report, no. 248. Champaign, Ill.: Center for the Study of Reading, University of Illinois at Urbana-Champaign, 1982.

Stein, Nancy L., ed. *Literacy in American Schools: Learning to Read and Write.* Chicago: University of Chicago Press, 1986.

Stotsky, Sandra. "Research on Reading/Writing Relationships: A Synthesis and Suggested Directions." *Language Arts* 60 (1983): 627–42.

Strahan, David B. "Problem Solving Strategies of Early Adolescent Readers: A Naturalistic Protocol Analysis." *Reading Improvement* 19 (1982): 183–93.

Street, Brian V. *Literacy in Theory and Practice.* New York: Cambridge University Press, 1984.

Sum, Andrew, and Bill Goedicke. "Basic Academic Skill Deficiencies of Young Women Potentially Eligible for Participation in

Project New Chance: Implications for Educational Remediation and Training." Paper prepared for the Children's Defense Fund, Washington, D.C., 1986.

Swanson, David C. *Buddy-Tutor Project.* Honolulu: Social Welfare Development and Research Center, University of Hawaii, 1974.

Taber, Sylvia Read. "Current Definitions of Literacy." *Journal of Reading* 30 (1987): 458–61.

Tanner, J.M. *Foetus into Man: Physical Growth from Conception to Maturity.* Cambridge, Mass.: Harvard University Press, 1978.

"Teaching Spelling." *Harvard Education Letter* 1, no. 5 (1986): 6–8.

Tierney, Robert J., and James W. Cunningham. "Research on Teaching Reading Comprehension." In *Handbook of Reading Research,* edited by P. David Pearson. New York: Longman, 1984.

Tierney, Robert J., and P. David Pearson. *Toward a Composing Model of Reading.* Reading Education Report, no. 43. Champaign, Ill.: Center for the Study of Reading, University of Illinois at Urbana-Champaign, 1983.

Titone, James S. "Reading One Solution." In *Educational Strategies for Preventing Students from Dropping Out of High School.* Palo Alto, Calif.: R & E Associates, 1982.

Toch, Thomas. "America's Quest for Universal Literacy." In "Cracking the Code: Language, Schooling, Literacy." *Education Week,* 5 September 1984.

Topping, Keith, and Sheila Wolfendale, eds. *Parental Involvement in Children's Reading.* New York: Nichols, 1985.

Torres, Arnoldo. "English-Only Movement Fosters Divisiveness." *Interracial Books for Children Bulletin* 17, no. 3/4 (1986): 18–19.

Tovey, Duane R., and James E. Kerber, eds. *Roles in Literacy Learning: A New Perspective.* Newark, Del.: International Reading Association, 1986.

Trelease, Jim. *The New Read-Aloud Handbook.* New York: Penguin, 1989.

Tuinman, J. Jaap. "Determining the Passage Dependency of Comprehension Questions in 5 Major Tests." *Reading Research Quarterly* 9 (1974): 206–23.

Turning Points: Preparing American Youth for the 21st Century. Washington, D.C.: Carnegie Council on Adolescent Development, 1989.

U.S. Congress. House. Committee on Education and Labor. Subcommittee on Postsecondary Education. *Illiteracy and the Scope of the Problem in this Country.* Hearings, 97th Cong., 2d sess., 1984.

————. Joint Committee on the Library. *Books in Our Future.* A Report from the Librarian of Congress to the Congress. 98th Cong. Washington, D.C.: U.S. Government Printing Office, 1984.

U.S. Department of Education. "Chapter 1 of the Education Consolidation and Improvement Act of 1981." Washington, D.C.: U.S. Department of Education, 1986.

U.S. Office of Education. *High-Intensity Tutoring Project: Analysis and Selection Kit.* Washington, D.C.: U.S. Government Printing Office, 1976.

Valencia, Sheila, and P. David Pearson. "Reading Assessment: Time for a Change." *The Reading Teacher* 40 (1987): 726–32.

VanLanduyt, Marybeth, and Thomas Zuhlke, eds. *Kenosha Model Training Manual: Academic Improvement through Language Experience.* Rev. ed. Kenosha, Wis.: Kenosha Unified School District, 1982.

Vaughan, Joseph L., and Thomas H. Estes. *Reading and Reasoning Beyond the Primary Grades.* Boston: Allyn & Bacon, 1986.

Venezky, Richard L., and Linda F. Winfield. *Schools That Succeed Beyond Expectations in Teaching Reading.* Technical Report, no. 1. Newark, Del.: Dept. of Educational Studies, University of Delaware, 1979.

Venezky, Richard L., Carl F. Kaestle, and Andrew M. Sum. *The Subtle Danger: Reflections on the Literacy Abilities of America's Young*

Adults. Princeton, N.J.: Center for the Assessment of Educational Progress, Educational Testing Service, 1987.

Vygotsky, L.S. *Thought and Language*. Cambridge, Mass.: MIT Press, 1962.

Waggoner, Dorothy. "Estimates of the Need for Bilingual Education and the Proportion of Children in Need of Being Served." *IDRA Newsletter* (Intercultural Development Research Association) (September 1986): 1–6.

Waters, Frances R. "Our Reading Buddy Program Really Works." *English Journal* 63, no. 8 (1974): 89–90.

Weaver, Phyllis, and Fredi Shonkoff. *Research within Reach: A Research-Guided Reponse to the Concerns of Reading Educators*. St. Louis: CEMREL, 1978.

Weber, George. *Inner-City Children Can Be Taught to Read: Four Successful Schools*. Occasional Papers, no. 18. Washington, D.C.: Council for Basic Education, 1971.

Weintraub, Sam, Helen K. Smith, Walter J. Moore, Kathleen S. Jongsma, and Peter J.L. Fisher. *Summary of Investigations Relating to Reading, July 1, 1983 to June 30, 1984*. Newark, Del.: International Reading Association, 1985.

Wellborn, Stanley N. "Ahead: A Nation of Illiterates?" *U.S. News & World Report* 17 May 1982, 53–56.

Wheelock, Anne, and Gayle Dorman. *Before It's Too Late: Dropout Prevention in the Middle Grades*. Carrboro, N.C.: Center for Early Adolescence, University of North Carolina at Chapel Hill; Boston: Massachusetts Advocacy Center, 1988.

"When Children Speak Little English: How Effective Is Bilingual Education?" *Harvard Education Letter* 2, no. 6 (1986): 1–4.

White, Howard D. "School Library Collections and Services: Ranking the States," *School Library Media Quarterly* 19, no. 1 (Fall 1990): 13–26.

Wigfield, Allan, and Steven R. Asher. "Social and Motivational Influences on Reading." In *Handbook of Reading Research*, edited by P. David Pearson. New York: Longman, 1984.

Wigginton, Elliot. *Sometimes a Shining Moment: The Foxfire Experience.* Garden City, N.Y.: Anchor Press, 1985.

Wiig, Elisabeth H. "Language Disablities in Adolescents: A Question of Cognitive Strategies." *Topics in Language Disorders* 4, no. 2 (1984): 41–58.

Wiig, Elisabeth H., and Wayne Secord. "Linguistic Competence in Early Adolescents with Learning Disabilities: Assessing and Developing Strategies for Learning and Socialization." In *Early Adolescent Transitions,* ed. Melvin D. Levine and Elizabeth R. McAnarney. Lexington, Mass.: Lexington Books, 1988.

Williams, Roger M. "Illiterate? Who, Us?" *Foundation News* 24, no. 1 (1983): 12–15.

Wilson, William Julius. *The Truly Disadvantaged: The Inner City, the Underclass, and Public Policy.* Chicago: University of Chicago Press, 1987.

Woods, Robert A., and Albert J. Kennedy. *The Settlement Horizon: A National Estimate.* New York: Russell Sage Foundation, 1922.

Yinger, J. Milton, Kiyoshi Ikeda, Frank Laycock, and Stephen J. Cutler. *Middle Start: An Experiment in the Educational Enrichment of Young Adolescents.* New York: Cambridge University Press, 1977.

Zakariya, Sally B. "To Boost Kids' Reading Skills, Pack Away the Workbooks and Bring on the Books." *American School Board Journal* 172, no. 8 (1985): 17–21.

INDEX

Judith Davidson headed youth literacy projects at the Center for Early Adolescence of the University of North Carolina at Chapel Hill from 1988 to 1991. She is currently a doctoral candidate at the University of Illinois at Urbana-Champaign.

David Koppenhaver is now the associate director of the Carolina Literacy Center, part of the Department of Medical Allied Health Professions at the University of North Carolina at Chapel Hill. He received his Ph.D. at the University of North Carolina at Chapel Hill with an emphasis on the literacy learning of those with severe physical impairments, such as cerebral palsy.

Founded in 1978, the Center for Early Adolescence of the University of North Carolina at Chapel Hill promotes the healthy growth and development of young adolescents in their homes, schools, and communities.